THE ARCHITECTURAL MODEL

THE ARCHITECTURAL MODEL

HISTORIES OF THE MINIATURE AND THE PROTOTYPE, THE EXEMPLAR AND THE MUSE

MATTHEW MINDRUP

The MIT Press • Cambridge, Massachusetts • London, England

This book was set in Calluna by The MIT Press. Printed and bound in the United States of America.

Library of Congress Cataloging-in-Publication Data

Names: Mindrup, Matthew, author.

Title: The architectural model : histories of the miniature and the prototype, the exemplar and the muse / Matthew Mindrup.

Description: Cambridge, MA : The MIT Press, 2019. | Includes bibliographical references and index.

Identifiers: LCCN 2018055025 | ISBN 9780262042758 (hardcover : alk. paper)

Subjects: LCSH: Architectural models—History.

Classification: LCC NA2790 .M515 2019 | DDC 720.9—dc23

LC record available at https://lccn.loc.gov/2018055025

10 9 8 7 6 5 4 3 2 1

For my son, Sebastian

CONTENTS

FIGURES

FOREWORD

MODEL INVESTIGATIONS

BY PAUL EMMONS

NOT FAR AWAY, in the front yard of a modest bungalow, attached on top of a four-by-four post is a replica of the house. It may have been made before the house to aid in its design and later put on view, just as models are displayed in the lobbies of grand buildings upon their completion as if to prove they are the result of human endeavor. Or, as either foreseeing or remembering, it may have been created after, as a ritualized celebration or magical protection of the house's existence. Is this a model? The two bungalows share a striking similarity, with porch, roof, and dormers, and are even identically painted in blue and white. Both are made of wood, but follow different assembly techniques. Is the appearance, the material properties, or the manner of execution important for one to be a model of the other? The house on the post is a miniature, so it seems to be a model. Or, since there are models as large or larger than reality, it could be the inverse—perhaps the inhabited house is a model of the tiny house, with the residents performing their lives in imitation of what is thought to occur in small.[1] Beneath the tiny house is a mailbox.[2] Does this function make it a full-size mailbox or signify a model house that also receives (and reads) letters?

These elements considered are only a few of the myriad of variable conditions that can be defining aspects of a model. Like Rabelais's 1542 list of 217 games played by Gargantua,[3] the listing of attributes of models is inevitably an exercise in excess. Here is the beginning of a Rabelaisian list, which readers are invited to expand:

> Models to look at, models to touch, edible models.
>
> Models as complete to admire behind glass, models to change/manipulate.

Models as miniatures, models as life-size, models as greater than life-size.

Models for building, models of building.

Models of concepts, models of things.

Models for thinking, models for making.

Models from electronics, models from materials.

Models as toys, models as tools.

Models to persuade, models to investigate.

Models of planes, models of masses.

Models of predetermined parts, models of found objects.

Models as drawings, drawings as models.

Models for dreaming, models for recording.

Models to interpret, models to assert, models to prove.

Many of these defining aspects of models are contradictory or even mutually exclusive. Ludwig Wittgenstein (1889–1951) is a philosopher of language who was initially educated as an aeronautical engineer and made numerous models, even designing a house for his sister in Vienna. He famously wrote: "You think philosophy is difficult enough, but I can tell you it is nothing to the difficulty of being a good architect."[4] His early philosophy was enthusiastically adopted by logical positivists, but his later work took a fundamentally different approach. Wittgenstein created the notion of "language games" to identify words' countless multiplicity of uses, their unfixedness, and their function as part of an activity. He first introduced the concept in a 1932 Cambridge University lecture.[5] In examining the range of things that fall under the category of "game," Wittgenstein concludes that there was no one thing which defines all games, and further that some games had nothing in common with others. Rejecting the assumption that a definition of game provides a common essence, he asserts that complex things like games share a "family resemblance." Some relatives share the same color hair, but not all, while some others may have the same gait when walking. When investigating meaning, the philosopher must attend to the variety of uses to which words are put, like different tools in a toolbox. Wittgenstein's insight applies particularly well to understanding architectural models. There are shared characteristics among certain models, while other models may not only lack that characteristic but even possess the opposite.

To overcome essentialist thinking, Wittgenstein developed a powerful but idiosyncratic working method: he looked to use for the meaning of words, declaring, "The meaning of a word is its use in the language."[6] Wittgenstein identified particular cases to "investigate" their working in order to use "description" to lead to deeper insights. For this reason, he wrote in short paragraphs, containing thoughts sometimes directly connected and at other times largely distinct.

Writers on architectural models have consistently shipwrecked, searching for a transhistorical or ahistorical essence in their attempts to define the nature of a model. Matthew Mindrup seems to be following a course set by Wittgenstein as he investigates particular models to reveal their own defining aspects in a family resemblance. He focuses on the ways in which models are used in order to understand their significance. Many authors of books on models tend to become beguiled by the sheer quantity of fascinating models and are tempted to simply assemble them into an ad hoc collection. Mindrup lists models by investigating their uses, describing the greater significance of models as a fundamental condition of human thought and creativity.

....

AMONG ALL THE CREATURES on earth, only human beings make use of models, because of their unique relation to the imagination—a designer's key attribute. It may be that Daidalos, the mythic first architect, introduced the first architectural model. After creating the Cretan labyrinth to contain the Minotaur for King Minos, he provides Ariadne with a clue: a ball of red thread that enabled Theseus to find his way out of the labyrinth after killing the Minotaur trapped at its center.[7] Daidalos was therefore forced to make his tragic winged escape from Crete, and King Minos, seeking revenge, tricked Daidalos into the open by offering a prize for anyone who could run a thread through a snail shell, a model of the labyrinth. Daidalos won the competition by tying the thread around an ant, inserting it through a small hole to the center of the shell, and enticing it out with a bit of honey on the shell's outer edge. The architect's cunning created a model that was his undoing.

Models are sometimes tools of thought and other times toys of play.[8] Wittgenstein observes that when a child pretends a chest is a house, "he quite forgets that it is a chest; for him it actually is a house."[9] Models can magically transport us to other times and places. Ultimately, models know more than even their creators intend.

ACKNOWLEDGMENTS

THE DREAM OF PUBLISHING a book addressing the use of architectural models has been taking shape in my mind for a number of years. I have been collecting material on the historical and contemporary use of architectural models for almost two decades. About two years ago, I began to take the production of this book more seriously and started putting pen to paper. During the course of this process, many people have stood by me and supported it.

My deepest gratitude goes to Roger Conover, executive editor at the MIT Press, for his immediate understanding of the book and its unique approach. Paul Emmons, Andrew Leach, Sandra Loescke, and Simon Weir have each provided useful critical feedback and comments on the chapters.

I used some of the material in this book for lectures at Virginia Tech, Carleton University, and the University of Sydney. My thanks go to those students who participated in these events. Their challenging questions and comments helped to fine-tune many of this book's important topics.

Finally, I would like to thank my parents for their continued encouragement and my wife, Franziska, for her unquestioned patience and support throughout the lengthy research and writing of this project.

INTRODUCTION

THIS BOOK EXPLORES THE HISTORY of the physical architectural model and the incredible value these objects maintain in the hands of their users. For over five hundred years architects have employed models as tools to test, refine, and illustrate their ideas about architecture in three dimensions. But these uses do not encompass the entire scope of models' utility to also signify, simulate, record, instruct, inspire, and generate architectural designs. What makes the physical architectural model an intriguing object of study is that all these different applications and their methods of construction have continued to evolve over time. Beginning with the earliest human artifacts, this book follows an intriguing narrative of discovery about the practical and cultural factors motivating the development of the model's different uses. Rigorously researched and informed by the latest academic findings, *The Architectural Model* is written to help orient the reader in the study of this important cultural object, its development, and its continued utility from antiquity up to the present.

The popularity of the physical architectural model is certainly proven by its longevity. As early as the Twelfth Dynasty (2055–1650 BCE) of ancient Egypt, three-dimensional models of architecture were employed not only in funerary and dedicatory practices but also as descriptive tools in design and construction.[1] The attractiveness of the model is that it, unlike drawings or other two-dimensional representations of buildings—also known from antiquity[2]—permits users to see before them an entire structure, the volumes of its spaces, and its constituent parts in three dimensions, including the size and location of the openings, its materials, and even its methods of construction. Although two-dimensional representations are equally important to the design and representation of architecture, models have a "hereness" that make the structures they describe tangible, present bodies. It is because of the physical model's ability to make visible a building in absentia that architects have continued to extoll its virtue.

Not the least familiar of these proponents is the fifteenth-century Renaissance architect Leon Battista Alberti, who recommended that architects construct plain and simple scale models as tools to aid in visualizing architectural ideas and above all to avoid faults.[3] For the next four centuries, Alberti's rhetoric was echoed by many others, including Vincenzo Scamozzi, Henry Wotton, Jacques-François Blondel, and Sir John Soane. Soane not only built models for his own designs but also collected those of antique Greek and Roman structures as didactic tools and, in one instance, also assembled a full-size column he called a *Pasticcio*—an architectural folly with no direct purpose.[4] The twentieth-century German artist and amateur architect Kurt Schwitters also used found materials to create art and architecture called *Merz*, and in 1922 he promoted it as a method for modeling and constructing new building designs.[5] As Schwitters explained, when a found object is used as material for creating a model of architecture, the efficacy of one over another depends on its ability to refresh an architect's imagination about the spatial or constructive principles of architecture. This approach was also fostered by another German architect from the twentieth century, Frei Otto, in his use of soap bubbles to anticipate the performance of his minimum surface lightweight tensile structures.[6] As these examples demonstrate, the role of the architectural model in design is not limited to the illustration of a preconceived architectural idea but also includes its use as a muse and generative tool.

Indeed, the selection and interpretation of a modeling material are fundamental to the entire nature of the architectural model. In certain kinds of modeling, such as that for model railways, reality is miniaturized and pebbles are used to depict stones and so forth. Unlike this naïve realistic approach, architectural models use materials such as wood or cardboard to represent building materials. The early twentieth-century German philosopher Edmund Husserl sought to explicate the process by which our experiences of things in the world are ascribed with an identity such as a model of architecture. The term Husserl employed when referring to this kind of temporary suspension of preconceptions is *Einklammerung* (also called *epoché* or "bracketing").[7] When a modeler "brackets" a modeling material, they cease to know it as a board of wood or piece of card, viewing it instead as a longitudinal, stiff mass of dry organic fibers having a unique weight and ability to transform. On the basis of these conditions, the modeler will approach their materials with an initial suspension of judgment by asking "what if?" and will speculate on whether a particular material is suitable for describing some aspect of an existing or proposed structure at diverse scales, levels of detail, or intelligibility.

It is surprising that despite the long-standing presence of models in architectural practice, as well as their familiarity in everyday life as toys, souvenirs, or even art, a historical survey of different uses for architectural models has rarely been undertaken. This task is made more difficult by variable terminology, as the Italian word *modello* became the dominant usage only during the fifteenth century.[8] Before that time, the terms *exemplum*, *muster*, *patron*, *Visierung*, *forma*, *disengno*, or even "model" could refer to both a two- and a three-dimensional representation of architecture.[9] A far greater obstacle for historians is that architectural models are typically constructed of perishable materials, were frequently destroyed, and in some cases were dismantled so that their parts could be recycled in depictions of other designs.[10] Notwithstanding their relative absence during the early Middle Ages, a significant number of models from antiquity have survived. Of these, many that had been preserved in civic, religious, or private archives and collections since the fifteenth century were brought together for two important international exhibitions in Venice during 1994 and Turin in 1999.[11] Although these exhibitions drew attention to Renaissance and Baroque models, they did not significantly widen research on their different uses. More recently, a few publications have begun to fill this lacuna in architectural research by exploring the employment of models for a particular project, in a specific geocultural region, or during a distinct period of time, while a handful of seminars and colloquia have encouraged interdisciplinary discussions.[12] Those works available in English from this field of research are mainly limited to brief chronological accounts introducing the use of models by a handful of contemporary architects or offer a concentrated topical survey of architectural modeling during the twentieth century.[13] These contributions to the history of the architectural model are valuable because they capture the model maker's thoughts and intentions that may otherwise be unknown; the microhistorical accounts provide the researcher with a concentrated picture of the model, its maker, and the use for which it was intended. Yet what they neglect to consider is that the uses of architectural models were developed not in isolation, for a particular project or by a single person, but in diverse locations and fields of cultural production.

One of the earliest attempts to create a historical survey of architectural models was made by Ludwig H. Heydenreich in "Architekturmodell," his encyclopedia entry for Otto Schmitt's *Reallexikon zur Deutschen Kunstgeschichte* (1937).[14] In it, Heydenreich proposed a classification of three principle types: *Entwursfmodelle* (design models), *Modelle nach gebauten Architekturen* (models of constructed buildings), and *Idealmodelle* (ideal models).[15] Under each of these categories, Heydenreich included a number of subclasses that covered most of the types known to architectural historians at the time. Few have challenged Heydenreich's classification, and there has been little reconsideration of the value of such a typological grouping.[16]

The difficulties facing any study of architectural models following a typology such as Heydenreich's is that these models evolved over time. Even Heydenreich's assertion that design models after the fifteenth century were created at a mathematical scale to the planned construction is not accurate. Already during the decade before Heydenreich published his encyclopedia entry, German architects were promoting the use of building blocks and found objects as modeling materials for inspiring new designs.[17] Further, as demonstrated by Sir John Soane's collection of plaster casts and models depicting existing structures from antiquity, they were not just souvenirs of the European Grand Tour but also didactic tools, which Soane he would use as sources of inspiration for new designs.[18] Equally significant for a study on the use of architectural models are the *Idealmodelle* that Heydenreich excludes from the practice of architects, since there is ample evidence that these artifacts were not simply artistic renditions of buildings in miniature but exemplars for the composition of architectural form.[19] Because the scope of Heydenreich's classification is limited to three-dimensional representations of buildings or their parts that are "hergestellt" (constructed) to depict a specific structure, important uses of architectural design models are excluded, thereby preventing a complete picture of their evolution in theory and practice from being established. For example, he omits Kurt Schwitters's use of found objects mentioned above, or those models co-opted from children's pedagogical exercises, such as building blocks that were famously adopted by Walter Gropius, Bruno Taut, and Herman Finsterlin as design tools during the twentieth century.[20]

What is problematic for historians of architecture is not just this shifting and evolution of the modeling material and its uses but the subtler areas of interpretation itself. This is to say, rather than following a simple chronological development of types, the different applications for architectural models result from a complex network of interpretation and reinterpretation. The French anthropologist and ethnologist Claude Lévi-Strauss provided a description of this complexity in his theory of human knowledge: he conceives it as an exchange between science and bricolage in which the former creates a tool to suit a particular task and the latter reuses that tool in new ways.[21] Umberto Eco's seminal text on human interpretation in the arts, *The Open Work*, shows how models may similarly acquire different applications in the representation of architecture.[22] Using the notions of "completeness" and "openness," Eco argues that a work of art, music, or literature was considered "complete" when its author ascribes to it an intention that the audience can re-create or understand in the way it was intended. In contrast, an "open work" was one that either the maker or the audience interpreted as "unfinished," incomplete, and open to interpretation.[23] An example of such a work, according to Eco, is scriptures: "The reader of the text knows that every sentence and every trope is 'open' to a multiplicity of meanings which he must hunt for and find. Indeed, according to how he feels at one particular moment, the reader might choose a possible interpretative key which strikes him as exemplary of this spiritual state."[24] Certainly, even an architectural model is also open to this same multiplicity of meanings that are not always intended or intentional. As the French philosopher Paul Ricoeur held regarding works of fiction or poetry, the architectural model may be considered open when its user disengages their assumptions about the world behind it, its historical causes, in order to speculate on new possibilities in the foreground. For Umberto Eco, this disengagement is particularly strong in the contemporary experience of art since, he reasoned, every reception of a work of art or architecture is both an interpretation and a performance of that work. A model of architecture is no exception to this diversity of applications, which reveals the limitations of any study on the physical model whose scope is unduly restricted.

This book aims to grapple with all the challenges and opportunities outlined above. Its main intention is to collect histories about the evolution and development of the architectural model's different uses from antiquity to the present into a single study. While tracing each of these histories, it also seeks to develop an interpretive framework for understanding each of its applications and their employment during different times and places. In particular, this book critically examines and reflects upon existing research about architectural models, architectural model collections, and the decisions of their makers in their historical context. In order to better distinguish the continuities and ruptures over time, the chapters are written as histories of the architectural model's different uses. The goal is to bring to the reader an appreciation both for the architectural model's diversity and for its importance over time.

The first half of this book considers those models of existing, fantastic, or proposed structures which a modeler creates for a patron, client, or builder to use in both imaginary and practical ways. Beginning with the earliest use of models as signs and surrogates for actual structures in ancient Egyptian or Greek dedicatory and funerary practices, the first chapter introduces the entire problem of the model as an interdependent relationship between sign, interpretant, and signifier.[25] Because many of these architectural models were created to reproduce an existing structure with a high degree of visual and proportional accuracy, they became valuable records for archaeological study and didactic tools in private collections and academies of architecture.[26] The second chapter considers models as a medium for architectural reverie, taking a closer look at the ways in which their materials or methods of fabrication enable them to become more than simple inert depictions of structures and to provoke imaginative architectural ideas. These examples demonstrate how a model's user, like a child playing with a toy, will undermine their own or their client's assumptions that it is a faithful depiction of a real structure to encourage the contemplative reverie of an architecture both possible and fantastic. These approaches are no less important than but certainly different from the sectioning and enlargement of models to bring a client or builder into the space of a proposed design. Early examples of these models and their use as prototypes for experimental designs in the twentieth century are discussed in the third chapter.

The study of the architectural model then changes focus, as the second half of this book explores those examples which exemplify the different methods employed by architects to utilize models as aids for designing buildings. The earliest and longest-enduring approach to an architect's use of the model as a design tool was inaugurated by Alberti, who, as already mentioned, promoted the model as an ideal tool for anticipating problems in physical three-dimensional form.[27] To this end, Alberti warned against overly decorated and refined models that might distract the user from a study and appreciation of the architect's solution, recommending instead that they be plain and simple.[28] This chapter illuminates the influence of Alberti's proposed modeling method on treatises and extant examples throughout central Europe and North America until the early twentieth century. It was during this period that changes in both political and aesthetic norms encouraged architects to look again at their modeling materials as a medium for thinking about new architectural form. In the examples surveyed in chapter 5, architects began to consider the propriety of their modeling materials as an informant and, when the structural or formal design was not yet determined, as a generative tool. In this cultural context, a use of the architectural model emerged that began to blur the distinctions between the making of art and of architecture, in what contemporary architectural handbooks refer to as a "concept" model.[29] The final chapter looks at the beginnings of these examples in allegorical, analogical, and anagogical forms of interpretation, which anticipate a use of materials that not only are transformed but also become an exemplar and source of inspiration for organizing materials, forms, and spaces into buildings, bridges, and other works of architecture.

These histories of the miniature and the prototype, the exemplar and the muse, demonstrate the value of architectural models in human culture. Because buildings cannot always be experienced directly, models have enjoyed a great popularity among their users as a surrogate for the structure itself or for the experience of its formal, tactile, and sensory complexity. In the hands of their maker, the manipulation, play, experimentation, and dreaming that occur with the aid of three-dimensional models opens the imagination to contemplate architecture in diverse ways. Whether it is used as a sign, record, didactic tool, informant, exemplar, medium, or muse, this book demonstrates the different ways in which the architectural model has evolved and acquired new uses over time.

1

MODELS OF EXISTING STRUCTURES

Large models, faithful to the originals in every respect, not only as to form and construction, but likewise to the various colours of the materials, would produce sensations and impressions of the highest kind, far beyond the powers of description, sensations and impressions which can only be surpassed by the contemplation of the buildings themselves, which, unfortunately for the artist, many causes frequently combine to prevent his enjoying.[1]

IN THIS EXCERPT from *Lectures on Architecture*, the nineteenth-century British neoclassical architect and educator Sir John Soane lauds the profound effect that he believed three-dimensional models of buildings can have on the human imagination. Showing his faith in their utility, Soane not only constructed scale architectural models of his own building designs but also amassed a personal collection of architectural fragments and models depicting extant and idealized versions of classical and Neolithic architecture. Today one can still visit Soane's collection in his house, a somber, symmetrically disposed, simple neoclassical stone and gray brick structure standing prominently alongside the Lincoln's Inn Fields park in central London. Almost immediately upon entering the house, one is struck by the sheer number and variety of books, drawings, artifacts, and especially models of ancient Greek and Roman structures on display. Already from the library and dining room at the front of the house, an astonishing number of stone or plaster cast vases, moldings, column capitals, and other architectural fragments in his collection can be seen standing in window openings and surrounding door frames, layer upon layer, leading from one room to another and into an interconnected series of spaces at the rear—the Dome Area, Colonnade, and Museum Corridor. Illuminated by skylights, every inch of this three-story gallery is filled with art, architectural drawings, artifacts, and scale architectural models, to which he dedicated an entire room (figure 1.1). To preserve his house and all its contents for the benefit of "amateurs and students" of architecture, painting, and sculpture, in 1833 Soane persuaded Parliament to pass an act establishing it as a museum upon his death, which occurred in 1837. More than mere decoration, Soane used his architectural collection as a source of inspiration and as a pedagogical tool for his students from the Royal Academy in London.[2] Soane's accumulation of these objects, and the ongoing interest in his house to this day, demonstrates the tremendous power that such objects and especially models of architecture can exert upon the inquiring mind.

But one need not be immersed in such collections of architectural fragments and models from antiquity to experience the power and utility they engender in everyday life. Some of our first encounters with architectural models are through humble architectural souvenirs—that is, those more or less proportionally accurate, miniature three-dimensional replicas of existing buildings and monuments that have been a feature of tourist sites for more than a hundred years (figure 1.2). An architectural souvenir, as the name suggests, helps us to remember our experience of a place or object, and can serve as "proof" of our having been there. Our collecting of souvenirs is not a modern phenomenon, however, nor are these souvenirs strictly architectural in appearance.[3] In one of their earliest forms as a pilgrim sign—a scallop shell or cast image of a saint worn around the neck and as a badge—they were purchased by medieval pilgrims to provide evidence for their visit to a religious site and to guarantee safe passage on their journey home.[4] Indeed, the object itself, whether a shell or a crude plastic Eiffel Tower, is little more than the hard, protective outer layer of an ocean mollusk or a miniature depiction of a structure associated with the city of Paris, respectively. Rather, it is the object's connection to one's experiences at the represented place that transforms it into a catalyst for storytelling and nostalgia.[5] Yet unlike the formal and spatial detail of a miniature scale architectural model, the souvenir will typically lack visual similitude to the represented building. As Susan Stewart notes, "The plastic replica of the Eiffel Tower does not define and delimit the Eiffel Tower for us in the way

that an architect's model would define and delimit a building. The souvenir replica is an allusion and not a model."[6] That is to say, for a souvenir—in this case an architectural souvenir—to "work," it need only display the identifiable, albeit memorable, features of a building or place to trigger a memory and thus nostalgia.

| 1.1 |

The Model Room at Sir John Soane's Museum, London, re-created according to C. J. Richardson's watercolor of ca. 1834/35 of the original room.

This chapter is concerned with the fascinating diversity of uses for models of existing structures. Whether employed as a souvenir, sign of dedication, simulation of a revered structure, or a pedagogical or didactic tool, these models take on an entire range of visual similitude from the crude to the highly sophisticated, in sizes from small to large. To retain their connection to an existing structure these models require a recognizable three-dimensional relationship with its formal, material, or spatial attributes. However, as is true of souvenirs, for some uses of these models the accuracy of this depiction is less important than the associations that its user(s) establish

|1.2|

Cast bronze souvenirs of the Grand Tour, 19th century.

with the re-presented place—the place presented anew in a different location, scale, or material. Those faithful renditions of an existing structure's measures and materials were retained for entirely different applications and found their way into collections like Soane's as tools for study and comparison. In order to explicate the different uses for these re-presentations of architecture, it is useful to survey how their size and visual or experiential similarity with the original developed over time. Beginning with their early use as surrogates for actual structures in funerary ceremonies, this chapter follows a trajectory of discovery through the development and proliferation of their uses as signs, simulations, records of construction, and pedagogical and didactic tools.

READING ARCHITECTURAL MODELS AS SIGNS AND SIGNATURES

When considering the variety of architectural models remaining from prehistory to the current day, the researcher confronts a large number whose meaning and use are intimately connected to structures that no longer exist. This is both a bane and a boon for the architectural historian. On the one hand, the model provides our most immediate insight into the way lost civilizations lived and thought about their built environment. On the other hand, because the original structures that these models depict are no longer present, inconsistencies between them and other extant evidence can raise more questions than they answer. Take, for example, some of the earliest remaining models of architecture, which are mainly formed of clay or stone to imitate the material or mass of a structure in everyday experience; these include models of houses, granaries, towers, and temples found in tombs or near important religious sites in central Europe and the Middle East. It is believed that these objects were "votive offerings"—miniature representations of architecture given in gratitude or devotion for the fulfillment of a vow or wish with the expectation of a good return.[7] As the re-presentation of a specific structure, the direction of the anticipated reward is unambiguously toward those individuals and objects associated with the place represented by the votive. For the model's users and in some cases also the community to which they belong, the accuracy of the model is less important than its visual and spatial semblance to the structure being "given." This triadic relationship between the model, act or gift, and devotion to a benevolent god is known as *semiosis*, and it is essential to the understanding of how the models examined in this section are used to signify or stand for a building or place in absentia.

The fields of communication and literary studies, as well as sociology, anthropology, and linguistics, have long accepted the relational nature of language as connected with signs. The Swiss linguist and semiotician Ferdinand de Saussure laid the foundation for the study of signs by proposing a dyadic relationship between a thing (the signifier) and its meaning (the signified). The American philosopher and logician Charles Sanders Peirce expanded Saussure's dichotomy, arguing that something which stands for something else does this for "someone in some capacity"; he thus proposed an interdependent triadic relationship between sign, object, and interpretant, for which he invented the term "semiosis."[8] This relationship is particularly relevant when one considers the use of early architectural model votives in which the house model obtains significance by standing for the actual house that is given to a god or goddess in expectation of a good return. Although architectural votives from antiquity continue to provide valuable insights into the appearance of past architecture(s) and in some instances also make it possible to hypothesize about the construction systems they represent,[9] the original significance of the model has come unstuck from its interpretant; as a result, the researcher experiences what Martin Heidegger refers to as "world withdrawal"—a distancing of the work from the events and systems of meaning from which it emerged.[10] The object therefore takes on the role of Umberto Eco's "open work," which permits multiple or mediated interpretations by the user.[11] It is the complexity of this relationship between sign, interpretant, and signifier in the use of models that will be discussed here.

This interdependence between model and user is already present in some of the oldest extant votive models found within or near burial sites of pre-Hellenic Aegean societies. Reducing the image of a structure to a model permits the user to hold the structure in their hands and literally give it to a god or wandering soul. From the lower Danube valley and the Balkan foothills is a 27 cm long hollow terracotta model from the Gumelniţa culture in Căscioarele, Romania, 4600–3900 BCE, depicting a large wall perforated by a regular pattern of finger-sized holes supporting four houses at the top (figure 1.3). Similar to this earthenware model is that of a round house, 2900–2460 BCE, found at the southeast corner of the Ninni-zaza Temple at Mari, Syria.[12] The purpose of the Gumelniţa and Syrian models is not certain, but they are assumed to have been used in a sacrificial ceremony to celebrate the completion of the structure.[13] Ancient Egyptians made similar models in clay; one example is of a house with a three-columned portico from 1750 to 1700 BCE, now held by the

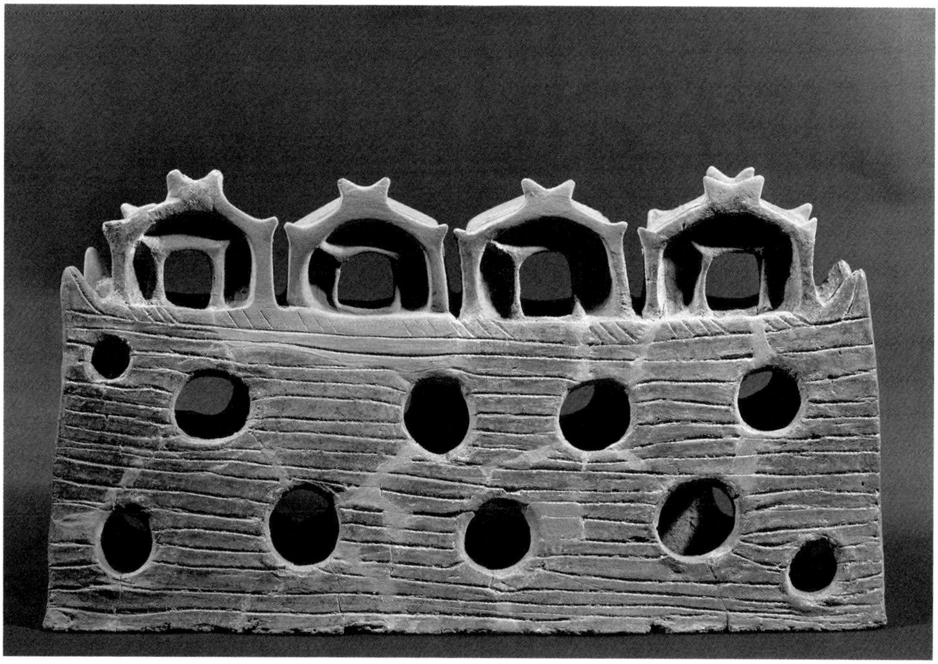

| 1.3 |

Model of a monumental building, Gumelniţa culture, Căscioarele, Romania, 4600–3900 BCE.

| 1.4 |

The "Arkhanes model" with new roof, 1700–1630 BCE.

Metropolitan Museum of Art, which was found near a burial site in middle Egypt. Initially thought to provide a dwelling place for wandering souls of the deceased, these models are now considered to be a type of offering vessel, designed to receive libations.[14] Special consideration should also be given to a terra-cotta house model believed to have served a ritualistic or votive purpose in the Minoan culture at some time between 1700 and 1630 BCE. Known as the "Arkhanes model," this miniature house has spatial and formal attributes proportionally scaled to a typical Minoan house and gave researchers a better understanding about the appearance of Minoan architecture.[15] Despite the differences between the Gumelniţa, Syrian, Egyptian, and Arkhanes models, these early examples all demonstrate a desire on the part of the modeler to shape material into the representation of a structure in order to signify specific acts of dedication.

Another important collection of antique votive models included in this survey is that of the small rectangular-shaped clay and limestone model buildings with sharply pitched roofs found near sanctuaries of female deities, particularly the Greek goddess Hera.[16] The German architectural historian Thomas G. Schattner has surveyed more than fifty of these three-dimensional miniature architectural

| 1.5 |

Terra-cotta house or temple model from Perachora, end of the 9th century BCE. Athens, National Archaeological Museum.

| 1.6 |

Jacob of Strasbourg, "Statues of Venus and Mercury with Models of the Conquered Cities," one of the fourteen images in *The Triumph of Caesar*, after 1503.

representations from the Greek world and identified them as models of houses. The two best-known examples come from Perachora (figure 1.5) and Argos from the end of the ninth and the seventh centuries BCE. As Schattner suggests, they were probably used as dedications to Hera, the protectress of the house and family, as votive models.[17] From the Roman period are terra-cotta models of a temple found at the Temple of Diana at Nemi from the fourth to third century BCE and a temple and lighthouse at Vulci from 100 to 50 BCE. Although all these examples are presumed to have a votive function, their relatively accurate depiction of contemporary architectural forms has enabled archaeologists to make assumptions about the appearance of temples and even the existence of a lighthouse at the port of Cosa.[18]

During the beginning of the first millennium, the construction of miniature architectural models of existing structures acquired a new

use: as a sign of imperial possession. An account of this use of a model to represent an existing structure or city is given by Appian of Alexandria (95–165 CE) in his *History of Rome*, where he notes that the presentation of models representing military conquest was an important part of triumphal marches.[19] Carrying a model of the conquered city demonstrated the empire's control over a territory that was being literally given to Rome (figure 1.6). Beginning around the fourth century CE, this use of a model to signify possession emerged in one of its most common applications in architectural history: as a sign to identify the individuals directly responsible for the establishment of a ruling body—the Roman Catholic church—in a new community.

These representations are a familiar motif in early Christian painting and sculpture throughout Europe and appear as symbolic attributes of human figures. In their earliest form, a model church is typically depicted in the hand(s) of or directly connected to an individual who was responsible for introducing the Christian religion or "ecclesia" to a community. An early example is found in the southern portal narthex of the Hagia Sophia, where the emperors Constantine and Justinian are depicted in a mosaic from 944 CE standing on either side of the Virgin Mary and the Christ child. Both emperors are holding models of structures dedicated to the Virgin Mary: Constantine is presenting the city of Constantinople and Justinian the Hagia Sophia.[20] A similar representation from the thirteenth century is that of Provost Heinrich in the window of a choir at Ardagger, Austria, kneeling while holding a model of the donated church.[21] Whatever the size of the human figures, the buildings are shown in relationship to them as a miniature. This ostentatious display of donors holding a model was at once a record of their act of giving, a demonstration of their control or power within the institution, and a reminder for later generations to pray for their souls.

Over time, an increasing precision of artistry in the model coincided with its extension into the third dimension as a means of identifying individuals closely associated with specific religious structures. These include patron saints to which the church is dedicated, like the fourteenth-century statues of St. Sebaldus in the St. Sebaldus church of Nuremberg, Germany, and also, as the architectural historian Ludwig H. Heydenreich observes, those individuals who funded the construction of specific churches during the twelfth and thirteenth centuries.[22] In the case of donors, the emphasis lies on the symbolic role of the model as a representation of the structure being offered to God. However, models like that of the St. Blaise cathedral held in the hands of Henry the Lion on his tombstone (1230) and that held by St. Elisabeth von Thüringen (1470) of the Elisabethkirche increasingly take on the appearance of the actual donated building (figure 1.7).[23] Because these models were created after the buildings were completed, they should be not associated with tools of contemporary planning processes but viewed as a demonstration of the increased artistry of the time period.[24]

| 1.7 |

Tombstone of Henry the Lion, Duke of Saxony and Bavaria, with his wife Matilda in the St. Blaise cathedral, 1230.

| 1.10 |

Jorge Fernández Alemán, sculptures of saints Isidoro and Leandro standing on either side of the southern façade of the cathedral of Seville, 1511.

thirteenth century, architects responsible for the construction of a cathedral are frequently portrayed holding one or more of the recognized tools of their trade, such as a compass, square, measuring rule, and plumb line.[29] Examples in Gothic cathedrals of northern Europe include Bruder Diemar holding a compass in the Regensburg cathedral (1270), Master William de Wermington on his gravestone at Crowland Abbey (1427), and Anton Pilgrim with compass and square in St. Stephen's Cathedral of Vienna (1513). In contrast, the tombstones for Hugues Libergier (1263) and Heinrich von Sampach (1382) depict the architect accompanied by a small representation of a cathedral. Sampach, who was the architect for the church of St. Marien in Mühlhausen, Germany, is depicted standing with hands folded in prayer next to a cathedral model.[30] Likewise, Libergier, who began the construction for the abbey of Saint-Nicaise in Reims, is shown not with only a small cathedral but also a rule, a compass, and square (figure 1.11).[31] If this image of a miniature cathedral upon Libergier's tombstone is not representing an architect's tool, a model, it must stand as a symbol of the cathedral created by the architect or as a reliquary

resembling one.[32] However, given the cathedral's scale and proximity to other proportionally accurate tools of the architect, it seems likely that it is indeed a representation of an architect's model now lost.

By the end of the sixteenth century, models used to identify an architect in cathedral sculpture began to appear in portrait paintings. In what is said to be the first portrait of a professional, the fifteenth-century Florentine architect Giuliano da Sangallo is portrayed with two of his tools, a pen and compass, in the painting's foreground (1482–1485).[33] A century later, in 1585, Vincenzo Scamozzi—an artist of unending assiduity discussed at more length in chapter 3 of this book—is painted taking measurements from the *paradeigma* of a Corinthian capital and thus is associated with its inventor, Callimachus (figure 1.12). By the eighteenth century, when a model is used to signify the architect's profession in a portrait it is rendered more accurately, representing a specific structure for which the portrayed individual was responsible.[34]

Identifying a building's authorship by portraying the architect standing next to or holding a model of a structure for which they were

| 1.11 |

Tombstone of Hugues Libergier (1229–1263) in the cathedral of Notre-Dame in Reims, France.

| 1.12 |

Paolo Veronese, portrait of Vincenzo Scamozzi, 1585.

| 1.13 |

Irving Penn, photograph of Mies van der Rohe and Philip Johnson with the model of the Seagram skyscraper project, 1955.

responsible became more common during the twentieth century. For example, when Frank Lloyd Wright is shown in a photograph standing with the Guggenheims at a press conference, the architectural model is not in their hands but near to or in front of the responsible architect. Likewise, when the American photographer Irving Penn photographed Mies van der Rohe and Philip Johnson with the model of the Seagram skyscraper project in 1955, Mies is in the foreground placing his hand on the model to demonstrate not patronage for the project—like that of saints Isidoro and Leandro for the Seville cathedral—but authorship of it (figure 1.13). Mies, who obtained the commission for the tower in 1954, invited Johnson to collaborate with him on the building, giving him special responsibility for the design of interiors above the lobby level. Twenty-five years later, Philip Johnson had an opportunity to demonstrate his own authorship of another project, the AT&T building, holding a model of it in his hands on the cover of *Time* magazine.[35] Unlike the earlier dedicatory or donor models, the models held by Mies and Johnson are used to signify not a structure being given to a god or protected by a benevolent saint, but its possession—an indication of authorship.

Perhaps the most important aspect shared by these examples is also the most obvious: they miniaturize an identifiable structure into a concentrated image of architecture to signify it. By reducing the size of a structure or place, the model acts as a surrogate for it, permitting individuals to literally hold the place to be given or possessed in their hands. This surrogate, however, does little to convey the experience of a place endowed with personal or cultural significance, which is the focus of the next section.

FROM COPIES TO SIMULATIONS TO SIMULACRA

While exiled in London in 1851, the German architect, art critic, and professor of architecture Gottfried Semper claims that he visited the "Colonial" section of the Great Exhibition, where he saw a full-size model of a simple Caribbean hut. The entire exhibition took place at Hyde Park, London, in Joseph Paxton's celebrated wrought-iron-and-glass Crystal Palace, which showcased reproductions of art and architecture alongside the industrial products of the world. Because great distances separated many of the visitors from the countries participating in the exhibition, models—here reproductions of existing structures, like the hut that Semper saw—were an ideal tool for bringing the experience of their architecture and industrial production to the eyes and hands of the visitors. For Semper, this opportunity was particularly fortunate, as he found confirmation for a theory he had developed about an original model for architecture. That is, in looking at this hut Semper was able to see that it contained the "four elements" which he believed constituted the first architecture: a central "hearth" (or fire pit), perimeter walls making up an "enclosure," a "roof" built with timber, and a "mound" or platform upon which the entire assembly was raised.[36] This sudden inspiration that

Semper experienced might also have occurred had he traveled to the Caribbean and witnessed the same structure in its native environment. Other architects claimed to have similar experiences; Le Corbusier, to name only one, connected his encounter with the lighting of the Serapeum at Hadrian's villa to his tower designs at Notre Dame du Haut in Ronchamp, France. Long before Semper's hut, during the Middle Ages models were created of important religious or culturally significant structures to provide a community with an opportunity to experience them at a distance. In contemporary practice, when these full-scale reproductions emphasize only their appearance they are frequently divorced from the scale, materiality, or context of the originals, and they become simulacra. This historical transformation, which is the focus of this section, is key to understanding the use and meaning of architectural models as simulations and simulacra today.

Some early architectural simulations of revered Christian structures were created in central Europe during the medieval period. Among these is the Holy House of Loreto, which was believed to be the actual house in Nazareth where the angel Gabriel announced to the Virgin Mary that she would conceive and become the mother of Jesus. According to legend, after that part of the Holy Land came under Islamic control in 1263, the house was flown by angels to the small town of Tersatto, Dalmatia (now Croatia), in 1291; it was moved three years later to Recanati and again in 1295 to a laurel grove known as Lauretanum, for which the Italian town Loreto is named. Since as early as 1296, the Catholic Church has sought to confirm the authenticity of the Holy House of Loreto by comparing its materials and measurements with those found at the house's original location in Nazareth. Because the religious importance of a relic is also attached to its location, miraculous transportation from place to place allowed it to retain its significance.[37] For early Christians, the visit to such an edifice or place could provide a sinner with an opportunity for forgiveness or, following a proper manipulation of the relic(s), certain desired effects of health or healing.[38] Yet long journeys during the Middle Ages were dangerous undertakings, during which entire groups of pilgrims could die in a shipwreck or be robbed by outlaws. In response, the church sought to re-create or, in the case of the Holy House of Loreto, relocate holy structures closer to home so that those who were not physically or financially able to complete such a pilgrimage might be able to benefit from visiting them. Because of its importance, copies of the Holy House were made in Gołąb, Poland (1628–1638), and Prague, Czech Republic (1626–1631), for the same reason it was relocated to Italy centuries earlier. However, a closer examination of the copies reveals that the materials, scale, and texture of the original have been simplified and altered. What these examples demonstrate is that neither the maker nor the user of a medieval copy expected that it had to reproduce the original's forms, artwork, materials, and methods of construction to provide an accurate simulation of the religious space.

When copies were being constructed in central Europe of the Church of the Holy Sepulcher, differences between original and reproduction were permissible as long as the figurative and symbolic attributes of the church were retained. Since it housed in a single structure important early Christian religious sites, enclosing the hill of Calvary and the place where Jesus Christ was buried, the Church of the Holy Sepulcher in Jerusalem became one of the most desired destinations for medieval pilgrims. Its great distance from Europe made travel to the Church of the Holy Sepulcher difficult even before the Muslims took control of Jerusalem in 1157, when the construction of copies became more popular. Priests were sent to Jerusalem to take measurements and make drawings of the Holy Sepulcher so that it could be reproduced "ad similitudinem s. Jerosolimitane ecclesie" closer to home.[39] However, these copies were not always precise with respect to the original's shape, size, or even design. In a study on the inaccuracies of the Holy Sepulcher's copies in central Europe, the German art historian Richard Krautheimer observes that when medieval architects sought to imitate the venerated site *typice* and *figuraliter*, they did not aim at reproducing an exact resemblance of the original.[40] Rather, these copies are reproduced approximately and vaguely, with just enough of the prototype's essential features to evoke its iconographic meanings—that is, it was circular to symbolize virtue and the eternal character of the church, or it had eight columns to signify the resurrection or twelve for the apostles.[41] In this way, the copy became a model concerned with simulating the experience of the essential spatial and symbolic characteristics of the original. By the thirteenth century, however, copies of buildings endowed with religious significance began to emphasize the reproduction of their formal and structural characteristics.

In the case of three thirteenth-century cathedral tower copies created in central Europe, the object of emulation was not the tower's symbolic attributes but, among other formal characteristics, the skeletal configuration of columns making up its corner piers. The particular tower in question was the *tour de l'horloge* of the Notre Dame cathedral in Laon, which was re-created in Switzerland at the cathedral of Lausanne and in Germany in a set of towers and a baldachin at the cathedral of Bamberg. The *tour de l'horloge* stands above the south transept of Laon's cathedral, and like the others at Laon it is characterized by a strong emphasis on the corner buttresses, which consist of a polygonal framework of columns containing sculptures of oxen emerging from the top—a record of their miraculous appearance aiding the completion of the tower's construction. The southwestern tower at the Lausanne cathedral of Notre Dame from the early thirteenth century appears to have been based on the second-level plan and elevation of the Laon tower, but it is visibly stouter and composed of only two almost identical levels with an arcade stretching horizontally across its entire façade. In Bamberg, a baldachin above the statue of the Holy Mary (1235) repeats the corner column motif found at Lausanne but also incorporates the double-story lancet window, creating an almost exact reproduction of the Laon tower's upper two levels in its base. The western cathedral towers embody the same framework of corner columns, with the upper floors going so far as to copy the Laon tower's oxen in its arches. However, unlike the tower baldachin, the western towers have an overall design of regression in which the High Gothic tower design in Laon is sublimated into the even floor-by-floor division and gabled roof of Bamberg's own Romanesque eastern towers. Unlike the copies of the Holy Sepulcher church, the discrepancies between copies of the Laon tower are important because those copies did not aim to reproduce iconographic content. Rather, they demonstrate a practice observed by thirteenth-century scholastics of craftsmen and artisans of the period of copying models or patterns.

Influenced by a growing knowledge of Aristotle, a new group of theologians set out to erect a logical structure for the concept of creation by attributing nontranscendental ideas to the artist.[42] One of these individuals was Robert Grosseteste (1168–1253), who was involved in the design of the Lincoln cathedral; he discussed the ideas of the artist in his *De unica forma omnium*. There Grosseteste refers to the original that the artist imitates as the *forma*, which he also calls *exemplar*. However, instead of viewing it as an object from which an artist makes an identical reproduction, he compares this *forma* to a cobbler's last.[43] As Grosseteste reasons, an architect forms his work through the imitation of a mental *forma* as an *exemplar* to which he gives physical shape in the same way that God created nature from universal *formae exemplares*.[44] In the absence of a physical last for the Laon tower copies, the mental *forma* of the architect can be compared to that of the cobbler, which Grosseteste showed in his commentaries on Aristotle's *Posterior Analytics* could be derived from our sensible experiences with things as an "inner *forma*."[45] In this way the work of thirteenth-century Scholastics can be used to show how in making a copy of the Laon tower, the *exemplar* that the architect imitates is not the physical form or motif of an original (the shoe of the cobbler) but an intermediate invisible *forma* (the last) inspired by it. This is quite different from the concept of an identical reproduction in the nineteenth or twentieth century, for the visual variety between the thirteenth-century copies of the Laon tower does not undermine the authority of the original but reinforces it.

Nine late sixteenth- and early seventeenth-century reconstructions of important sites in the Piedmont and Lombardy regions of northern Italy called Sacri Monti (sacred mountains) present a variation of this central European modeling practice by emphasizing the reproduction of a structure's topographical and spatial characteristics. Intended to reevoke the "New Jerusalem," Sacri Monti are devotional complexes standing on the slopes of a mountain that offer pilgrims an opportunity to visit the Holy Places by re-presenting smaller-scale copies of buildings and locations associated with the story of Christ, from the Annunciation to the Ascension. With the help of rich local families, Sacri Monti were promoted by Father Bernardino Caimi, who sought to re-create the holy sites at Varallo, "so those who could not make the pilgrimage could see Jerusalem right here."[46] Fra Bernardino was responsible in particular for the Sacro Monte di Varallo (sacred mountain of Varallo), whose topography he claimed resembled that of the Holy Land. Yet as Samuel Butler has observed in his study on the Sacro Monte di Varallo, "The resemblance between Varallo and Jerusalem is too far-fetched to have had any bona fide effect on a man of travel and of affairs[;] … there is indeed, a river,—not to say two—and there is a river also only twenty-five miles off Jerusalem; doubtless at one time or another there have been crucifixions in both."[47] The pilgrims climbing the mountain, moving from chapel to chapel, were spectators participating in the reenactment of specific spatial and topographical events recounted in the life of Christ. Comparable to architectural renditions of the Stations of the Cross, each chapel contained an actual scene from the life of Jesus Christ, including polychrome life-size figures, fresco paintings, and props in the same space as that occupied by the viewer. In this way, David Leatherbarrow sees the sequence of architectural events on the hillside as a large-scale "theatre of memory" for "spiritual exercise."[48] For Leatherbarrow, the choreography of these structures and their contents embody rules like those set down by Frances Yates in her classic study *The Art of Memory* (1966) for making mental images that would lodge in the memory of the pilgrim.[49] Unlike copies of the Holy Sepulcher and Laon Tower, emulation is now directed toward the topographical and spatial sequencing of the chapels. At the Sacro Monte di Varallo in particular, the pilgrim who ascended the mountain would encounter the first set of chapels in a sloping garden narrating the story of Christ, from the Annunciation until his arrival in Bethlehem, while those chapels located at the summit are built in an urban context of palazzo and porticos to emulate the urban character of Jerusalem around which the events of Christ's later life occurred.

Today, similar inconsistencies between the materials and measures of original and copy can be found in reconstructions of the Washington, DC, Vietnam Veterans Memorial. Originally designed by Maya Lin in 1981, the war memorial is a V-shaped configuration of two black granite and concrete retaining walls, set into a grassy slope, upon which are inscribed more than 58,000 names of veterans killed in the war. The path alongside each wall is not flat, however, but slowly descends. As the visitor walks down the path the wall becomes taller, accommodating an increasing number of names until the visitor suddenly sees themselves in the mirror reflection of the stone. Just two years after its completion, both traveling and permanent copies were being constructed so that the experience of the memorial could be shared with those unable to travel to Washington to see the original. Although the copies use the same material and formal arrangement of Lin's original design concept, in most replicas the experience of the path created by the walls is lost. The copies are bent slightly inward and retain the pyramid shape, but they are not set into the earth. Thus, visitors will tend to walk on a flat surface while the wall rises up to the sky, and their mimetic experience of the visitor descending and ascending alongside the casualties of the war will be altered. Whether the user is familiar with the intended experience of the original structure or not, the copies of the memorial wall demonstrate how the desire to enable others to experience or for a community to possess a revered structure surpasses the need for it to faithfully reproduce all of the original's measures, materials, forms, and structure.

A similar disregard for reproducing a building's scale and structural attributes appears in a one-fifth-scale reproduction of China's Pavilion for the 2010 Shanghai Expo built in Funing County in China's Jiangsu Province (figure 1.14). Not unlike the medieval copies of the Holy Sepulcher and Renaissance Sacri Monti, the copy of China's Expo pavilion is a simulacrum. Here the copy is concerned only with the external appearance and has none of the original's structural or spatial attributes. For the French sociologist and philosopher Jean Baudrillard, this loosening in contemporary culture of the requirement for an accurate copy belongs to a second order of simulacra, created when advances in mechanical reproduction generate images that mask and pervert the primacy of the original.[50] In these instances, a gap between the original and its copy is permitted, allowing for artistic volition and novelty. For example, in the

| 1.14 |

One-fifth-scale model of China's Pavilion for the 2010 Shanghai Expo, Funing County, Jiangsu Province.

| 1.15 |

Papier-mâché model of the church of St. Maclou in Rouen, France, 1521.

| 1.16 |

Model of the Marienkirche on the Harlunger Berg near Brandenburg, Germany, 1722.

their way into private collections, municipal archives, and academies of architecture as didactic tools.

Already during the early sixteenth century, models of historic, innovative, or civic structures, machines, or other mechanical devices were being collected as important tools for future generations wishing to study buildings, compare them, and retain knowledge about them. These models were used not merely as decorative objects but also for visual and didactic study. In 1565 Samuel Quiccheberg, the Belgian scientific and artistic adviser to Albrecht V, the Duke of Bavaria, published *Inscriptiones vel tituli theatri amplissimi* to demonstrate the pragmatic value of collecting historically, culturally, geographically, zoologically, and artistically significant specimens in specially appointed rooms and cabinets, variously called *Kunstkammern*, *Wunderkammern*, and *Kunstschränke*.[59] In his treatise, Quiccheberg demonstrates that organizing objects made knowledge of them more accessible and that juxtaposed or grouped objects could tell a story. Of particular interest was Quiccheberg's recommendation to collect architectural and engineering models, "[t]iny models of machines, such as those for drawing water, or cutting wood into boards, or grinding grain, driving piles, propelling boats, stopping floods, and the like; on the basis of these models of little machines and constructions, other larger ones can be properly built and, subsequently, better ones invented."[60] In 1563 construction began on a *Kunstkammer* to house a collection that Albrecht V had been amassing in Munich since the beginning of his reign in 1550. Quiccheberg's treatise was likely the conceptual force shaping the project.[61] There were certainly architectural models of existing structures in the Munich *Kunstkammer*. In particular, city models of the duchy's *Residenzenstadt* (seat of government) produced by the woodturner and model maker Jakob Sandtner between 1568 and 1572 gave material presence to these administrative strongholds in the center of the Bavarian state, Munich (figure 1.17).[62] The value of these models was as both a symbolic demonstration of the duke's administrative power and also a tool for military action.[63]

A short distance away from Munich, the Free Imperial City of Augsburg capitalized on its collection of architectural models as didactic tools for technical solutions and advancements in engineering and building construction. Free from aristocratic rule since 1276, Augsburg began collecting models in 1620 when the architect and

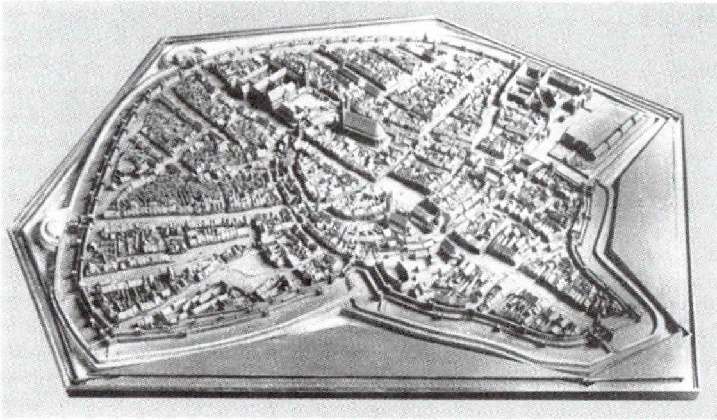

| 1.17 |

Jakob Sandtner, model of the city of Munich, 1570.

| 1.18 |

Model of the Perlach Tower with Elias Holl's scaffold, 1614/15.

designer of the town hall, Elias Holl, founded its municipal model chamber less as a means of symbolic pride or military control than as a storehouse of tools to record important structures and methods of construction.[64] These models included proposed and completed structures and structural engineering models. No less interesting are the models of temporary constructions and of the devices used during the building process, such as the model of the Perlach Tower (1614/15) with a scaffold by Elias Holl (figure 1.18), as well as of the scaffold used from 1747 for the vaulted ceiling of the Sankt Anna Kirche. Also included in this collection are those models called "master pieces," which were produced by handicraft workers—carpenters and masons who were required to construct models not to copy existing structures but to apply existing construction methods in order to demonstrate their mastery of skills in a particular trade.[65] These comprise a variety of technical models for water supply and mill construction that were originally installed in the new water towers for interested

| 1.19 |

Model of a pump works, Augsburg, mid-18th century.

travelers who came to learn from the *Brunnenmeister* (master of the waterworks) (figure 1.19).

It was during this period that the École des Beaux-Arts was founded in France and began amassing its own collection of architectural models and model fragments. This school was established in 1671 by Jean-Baptiste Colbert, a minister to Louis XIV, as the Académie Royale d'Architecture (Royal Academy of Architecture), to provide an education in architecture to individuals who might advise the king on matters concerning the design of royal buildings. Rather than study technical solutions, the Académie was—in the words of François Blondel, its first professor and most distinguished theoretician—intended to assist in the "rétablissement de la belle Architecture" (restoration of beautiful architecture).[66] What Blondel wanted to "restore" was the Roman architecture lost to the world since the fifth century, revived during the Renaissance, and only beginning to be understood in France during the seventeenth century. Included in the models collected at the Académie since its founding until its suppression in 1793 are those of important works, presented to the king at the outset of a project, and also full-scale plaster casts of architectural ornament from classical antiquity—a collection that was substantially expanded in the eighteenth and nineteenth centuries by the Académie's postrevolutionary manifestation, the École des Beaux-Arts.[67] The purpose of these objects was to make possible comparative study so that the school's students could take inspiration from them in their own designs.[68]

Already during the seventeenth century, architects were amassing their own collections of technical models of construction methods and actual fragments or plaster casts of architectural ornament. The German architect Joseph Furttenbach (1591–1667) owned, among other objects, models of bridges, mills, and waterworks, and he installed his own *Kunstkammer* in his house.[69] As the drawings in the Parisian aristocrat Joseph Bonnier de la Mosson's cabinet of curiosities (1744) demonstrate, it was also common for French noblemen to collect objects and devices for scientific study, including architectural models of existing, fantastic, or biblical structures and technical construction models such as cranes or bridges (figure 1.20).[70] In 1774, sixteen models from Blondel's own collection "concerning the theory of penetration of matter in view of cutting stone, the arch of a door from Marseille, models of *trompes*, volutes, roof trusses" were given

to the Académie Royale d'Architecture as "teaching material."[71] Concurrently, private and academic "teaching" collections came to witness the introduction of a new species of architectural model: scale re-presentations of antique constructions made of cork.

Since the eighteenth century, the culmination of an architect's education was a Grand Tour of cultural sites in Europe to study and obtain records of ancient monuments. The primary destination for the traveler was Italy—especially the artistic patrimony of Venice, the archaeological sites surrounding Naples, and most importantly Rome. Unlike distracted contemporary tourists, travelers on a Grand Tour preoccupied themselves with the documentation and collection of antique and modern monuments by creating measured drawings and plaster casts.[72] One of the largest private collections of drawings and objects of antique monuments belonged to Sir John Soane, mentioned at the beginning of this chapter. Having won a

| 1.20 |

Jean-Baptiste Courtonne, section of drawing from Bonnier de la Mosson's cabinet of physical and mechanical objects, 1744.

Gold Medal for Architecture in 1776, Soane was awarded a traveling scholarship paid for by King George III that enabled him to spend two years in Italy. Like many of his European peers (especially architects),[73] Soane amassed a collection of plaster casts, architectural details, measured drawings, and models first at his country house (Pitzhanger Manor, Ealing) and later in three connected houses at 12–14 Lincoln Inn Fields, London, where eventually collection and house became indistinguishable.

Soane's house exemplifies the value of architectural model collections for architectural practice and education during the late eighteenth and nineteenth centuries. Other academic and professional collections of models and plaster casts include those of the École des Beaux-Arts (already mentioned), of the Technische Hochschule in Munich (destroyed during the Second World War; figure 1.21), and of Cornell University in the United States. During the Napoleonic wars

with France, travel to Europe was notoriously difficult, and private collections like Soane's became a replacement for those who were not able to undertake a Grand Tour. Interspersed throughout the domestic spaces of Soane's house were an architectural office that later doubled as a studio for training apprentices, an archaeological museum, an archive of drawings and folios, a professional and scholarly library, an art gallery of folding wall panels, and a room-size display of architectural models.[74] Many models in collections like Soane's were constructed of cork—a material that lent itself well to mimicking the porous surface structure of travertine and tufus-formed remnants of actual antique constructions. Soane owned fourteen cork models, including one of the Temple of Vesta at Tivoli (figure 1.22) that inspired his northeast corner of the Bank of England.[75] During his tenure as professor of architecture at the Royal Academy of Arts in London, Soane argued that historical models could be set alongside

| 1.21 |

Teaching collection of the Technische Hochschule in Munich, 1917.

| 1.22 }

Giovanni Altieri, cork model of Temple of Vesta in Tivoli, Italy, 1770s.

contemporary designs to reveal not only how buildings were to be composed but also how technology was constantly reinvented by different civilizations at various stages.[76] Soane's collection is one of the few still remaining in its original configuration, thereby providing valuable insights into the collection, display, and use of models in pedagogical and design practices during the nineteenth century.

In other spheres of cultural edification, the miniature re-presentation of architecture was an important tool during the nineteenth century for the education of taste. To help individuals comprehend fundamental geometric principles and specifically develop a sensibility regarding their use in architectural composition, the German mathematician, teacher, and technician Heinrich Rockstroh promoted the modeling of German houses and agricultural structures with folded paper (figure 1.23).[77] Rockstroh's book *Anweisung zum Modelliren aus Papier oder aus demselben allerley Gegenstände im Kelinen nachzuahmen, Ein nütlicher Zeitreib für Kinder* (1802) echoed Johann Heinrich Pestalozzi's pedagogical theory that a lesson can be successful only when the head, heart, and hands of the pupil are all spoken to. Rockstroh proposed that children should cut and fold simple paper models of identifiable architectural structures in order to develop a sensibility regarding the compositions of geometrical shapes such as equilateral triangles, pyramids, and cubes.

| 1.23 |

Heinrich Rockstroh, preparatory drawings for cutaway models of houses, from *Anweisung zum Modelliren aus Papier oder aus demselben allerley Gegenstände im Kelinen nachzuahmen, Ein nütlicher Zeitreib für Kinder*, 1802.

| 1.24 |

Hermann Finsterlin, *Das Stilspiel*, 1921/22.

Because of its later influence on architectural design practices, another didactic activity developed during the first half of the nineteenth century by the father of kindergarten, Friedrich Fröbel, is worth examining. In supervised play with precut simple geometrical building blocks, organized into didactic exercises of increasing complexity called "gifts," Fröbel saw a means of enabling children to perceive a relationship between the whole and part of such structures as a bath, house, or church and of providing them with an opportunity to use, apply, or modify what they had learned.[78] Shortly after the end of the First World War, in 1921, the German expressionist architect Hermann Finsterlin began to experiment with the application of similar principles in a block set he created called *Stilspiel* (play with styles). Unlike Rockstroh's paper models or Fröbel's wooden gifts, Finsterlin's building blocks were not simple geometrical forms but were derived from identifiable architectural structures, including a Gothic cathedral, pyramid, mosque, and Greek temple (figure 1.24). As

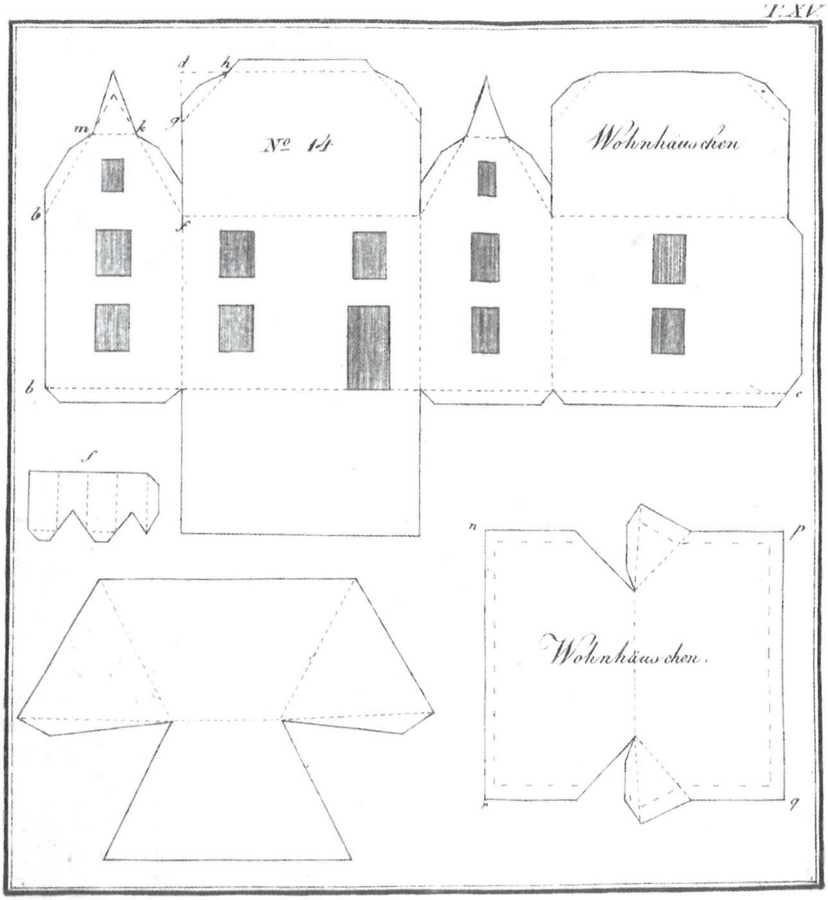
T.XV
Nº 14
Wohnhäuschen
Wohnhäuschen.

is clearly indicated by the subtitle to Finsterlin's article "Die Genesis der Weltarchitektur oder die Deszendenz der Dome als Stilspiel: Ein Lehr-, Spiel- und Versuchsbaukasten" (The genesis of world architecture or the evolution of the cathedral as stylistic game: A teaching-, play-, and experimentation building blocks set), they were intended to function both as a children's toy and as a design tool for architects, who he suggested "would like to seize the impartiality of the child to rid themselves of their cultural inhibitions."[79] Like a child at play with a found object, the architect who works with assemblages of building blocks as an architectural modeling method is encouraged to speculate by inserting their imagination precisely between wondering at and asking "what if." The implications of this method for designers will be discussed further in chapter 6 of this book.

……………………

STILL TODAY, ONE CAN witness in the early semesters of their education architecture students tasked with modeling the forms and spaces of distant structures. For most institutions, these activities are not intended to teach students to copy structures as ideals or to enforce a given style on a generation of architects. Rather, by constructing the formal and spatial characteristics of a revered work of architecture, students are enabled to experience a distant structure and absorb its formal and spatial characteristics through their eyes and hands—memories that they draw on when constructing models of their own designs. In the tradition of the eighteenth- and nineteenth-century Grand Tourist, these exercises demonstrate a reversal of Winston Churchill's 1944 argument that "[w]e shape our buildings, and afterwards, our buildings shape us":[80] an architect studying existing structures might suggest that "our buildings shape us and afterwards we shape our buildings." It is this exchange between model, building, and user that makes the signification, simulation, and projection of architecture possible. The use of architectural models to visualize and inspire new designs is the subject of the chapters in the second half of this book.

2

DREAMING BY THE MODEL

BUTLER. Did you notice ... did you notice that there is a model within that room in the castle? A model of the model?

JULIAN. I ... I did. But ... I didn't register it, it seemed so ... continual.

BUTLER. (A shy smile.) You don't suppose that within that tiny model in the model there, there is ... another room like this, with yet a tinier room within it, and within ...

JULIAN. (Laughs.) ... and within and within and within and ... ?

No, I ... rather doubt it. It's remarkable craftsmanship, though. Remarkable.

BUTLER. (Crosses to sideboard, puts spoon in U. drawer, shuts drawer.) Hell to clean.[1]

IN THE ABOVE EXCERPT from the American playwright Edward Albee's allegorical drama *Tiny Alice* (1965), the discussion focuses on a large architectural model of the very castle within which it sits. Miss Alice is the owner of the castle, and the architectural model depicts the castle itself in remarkable detail. The characters interact with this model; they wonder and make observations about it, referring to the model and the mansion as the same thing. As the play gathers momentum, the model begins to take on more importance when Julian, a priest whom Miss Alice wishes to seduce into marriage, discovers that the model in the library contains an even smaller model of the mansion it depicts—the home of a presumably smaller Alice of whom Miss Alice is only a re-presentation. In this replacement of reality by its re-presentation, imaginative play with the model is conflated with the actual activities of the mansion's inhabitants. This exchange is made most explicit when a fire breaks out in the model's chapel, causing the characters to rush off to put out a fire in the chapel of the real mansion. Albee's play reveals an important characteristic about the use of a model: it is a tool by which the imagination may contemplate architecture infinitely in regress, since, as the play demonstrates, "reality" is also a model.

Perhaps the most famous precedent for Miss Alice's imposing house within a house was a dollhouse created by the English architect Edwin Lutyens for Queen Mary between 1921 and 1924 (figure 2.1). Just as Miss Alice's model was a miniature reproduction of her own home, so too the Queen's Doll House incorporated miniature replicas of the items in Windsor Castle, including some of the queen's own possessions that actually work, among them shotguns that "break and load," monogrammed linens, electric lights and lifts, running water, a flushing toilet, a garage of cars with engines that run, and a collection of original works of art and literature. Designed in the style of Sir Christopher Wren or Inigo Jones, the Queen's Doll House was filled by Lutyens with thousands of objects made by leading artists, designers, and craftsmen, nearly all on the tiny scale of 1:12, making it an ideal representation of an early twentieth-century aristocratic home.[2] Because the Queen's Doll House included many of the items found within the queen's everyday life, it endowed users—which at least for a time included the queen herself—with the possibility of imagining both real and fictional events that might take place in their daily life.

| 2.1 |

Queen Mary's Doll House, as seen from the northeast, 1935.

Throughout the nineteenth century, dollhouses like the one for Queen Mary were promoted as teaching tools for cultivating ideas about moral order and taste in young women who would one day keep and furnish their own houses. These models were meant to represent the interior of a house and many of its familiar contents in extraordinary proportional detail—literally creating a house within a house. Whereas a young woman could manipulate the objects within the house in order to act out different events of everyday life, architects also construct and alter their models to permit the playful contemplation or reverie that different formations and transformations of the materials, forms, or structural elements might elicit.

This notion of the model as a vehicle of imaginative play is central to its use as a tool for enabling someone to think about a structure that is not immediately present. The importance of this activity in the development of cultural objects is well expressed by the Dutch historian Johan Huizinga in his seminal work *Homo Ludens* (1938). For Huizinga, play is a voluntary and meaningful activity, segregated from the obligations of practical life.[3] He argues that culture develops thanks to the capacity of living beings—animals and humans—to change their experience through the freedom to create new play "realities." As Huizinga explains, "Play only becomes possible, thinkable and understandable when an influx of mind breaks down the absolute determinism of the cosmos." He proposes the existence in play of a "magic circle," within which a group agrees that "the laws and customs of ordinary life no longer count. We are different and do things differently."[4] This is to say that when a child is alone playing with dolls, they become the doll—or, as Huizinga's most famous interlocutor, Roger Caillois, observes, the child "forgets, disguises, or temporarily sheds his personality in order to feign another."[5] This notion of play also occurs when one is dreaming, whether in reverie about architecture or in sleep. In terms of the architectural model, the word "dream" thus refers to the imaginative contemplation of its materials, forms, and spaces as an actual or proposed spatial, material, and structural architecture.

This chapter focuses on the model as a medium for architectural reverie, and its title pays homage to Elaine Scarry's *Dreaming by the Book* (1999)[6]—a study on the construction and manipulation of images according to rules or "formal practices" provoked by the text.

Like a book, the architect's model can also offer its user an opportunity to explore imaginary ideas, however impractical or unbuildable, by creating, as Jun Yanagisawa remarks about the use of models by Toyo Ito, "a labyrinth of reality and fiction."[7] When left incomplete, a model invites the user to speculate on the missing parts, while a proportionally inaccurate model can deceive a client who is unfamiliar with the rules of scale about the size or structural congruency between it and the to-be-constructed architecture. Conversely, in the hands of an architect, the exchange of one modeling material for another or the assemblage, juxtaposition, and recombination of existing models and their parts can incite the imagination to contemplate new and unexpected ideas. Despite their differences, these activities with models have a common goal: to encourage the model's users to dream about an architectural idea that they may not be able to envision on their own.

THE ONEIRIC MODEL OF ARCHITECTURE

Most architects can easily tell when a model presents a faithful or false rendition of structure at a larger scale. That is to say, when working on a scale architectural model, the architect knows that it represents a fiction since the depicted building does not (yet) exist; but they will still select and transform their modeling materials as if these were the real building materials at the prescribed scale. The conflation of the faithful and the false, the real and the fictitious, is the locus of an architect's imagination, which must dream fictions in the space of reality. This is certainly the case for the citizens of the imaginary city of Fedora, a gray stone metropolis in Italo Calvino's book *Invisible Cities* (1972); in its center is a metal building, every room of which contains a crystal globe, each holding the model of a different Fedora.[8] The inhabitants of Fedora visit this metal building and choose the miniature model that matches their desires while imagining what Fedora would have become if for one reason or another it were not the city it is. In Calvino's tale, Fedora's citizens demonstrate a use of the scale architectural model to invite imaginative reverie. It is because these models of a familiar place are constructed according to a proportional relationship between the human body and the proposed architecture that the visitor is able to imaginatively inhabit them. For an architect, this proportional ratio is essential to a playful imagination of architecture. By juxtaposing the "real" and the imaginary, an architect's models, like those of Fedora, become oneiric (dreamlike) when they are foiling their user's attempts at finding a resting point in the real.

The term "oneiric" has its root in the Greek *oneiros*, meaning "dream." In Greek mythology, the Oneiroi belong to a class of guiding spirits or tutelary deities known as daemons and are responsible for dreams.[9] In Homer's *Odyssey* 19.562–567, dreams travel through one of two gates: the first is transparent, made of polished horn, and the second is opaque, made of sawn ivory. Dreams that passed through the gate of horn were believed to be prophetic and sent by the gods, while dreams that came through the ivory gate were considered false and would not be fulfilled. For the Greek architect, it is Phantasos, a son of Sleep, who in dreams personifies inanimate objects like earth, rock, water, wood, and even architecture.[10] The scale architectural model may be included in this list and compared to what passes through the gate of horn, since its spatial, material, and formal characteristics are a guide—as suggested by the early German term for "model," *Visierung* (guide, gunsight)—used by the imagination to project the depicted structure, whether existing or proposed. But an architect may also choose to temporarily suspend their contemplation of a scale model as a miniature representation of real materials, structure, and space in order to invite reverie about the place it describes. Like those dreams that pass through the ivory gate, a model created by the architect may intentionally not present a faithful rendition of a proposed or existing structure but rather be left incomplete, inaccurate, or composed of modeling materials that can be easily exchanged and rearranged. In this "oneiric" state, the model invites speculative reverie about the missing parts, methods of construction, and new configurations of form that are essential to dreaming about architecture and the discovery of new architectural ideas. This section explores the different ways in which models and modeling materials have been used since antiquity to encourage dreaming about architecture.

An early example of an oneiric model of architecture is the early Egyptian funerary model. Since as early as the predynastic period (pre-3000 BCE), ancient Egyptian pharaohs were accompanied in their tombs by proportionally accurate models of everyday structures.

| 2.2 |

Model of a granary with scribes, ca. 1981–1975 BCE.

With the exception of some barges, these funerary models are isolated from their contexts and depict just enough of an entire structure to show the activities that occur in or at them, enabling them to be identified as granaries, gardens, and bakeries or textile-weaving shops, slaughterhouses, and so on (figure 2.2). These models, however, should not be confused with ancient Egyptian toys such as spinning tops, wooden dolls, carved animals, or several types of board games.[11] Rather, they were important tools for the *ka* or life-force of the pharaoh, which required a body to survive—either the preserved mummy or a model of the pharaoh known as a *ka* statue. Because the *ka* required the same sustenance in death as in life, after an Egyptian pharaoh died, food was delivered regularly to their *ka* statue while models of everyday life—people working in rooms—were placed in their tomb to perform the same functions. These were not teaching tools or representations of proposed designs but imaginatively habitable substitutes—approximate representations of everyday structures for the pharaoh's *ka*. In the same way that the pharaoh could dream with a model in life, it was believed that the *ka* could continue its reverie of everyday activities after death. Without roofs and devoid of additional information about their location in reference to other models included in a tomb, they take on a function similar to that of pieces of furniture in a nineteenth-century dollhouse, able to be combined and rearranged according to the different narratives imagined by their user.

An Egyptian funerary model or dollhouse may look like a miniature depiction of architectural materials and their assembly, but modeling materials have their own scales and limitations that don't always correspond to those of the structures they portray. Already during the Roman period, architects knew they could undermine an audience's assumptions about the model as a faithful rendition of architecture and used this method to obtain commissions. In book 10 of his treatise on architecture, Vitruvius provides one account of this activity as he describes how an architect from Aradus, named Callias, won the job of city architect through the deceptive use of an architectural model. While visiting the city of Rhodes, according to Vitruvius, Callias presented models of a crane and a city wall arranged to show the crane lifting a third model, an approaching siege tower, over the wall and into the city. The audience was impressed by the skill that Callias demonstrated by his model and immediately hired him as their city architect. However, when asked to build his crane in order to save the city during an actual siege, Callias was forced to confess that he could not, since the structural and mechanical properties of materials at one size cannot necessarily be duplicated at another. As Callias explained, "There are some things that achieve large-scale results like those with small models. And then there are other things for which models [*exemplaria*] cannot be made at all and they must be built to scale in the first place."[12] In Vitruvius's example, the audience assumes that the architect's model is a faithful representation of an actual crane lifting a siege tower over a city wall. The citizens of Rhodes were drawn in by Callias and his model—a case illustrating not the willing suspension of disbelief but the persuasiveness and power of models to inspire. Generally, this act of faith in models exemplifies Huizinga's "magic circle," an agreement among the participants to believe that the model being presented to them in miniature is a true representation of architecture at full size.

Even when a reduced-scale architectural model is a faithful rendition of an existing or proposed building, it can be the locus of contemplative reverie, because it simultaneously represents the real and the fictitious. The fact that the model must be built in order for it to exist emphasizes the model's role as an important tool for imagining architecture. As a physical construction, the model is real. Yet because modeling materials are not building materials, it is a fiction and the architect must interpret its spatial, structural, or formal aspects as a faithful depiction of a real building. It is in this interplay between real and fiction that an architect may also decide to suspend their use of modeling materials as true portrayals of a proposed structure in order to encourage their own musings about a possible place.

One approach that early twentieth-century German architects explored as a method for imagining new architectural ideas was to use children's building blocks as a modeling material.[13] A familiar example of this practice is Herman Finsterlin's 1921 *Stilspiel* (play with styles) building blocks set, discussed in chapter 1, which was based on identifiable examples of world architecture. In Bruno Taut's short-lived architectural journal *Frühlicht*, Finsterlin promoted *Stilspiel* as both a children's toy and a design tool for architects, who he suggested would like to adopt the impartiality of a child and rid themselves of their cultural inhibitions by finding inspiration for new architectural ideas in the decomposition and recomposition of Gothic cathedrals, pyramids, and so on.[14] In the same issue of *Frühlicht*, the amateur architect and Merz artist Kurt Schwitters promoted a similar use of "beliebiger Materialien" (found materials) to refresh an architect's imagination.[15] Using his model *Schloss und Kathedrale mit Hofbrunnen* (Castle and Cathedral with Courtyard Well) as an example, he argued that the selection and use of a found object as a modeling material depended on how well it can lose its original identity and take on the "representative material as well as constructive possibilities" of the proposed building.[16]

In 1978 the Italian architect Aldo Rossi created a model he called a *Teatrino Scientifico* (Little Scientific Theater), making use of a similar opportunity afforded by juxtaposing multiple scales and dimensions of both existing and projected designs (figure 2.3).[17] Conceived as a machine for architectural experimentation, this model was called "scientific" by Rossi to recall eighteenth-century Italian anatomical

theaters like those in Mantua and Padua.[18] Like a cabinet displaying a collection of objects, Rossi's *Teatrino Scientifico* contains models of his 1974 Milan Gallaratese Housing project in the foreground and a pictorial representation of various structures in the background, including his design for the 1972 Modena Cemetery. As Christian Hubert notes, "Rossi's work continuously presents and represents. His analogical enterprise, like Surrealism, juxtaposes the 'real' and the imaginary, allowing for a continual interplay, a constant substitution.

| 2.3 |

Aldo Rossi, *Teatrino Scientifico*, 1978.

And like Surrealism, his work foils any attempt to find a resting point in the real."[19]

In creating a model of architecture, the architect may choose to undermine their own assumptions about it as a proportionally accurate representation of structural performance in order to invite speculation and reverie about new form. As Callias observed and Galileo proved with his square cube law, the functioning of materials at a small scale is not a proportional imitation of the same materials at a larger scale.[20] The American architect Frank Gehry knowingly exploited this lack of congruence in his use of crumpled, bent, or twisted paper and card when he created preliminary models for such projects as his 2004 Brooklyn Arena or MIT Ray and Maria Stata Center projects, to name only two (figure 2.4). In themselves, the forms created by crumpled and bent paper or card have their own scale. Like the model crane that Callias presented to the citizens of Rhodes, Gehry's paper constructions are meant to intentionally suspend his own assumptions about the model as a proportionally accurate representation of material or structural performance. For Callias, the aim was to dupe the audience. By contrast, by exploiting the oneiric possibilities of his modeling materials, Gehry is free to speculate and engage in the contemplative reverie of architectural possibilities.

An example of this approach to the oneiric model is found in the work of the American architect Lebbeus Woods. A self-described "experimental architect," Woods developed a body of architectural and urban propositions that challenges tectonic possibility "with the purpose of gaining experience for its own sake."[21] Inspired by disaster-stricken cities, Woods created a vast collection of intricate drawings and models of splintered architectural surfaces and twisted wiry masses he likened to "scabs" over the "wounds" of buildings damaged by war and natural catastrophe. Woods views his designs as "experimental architecture" and is not concerned with matters of style or buildability.[22] Those investigations expressed in model form, such as the Meta-Institute from 1996, Siteline Vienna from 1998, or Nine Reconstructed Boxes from 1999, show large portions of structure supported by cardboard, polystyrene, and wood, which, in their proposed guise as concrete, steel, and glass, would be precariously vulnerable to the forces of wind and gravity. But for Woods, the act of drawing or modeling his architectural ideas is as much an act of testing their

| 2.4 |

Frank Gehry, Brooklyn Arena study of basswood, paper, gatorboard, pushpins, 1:40 scale, 2004.

viability as of building itself.[23] Rather, by undermining the accuracy of the building structure's simulation in the model's structure, Wood's designs become oneiric, providing the user with, as Lebbeus Woods and his collaborator Christoph Kampusch explain, an "opportunity to experience a type of space we haven't experienced before."[24] In reference to these qualities, the philosopher Karsten Harries observes that "the conspicuous strangeness of what we see disturbs and distances us from the familiar. Such distance invites more thoughtful consideration of what architecture has come to be and mean, and its ruling ethos."[25] Woods's designs demonstrate that oneiric models, as works of fantasy, may be an end in themselves. Callias's crane belongs to a similar use of the architectural model, since it was never intended to be built but was meant to merely provoke wonder and admiration in its audience. In contrast, those models or modeling methods employed by Gehry, Finsterlin, or Schwitters are intended not to deceive a client but to inspire the imagination of the architect to speculate about new architectural possibilities. A similar role will be attributed to models of architectural ruins and fragments discussed later in this chapter.

THE CATHEXIS OF MODELS AND THEIR MATERIALS

Over the past thirty years, the Office of Metropolitan Architecture (OMA), a Dutch architectural firm, has cultivated a unique design process synonymous with visualizing and testing architectural ideas in physical models. Inside the OMA office, design is a collaborative activity defined by minute material operations, using models and plans, in which concepts are questioned at every stage of design. OMA architects have the freedom to choose their materials, methods, and working hours, but everything starts with models. They have developed a preference for blue Styrofoam as a modeling material to engage in a bottom-up, labor-intensive, research-led way of questioning everything. A former OMA collaborator, Fenna Wagenaar, explains that "you can do anything with Styrofoam—cut it with a knife, dissolve it with spray paint, glue it, warp it with a hot glue gun, burn holes in it with your cigarette, and transport it on a plane. The material is easy and quick to work with. No OMA without it. ... In Rotterdam ideas are never judged before they are materialized."[26] The numerous models on display or in the archives of OMA's Rotterdam office attest to designers' affinity for the imaginative potential of blue foam in their architectural practice.

The preoccupation of an architect with a particular modeling material or idea as a medium for designing architecture is not unusual. One can observe similar types of fixation in Louis Kahn's interrogation of the brick as a fundamental building element or Adolf Loos's focus on etiquette as an approach to design purity. In psychoanalysis, Sigmund Freud labels this investment of mental or emotional energy (the psychic energy of the libido) in a person, object, or idea with the German word *Besetzung*, literally "occupation" or "charge, energy, interest." For his English translation of Freud's complete works, James Strachey chose to render *Besetzung* as "cathexis." Originally deriving from the Greek word *kathexis*, or "holding," cathexis can ultimately be traced back (through *katechein*, "to hold fast, occupy") to the Greek verb *echein*, "to have" or "to hold." Freud used different metaphors to describe what he meant by cathexis, including the occupation of a place with troops. This trope suggests that the libido is sent out to "seize" an external object, idea, or person as an army would seize and occupy a city. In architectural terms a designer may cathect a model, modeling material, or the forms it produces for a variety of reasons, sometimes personal and sometimes religious.

An early example of the overwhelming fixation of the architectural imagination on a material is given by Abbot Suger, a twelfth-century French clergyman, historian, and adviser to Louis VI and VII. Suger is best known in architectural history for documenting the rebuilding of the abbey church of Saint-Denis—an important structure in the development of Gothic architecture. In his memoirs, Suger recorded the work on the cathedral, providing one of the most celebrated descriptions of cathecting the "multifarious wealth of precious stones" to heighten religious experience. When these materials were used in the making of a Gothic reliquary or other religious object, Suger claimed, they would cause him to "reflect, transferring that which is material to that which is immaterial" and to be "transported from this inferior to that higher world in an anagogical manner."[27] This "anagogical" perception of art and architecture essentially derived from a dictum attributed to the early Christian theologian Origen of Alexandria: "the visible world contains images of heavenly things in order that by means of these lower objects we may rise to that which is beyond."[28] Because of the important role played by reliquaries and other religious objects in religious experience, they came to have a profound influence on the design of the cathedral's macro-architecture.

Beginning in the mid-thirteenth century, one can observe an important exchange between the formal vocabulary of the cathedral and the architectonic designs of the church reliquaries, monstrances, and censors it housed—that is, the cathedral's micro-architecture. A survey of the development of cathedral micro-architecture north of the Alps reveals a progressive sublimation of architectural forms but not of the structural principles of their larger ideals, like those displayed in the two-aisled basilica shrine of the Three Kings (1181–1230) by Nicolas de Verdun at the Cologne cathedral (figure 2.5).[29] Beginning in the thirteenth century, the use of Gothic arches, pinnacles, and spires in screens, stalls, lecterns, and small reliquaries like that at the shrine of St. Taurin in Evreux (1240–1255) had become more sophisticated (figure 2.6).[30] Likewise, stone structures such as the rood screen at St. Elisabeth in Marburg (1308–1331) show how the design procedures of the goldsmiths had been integrated into nonstructural objects.[31] In the Three Towers reliquary of Aachen (1390) or the 12-meter Sacrament Tabernacle by Matthieu De Layens of St. Peter's Church in Louvain (1450–1490), more delicate and elongated versions of Gothic design combinations were invented and employed (figure 2.7).[32] In these examples, the squares, triangles, and polygons used in the design of the micro-architecture were no longer limited by their predictable geometrical rotation in the design of Gothic cathedrals and their parts. Rather, the fantastic descriptions in medieval literature of buildings and particularly of the heavenly Jerusalem fueled the craftsmen's efforts to perform sophisticated experiments with architectural form in order to construct micro-renditions of these gigantic imaginary edifices.[33] A similar if not identical manipulation of geometrical forms occurred in the arts of goldsmithery and architecture, as shown by the use of similar drawing techniques for reliquaries, monstrances, and baldachins that blur the distinctions between the making of the micro- and macro-architecture (figure 2.8).[34] No longer were designs in stone limited to simple forms. As illustrated by Lorenz Lechler's 1486 design for a tabernacle at St. Dionysius in Esslingen or by Anton

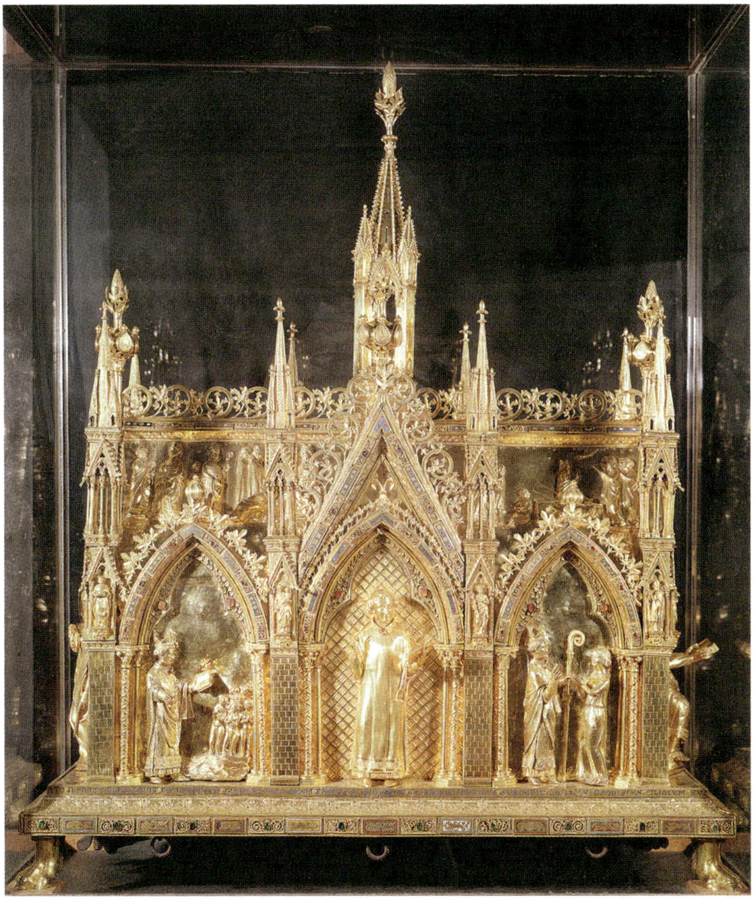

| 2.5 |

Nicolas de Verdun, Shrine of the Three Kings, Cologne Cathedral, Cologne, Germany, 1181–1230.

| 2.6 |

Reliquary of St. Taurin, Church of Saint-Taurin, Evreux, France, 1240–1255.

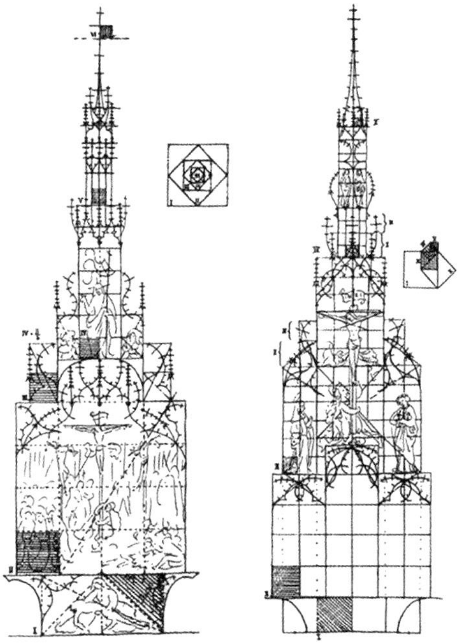

Pilgrim's 1513 organ podium at St. Stephen Cathedral in Vienna, complex, starlike ornamental rotations of squares and heavy, undercut, double-curved stonework create a surreal organic abstraction rising from the building's floor and wall planes. The heavy iron reinforcing used to support the cathedral spires, such as those of Freiburg (1354) and Cologne (planned 1310–1320), demonstrates the overwhelming cathexis with which Gothic architects endowed the spatial and formal characteristics of the micro-architecture in stone. The fifteenth-century Milan goldsmith and architect Antonio di Pietro Averlino, better known as Filarete, gives historical credence to this exchange of scales in the design of Gothic architecture, suggesting that because of a lack of practical skill, Italian architects turned to goldsmiths and painters from north of the Alps, who carried the Gothic forms of tabernacles and censers over to architecture.[35]

| 2.7 |

Matthieu De Layens, Sacrament Tabernacle, St. Peter's Cathedral, Louvain, Belgium, 1450–1490.

| 2.8 |

Elevation of a baldachin (left) and a monstrance (right).

South of the Alps, small-scale architectures retained their role as experimental exempla for cathedral architecture during the fifteenth and sixteenth centuries. Of these the most important are what Alina Payne has referred to as *Kleinarchitektur* (small architecture)—chancels, altars, tombs, tabernacles, freestanding chapels, pulpits, baptismal fonts, sarcophagi, fountains, and so on.[36] These small architecture-related objects are different from the cathedral reliquaries and scale architectural models being produced in Italy during this time. Unlike a scale model of the cathedral, *Kleinarchitektur* is made not of substances that represent something else (stone) but of the actual materials of architecture—limestone, marble, granite, mosaic, and so on. *Kleinarchitektur* therefore provided architects with an opportunity to experiment with materials, carving techniques, and the assemblage of the forms at full scale, enabling them to assess rather than speculate on the surface effects and texture that might be applied to the larger cathedral edifice. These refinements were emulated in, for example, the windows of the Palazzo Ducale in Urbino, which, as Payne claims, "recall the look of jewellery more than the look of imperial Roman building details."[37]

A notable instance of the obsession with the use of architectural models during the late eighteenth century is found in the decorative confectionary architectural *pièces montées*—table settings created for formal banquets—made by the French confectioner Marie-Antoine (Antonin) Carême. His father was a common laborer who abandoned Carême when the boy was only ten years old.[38] The details of Carême's induction into the culinary arts are unclear, but at the age of seventeen he obtained an apprenticeship with Sylvain Bailly, a well-known pastry chef who taught him to make pastry and encouraged him to learn how to read and then write and study in the Cabinet des Gravures (Department of Prints/Engravings) of the Bibliothèque Nationale.[39] At the library, Carême became infatuated with the architecture of Egypt, Greece, and Italy, and despite lacking architectural training or practice he began to conceive how he could use the materials of a pâtisserie to create his own designs in confectioner's paste, nougat, marzipan, and spun sugar as *pièces montées*, which Bailly would display in his pâtisserie window. The success of Carême's method of constructing architectural models won him the title "The Palladio of the Kitchen," and in 1815 he published 124 designs for *pièces montées* preceded by a treatise on architecture in a volume titled *Le pâtissier pittoresque, précédé d'un traité des cinq ordres d'architecture* (The picturesque pastry chef, preceded by a treatise on the five orders of architecture) (figure 2.9).[40] In it Carême argued for an association between architecture and pastry, proposing that "[t]he fine

arts are five in number—namely painting, sculpture, poetry, music, and architecture—the principal branch of the latter being pastry."[41] Indeed, the development of Carême's confectionary structures coincided with the revival of interest in the classical period. Confectionary architectural table settings were copied all over Europe, and their inclusion at a dinner party was believed to have an elevating effect on its participants, inspiring them to engage in erudite conversations about historical monuments and works of art.

In such instances, when a model has or is believed to have a powerful effect on its viewers, it can be said to take on the characteristic of a fetish. This is not a fetish in the Freudian sense (a strong cathexis that results from a man's displacement of castration anxiety onto the nongenital parts of a woman's body). Rather, it is more akin to a form of quasi-religious idolatry whose antecedents are found in premodern West African culture. In a series of three articles on the fetish, William Pietz explained that the term derives from the Portuguese pidgin word "fetisso,"[42] which emerged during the late sixteenth century when Portuguese and Dutch traders used it to describe objects thought by the West Africans to be endowed with "quasi-personal powers" that could have an effect on the material world.[43] At the end of the eighteenth century, the German philosopher G.W.F. Hegel saw a connection between the African fetish and European concepts of magic and idolatry.[44] According to Hegel, fetish objects in African culture could be anything that they arbitrarily imbued with imaginary power. As Hegel observed, if the fetish failed, it would

| 2.9 |

Antonin Carême, "Pièces montées," from *Le pâtissier pittoresque*, 1815.

| 2.10 |

Carl Joseph May, cork model of the Arch of Constantine, ca. 1792–1814.

be abandoned for another, and Africans thereby retained power over what they imagined held power over them: "The substance always remains in the power of the subject."[45] To call a model its materials or methods of construction a fetish is to imply that its user ascribes to them a transformative power on the basis of irrational, acausal criteria.

The increasing popularity of the European Grand Tour during the late eighteenth and early nineteenth centuries coincided with the displacement of pastry *pièces montées* by more durable and technically accurate cork models. This exchange of pastry for cork resonates with the use and disuse of fetishes that William Pietz and Hegel observed in West African culture. So inspired was the *Hofkonditor* (court confectioner) Carl Joseph May (1747–1822) by cork as an ideal medium for establishing a scholarly alliance between material and spiritual foods in dinner conversations about cultural topics that he took up the

| 2.11 |

Carl Joseph May, model of the tomb of the Horatii and Curiatii, 1813.

profession of cork modeler and, presumably because of this work, was later appointed *Baurat* (building adviser) (figures 2.10–11).[46] For all of his skill, however, May was known to copy models of models—and in one instance also the errors and signature of the most successful architectural cork modeler in Italy, Antonio Chichi (1743–1816).[47] Because the model was a fetish object, its inauthenticity did not seem to have diminished its perceived ability to inspire erudite conversation.[48] Their artistic and technical quality ensured that cork models found their way into private hands and public academies as didactic tools. The next section shows how these models were thought to endow their user with a propensity for furnishing innovative architectural solutions.

COLLECTIONS

In *The Savage Mind* (1962), the French anthropologist Claude Lévi-Strauss proposes the concept of bricolage as a mode of acquiring knowledge that resonates with the collection and use of architectural models. Lévi-Strauss claims that no fundamental differences exist between the ways that modern humans and "primitive" peoples think and acquire knowledge. To support his argument, he introduces the concept of the "savage mind" as an ever-present alternative to the "scientific mind." For Lévi-Strauss, a craftsman uses materials and tools in a normative or "scientific" way, while a bricoleur, possessing a "savage mind," assembles found objects—often the products of the craftsman's work—in new ways and makes do with whatever is at hand. Lévi-Strauss argues that craftsmen may be fully in control of their materials and tools, but their approach to making prevents them from seeing beyond the conventional range of preconceived uses. By contrast, bricoleurs will acquire objects they deem useful without knowing their ultimate purposes.[49] An architect may similarly keep a collection of models of existing or proposed structures. These objects are not denuded of their utility as depictions of specific designs, but in the context of the collection they become tools that can be assembled and reassembled in ways both accidental and intentional so that the architect may imagine new architectural solutions.

One example of this practice from the nineteenth century is Sir John Soane's house-cum-museum, mentioned in chapter 1. In 1827, a book review of John Britton's *The Union of Architecture, Sculpture, and Painting* in *Gentleman's Magazine* called Soane's house "an edifice intended solely for his own domestic uses, private tastes, and particular attachments."[50] Indeed, Soane's house contained over one hundred scale architectural models of buildings Soane himself designed, twenty plaster models of antique buildings envisioned in their original or ideal state, and fourteen cork models of ancient buildings in their current ruined condition. Many of these items were carefully displayed in a designated model room on a single pedestal so that the models of his own buildings could dwell on equal terms with the architecture of antiquity.[51] As a collector of architectural models, Soane is different from Walter Benjamin's collector of books, who develops a magic circle of ownership around the activity of collecting.[52] Rather, Soane collected his models in order to learn from them, teach with them, and find inspiration in them for his own designs. As noted above, his cork model of the Temple of Vesta at Tivoli by Giovanni Altieri certainly falls into this category, and Soane used it as a stimulus for the "Tivoli Corner" of his Bank of England design.

Perhaps cork models of ruined antique structures came to acquire such value for architectural collections because of the connection of the ruin to the German Romantic movement. As a philosophical and artistic movement, Romanticism was in part a reaction to Enlightenment philosophy and scientific thinking, which fostered the idea that all persons possess a similar faculty of reason that can reflect, analyze, and grasp the universe's logical order, assumed to be known a priori.[53] A handful of individuals inspired by similar interests in philosophy, literature, and art gathered in the German town of Jena around Friedrich Schlegel and called the products of their new movement "Romantic." For these individuals, the creation and experience of art could parallel nature's creative processes and play a decisive role in gaining a sense of an invisible foundation common to all things.[54] Enthused by this potential of artistic experience, the Jena Romantics embraced the use of glimpses, fragments, and intimations rather than reproductions mirroring nature's externality, which they viewed as eternally becoming.[55] The tensions between intention and accident, past and present, nature and spirit are brought together in the ruin as contradictory strivings of the same creative force, and thus its cork model is especially appealing for the contemplative reverie of nature's becoming. For those engaged in the creative visualization of an idea, the plaster cast fragment or cork model of an architectural ruin may act like a passage of poetry from which words or lines are missing, an absence inviting the imagination to construe alternate ways of making it whole. In the context of a collection, model ruins and full-size architectural fragments afford similar opportunities for the imagination to construe conclusions and postulate new connections.

When gathered in a collection such as Soane's, models of ruins, architectural fragments, and models of existing structures can permeate an architect's design process and lead to surprising results. Soane's collection of plaster casts of architectural fragments and cork models of classical antiquity show he was an experienced designer who knew that the design of architecture rarely goes according to plan and that situations will arise that require inspiration. To take advantage of potential moments of creative inventiveness, Soane located his office in the middle of his collection, which, in this contemplative environment, must have inspired his sudden assembly of a column known as a pasticcio by using a number of architectural fragments in the Monument Court.

Like Soane, the early twentieth-century Swiss architect Le Corbusier was an avid collector of another sort of architectural model, not plaster casts or architectural fragments from antiquity but found natural objects that he used to stimulate his architectural imagination.[56] Perhaps the most famous object in Le Corbusier's collection was a crab shell he found while roaming a Long Island beach in the 1940s. According to Le Corbusier's own account, it was this empty crab shell's strength as a geometric form—two curvilinear surfaces joined at the edges—that inspired the roof of his Notre Dame du Haut chapel in Ronchamp, France (completed 1955).[57] The crab shell was among Le Corbusier's collection of *objets à réaction poétique*, which, he explained to students in 1942, "form the vast panoply of spokesmen who speak the language of nature. They are caressed by your hands, your eyes gaze upon them, they are evocative companions"[58] (figure 2.12). For Le Corbusier, an object's having poetic potential must prompt speculation, engaging the body and mind to contemplate the efficacy of its forms, which may lie entirely outside the architect's accustomed architectural vocabulary. Like Gehry's oneiric paper models, Le Corbusier's *objets à réaction poétique* have no recognizable architectural purpose until the architect ascribes one to them, imparting imaginative direction. As Louis Pasteur remarked in a speech to the Faculty of Sciences at Lille, "fortune favors only those minds which are prepared."[59] To recognize an everyday object or event as inspiration for architecture, a designer must be actively engaged in a problem. Le Corbusier's appropriation of the crab shell demonstrates that accidental moments of creativity depend on the designer having experiences—like those afforded by a collection of architectural models—with which they can make hypothetical associations.

The kind of hypothetical associations in which Le Corbusier engaged with his *objets à réaction poétique* are taken up by Charles Sanders Peirce in his discussion of how human beings come up

| 2.12 |

Le Corbusier, "Objets à réaction poétique" (objects of poetic reaction), 1925–1965.

with ideas by comparative association. Peirce described the formation of a hypothesis as "an act of insight" that seeks to explain an observed phenomenon. To elucidate his concept of hypothesis formation, Peirce coined the term "abduction," which describes a kind of inference when the subject, confronted with an observed fact that requires explanation, finds an "idea of putting together what we had never before dreamed of putting together which flashes the new suggestion before our contemplation."[60] To enable our imaginations to take advantage of this shift back and forth between analytic and associative modes of thought, Peirce recommended "musement," a practice in which the mind casts aside all serious purpose and searches in "pure play" for "some connection" between objects, especially between two of the three Universes of Experience (mere Ideas, Brute Actuality of things or facts, and Signs).[61] The term "musement" evokes the ancient Greek concept of the Muse—a goddess who, as Plato says, is the source of poetic inspiration and overwhelms the artist with divine madness.[62] Yet what Plato attributed to a mythological being is for Peirce a human ability to engage in the lively contemplation of experiences "with speculation concerning its cause."[63]

In practice, architects frequently develop a preference for specific forms, materials, or methods for inspiring architectural reverie. At times, a collection of models is a useful tool for an architect who is seeking to refresh their architectural vocabulary. To invite accidental inspiration, an architect may seek to suspend their assumptions about a sought-after design solution and speculate on the efficacy of those forms and methods of construction found in collections of architectural models. This is certainly how Soane and Le Corbusier used their own compendia of ideal prototypes.

....

THIS CHAPTER REFLECTED on various ways in which the reading of physical models elicits the imaginative contemplation of architectural ideas. In constructing a physical model of architecture, its user seeks to visualize an existing or to-be-constructed building in physical form. Yet not all approaches to modeling architecture are ideally suited for inciting architectural reverie. As a result, because a particular model or modeling material may be more efficacious than another, a user may cathect on it as a medium for design or as a tool for facilitating some form of cultural or religious experience. When a cathexis is particularly strong, the model's maker may ascribe to it an imaginary power to influence the success of a sought-after design solution or a user's experience of it. In these processes of model construction, the designer of a to-be-constructed building will come to view the model as a true representation of material and structural performance. Yet, during the model-making process, the designer could decide to deliberately create an inaccurate model in order to deceive a client or to encourage the user to contemplate a fantasy as the real. Taking a similar approach, an architect may temporarily suspend their own assumptions about the scalar relationship between their modeling materials and building materials to invite their imagination to consider alternate solutions. This temporary suspension of treating the model as a real representation of reality is a fundamental trait of a playful architectural imagination. It is particularly useful when searching for connections between collections of incomplete models or their parts. In such cases, the imagination is enlisted to ask the modeling materials not "what is?" but "what if?" The following chapters will explore different ways in which architects have sought to use models and their modeling materials as a means of conveying their ideas to others and as a tool for developing design solutions.

3
DESCRIPTIVE TOOLS

IT WAS EARLY IN THE WINTER of 1418 that the Florentine *orafo* (goldsmith) Filippo Brunelleschi submitted his model to a competition for a project that would define his career as the most renowned architect and engineer of the Renaissance: the construction of a cupola over the 43-meter-diameter octagonal space of Santa Maria del Fiore, the Duomo (cathedral) of Florence, Italy. In architectural history, this event is also significant for the emergence of the architectural model as a tool preferred by clients and builders for studying an architect's design(s) in three dimensions.[1] A detailed record of this new role is provided by the payment receipts for wood and brick models, representing designs for the centering and construction of the cupola itself, that were submitted to the competition. However, unlike the other competitors, Filippo Brunelleschi refused to explain his large brick model to the members of the Opera del Duomo (Cathedral Works Commission), simply claiming his unique expertise in the matter.[2] As the sixteenth-century Italian painter, architect, and historian Giorgio Vasari recounts, Brunelleschi tendered a different sort of model to secure the commission: namely, a simple egg.

According to Vasari, the members of the Opera del Duomo were skeptical of Brunelleschi's proposal, since he refused to explain his method for constructing the heavy double-shelled dome without centering—the structure needed to support an arch or dome until the keystone or keystones are added. Of the varied solutions for constructing the cupola, including one that proposed filling the entire space with a mixture of earth and coins, none had seemed effective to the Opera.[3] Brunelleschi alone declared that the cupola could be vaulted at a much lower cost and quite easily without any supporting armature.[4] Yet, when the city officials and competitors asked him to explain his intentions in detail, as had the other competitors, he refused. To further clarify his position, Brunelleschi proposed to both foreign and local masters that whoever could stand an egg upright upon a marble slab should execute the project, since this test would reveal each man's intellect. All the masters tried to make the egg stand upright, but no one could find a way to do it. When asked to show them how it is done, Vasari claims, "He graciously took the egg, cracked its bottom on the marble and made it stand upright. The artisans loudly complained that they could have done the same thing, and laughing, Filippo answered that they would also have learned how to vault the dome if they had seen his model and his plans."[5] And so it was resolved that Brunelleschi should be commissioned to carry out this work and be asked to give more details. When the dome was completed it had the shape of half an egg slightly flattened at the top, but one should not infer that the egg was a visual model describing the cupola's construction. Rather, Brunelleschi's egg is a lesson in the rules an architect must establish with the users of any architectural model concerning the relationship between its formal, spatial, or constructive characteristics and the depicted structure.

Because even a faithful three-dimensional depiction of architecture in all its measures and materials can be incomprehensible to an inexperienced user, one of the first agreements that must be made between the maker and user of a model is its size relative to the body of the building. An early example of this accord between model and building appears in a story about the use of a model to measure the height of a pyramid. According to the Greek historians Hieronymus of Rhodes (third century BCE) and Plutarch (45–120 CE), during the sixth century BCE the Egyptian pharaoh Amasis wished to build a pyramid higher than that of Cheops. To do so, Amasis needed to know the measures of Cheops's pyramid, and he consulted the Greek mathematician Thales of Miletus to solve the problem. Unfortunately, none of the works of Hieronymus survive, but Diogenes Laertius recounts his claim that Thales "measured the height of the pyramids by the shadow they cast, taking the observation at the hour when our shadow is of the same length as ourselves."[6] Plutarch also relates this tale in his *Moralia*, which includes a work of historical fiction known as the *Dinner of the Seven Sages*. In it, the character Neiloxenus tells Thales that the king

> was immensely pleased with your method of measuring the pyramid, because, without making any ado or asking for any instrument, you simply set your walking-stick upright at the edge of the shadow which the pyramid cast, and, two triangles being formed by the intercepting of the sun's rays, you demonstrated that the height of the pyramid bore the same relation to the length of the stick as the one shadow to the other.[7]

What Thales' solution demonstrates is the human mind's ability to reach that which lies outside immediate experience by considering an indirect approach to finding the solution. Because the height of the pyramid is inaccessible, Thales creates a proportional scale.

Scale is a human concept for comparing, measuring, or manipulating objects and events in the physical world. A scale architectural model is more than just a representation that is larger or smaller than the structure being portrayed: it is a rule that tells the model's users there is a consistent, measurable relationship with its object at a specific, proportional ratio. When a client cannot read an architectural drawing, a miniature scale model provides an immediately tangible three-dimensional depiction of the form, the space, and even the materials of a proposed structure.

Owing in part to their simplicity but also to their durability, a few extant stone models from ancient Egypt and Rome attest to their use as descriptive tools for the client to study or for workmen to copy. In these early examples, one can discern an effort to simulate not only the measures of the object represented in miniature but also its material and constructive principles. Although three-dimensional architectural models were relatively scarce during the Middle Ages, written accounts attest to their use for the Milan and Florence cathedrals in the fourteenth century. Even at this early stage of development in the use of scale models during the Renaissance, architects had already begun to develop techniques for opening the model in order to permit the user to imaginatively and bodily inhabit its space. Later, the scale architectural model came to acquire an important role in architectural practice as a tool for demonstrating visual and structural performance at full size. This chapter explores the development and continued use of the physical scale model as a tool for architects to describe their designs to others.

SCALE AND MATERIALITY OF EARLY ARCHITECTURAL MODELS

In the planning practice of architecture, both the client and builder use the architect's model with an expectation that it is a tangible three-dimensional representation of a proposed structure. But the needs of these two individuals are quite different. In most cases, the appearance, utility, and cost of the architectural form, structure, or spaces will be of far greater concern to a client than to a builder, who would require a detailed description of the shape and dimensions of the individual parts or the materials in order to determine their sourcing and methods of transformation. To meet these expectations, the architect must establish a set of rules to aid a client or builder in understanding the model as a measured representation of architecture. These include the use of a basic measure to establish a scalar relationship between model and building. However, one also witnesses in models created before the fifteenth century a naïve realistic expectation of a correspondence between the architect's modeling materials and those used to construct the actual edifice. Collectively, they suggest that clients and builders believed that the veracity of early architectural models depended on such a correspondence.

This congruency between model and building is already present in the extant examples from the early dynastic period of ancient Egypt. Surveys of temples and pyramids from this era demonstrate that a standard unit of measure was employed to designate the location of the walls, columns, openings, and other material dimensions.[8] This practice is evidenced by depictions of a foundation ceremony called the "stretching of the cord" from the Second Dynasty (3890–2686 BCE) on.[9] A grid of red lines on an elevation drawing of the Gurob Shrine from the Eighteenth Dynasty (1549/50–1292 BCE) demonstrates the use of a module to lay out the measurements of forms and materials in an architect's design so that it can be realized in a larger construction.[10] A recent study by Ulrike Fauerbach of more than twenty-four miniature stone columns and column capitals from the late Pharaonic period testifies to the use of proportionally accurate models to

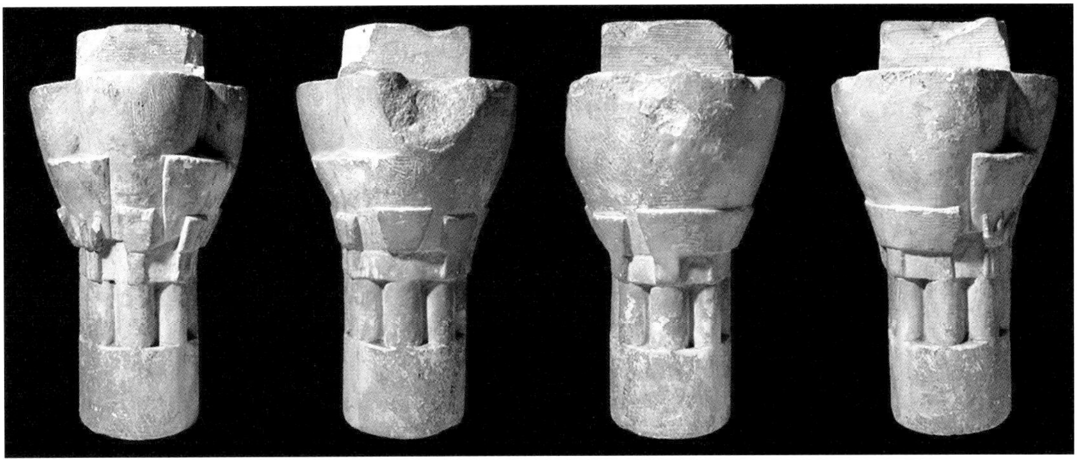

describe three-dimensional designs in miniature. The objects studied were constructed out of limestone, which permitted the modeler to obtain a high level of detail at a much smaller scale than would have been possible using the sandstone of the temples.[11] Although the origin of the models is generally unknown, some that were found together were constructed at the same scale, and marks etched or drawn with ink on their surfaces indicate the use of a compass for delineating the to-be-cut designs.[12] Several of these models demonstrate four steps for constructing a capital by rotating it on its own axis, while others show two variations of floral elements on either side (figure 3.1). Fauerbach concludes that these models were unlikely to have been made as ritual objects, since the variations would have been considered defects.[13] Rather, because the column and column capital models were designed and constructed using the same method as their full-size counterparts, they were more likely used as tools to describe proposed designs or their methods of construction so that, once approved, they could be reproduced by craftsmen at a larger proportional scale.

|3.1|

Four sides of a limestone open-lotus column capital, ca. 600–300 BCE.

A frequently referenced limestone and wood model of a funerary apartment from the Twelfth Dynasty (2055–1650 BCE) is another important demonstration of the use of models in ancient Egypt as a tool to describe a structure's function. This model was discovered by the German archaeologist Rainer Stadelmann carefully buried in the floor of a valley temple near two pyramid complexes built by King Amenemhat III at Dashur and Hwara. From the presence of the wood

block, Stadelmann deduced that the model was used to demonstrate how one of three stone blocks would slide across the funerary apartment's passageway to seal it for eternity (figure 3.2).[14] After examining it, Fauerbach has recently concluded that the model does not have a consistent proportional congruency with a funerary apartment at the pyramid complex but does adequately describe the spatial relationships between rooms, turns, slope, and in particular the closure system.[15] In practice, such a model would probably be too costly or time-consuming for an architect to carve for personal use. Moreover, an orthographic drawing might have difficulty conveying the three-dimensionality of the sliding mechanisms, making this model an ideal explanatory tool for a patron or craftsman. As long as its maker made clear that it shows only the major features of the proposed design, the model would be a useful way to persuade a patron that a design was effective. Because it was interred close to the construction site—like those models and tools buried in foundation deposits—its users may have believed that this model was endowed with the power to magically maintain the building for eternity.[16]

| 3.2 |

Limestone model of an Egyptian funerary apartment, ca. 1800 BCE.

Compared to the handful of examples from ancient Egypt, miniature scale models from ancient Greek architects are by and large absent from archives and museums, which instead demonstrate the prevalence of full-scale *paradeigmata*. Typically produced by the architect in charge of a building project, a *paradeigma* was a three-dimensional architectural element such as a column capital that acted as an exemplar or specimen that was to be copied multiple times. The Greek historian Herodotus provides one of the oldest records attesting to the use of *paradeigmata* in the reconstruction of the Temple of Apollo at Delphi. In Herodotus's account (5.62), the Alcmaeonidae, an

Athenian aristocratic family, were said to have substituted the finer Parian marble for the originally proposed tufa stone, thereby making it more beautiful than the *paradeigma* showed.[17] During building construction, Greek architects made use of full-size three-dimensional representations of architectural details constructed of stone, wood, or wax.[18] The *paradeigmata* produced for ancient Greek municipalities to maintain the quality of building construction exemplify this practice. These models include stone *paradeigmata* of clay roofing tiles found at three different Greek cities (figure 3.3).[19] A *paradeigma* may be not only a detail, like a column capital, but also a significant part of an entire edifice that is used as a standard example to be copied. This is certainly the case for a 5-meter-long section of the Tunnel of Eupalinos found in Samos, Greece, from the sixth century BCE, where the word *paradeigma* is written on the wall, indicating its role in the construction of the 1,036-meter-long aqueduct.[20] Like the roof tiles, the tunnel was an individual example from which multiple copies were intended to be made.

| 3.3 |
A roofing tile standard in the Agora at Athens, 1st century BCE.

The historical development of the Corinthian capital shows that the *paradeigmata* of ancient Greece were not always created by an architect but were sometimes found in nature and interpreted as a model of architecture. The earliest use of the Corinthian order is believed to have been at the Temple of Apollo at Bassae, where a single Corinthian column stood in the center of the temple's naos.[21] Unlike the roofing tile or tunnel section mentioned previously, this capital is neither a *paradeigma* nor one of its copies but a unique work of architecture. A historical account, however dubious, for the beginnings of the Corinthian order is provided in book 4 of Vitruvius's treatise on architecture. As Vitruvius relates, while strolling past the tomb of a young maiden from Corinth, the architect Callimachus happened upon a basket standing above her grave that was covered by a roof tile and had an acanthus plant growing up along its sides. Impressed by the novel arrangement, Callimachus "began to fashion columns for the Corinthians on this *exemplar* [*paradeigma*], and he set up symmetries, and thus he drew up the principles for completing works of the Corinthian type."[22] In Vitruvius's account, Callimachus is not supplied with a *paradeigma* but interprets what he finds in nature. Indeed, Vitruvius views architecture as an imitation of nature whose greatest work of art, the human body, is beautiful because of the mathematical and proportional symmetries embodied in it. For Vitruvius, architecture is beautiful when it is the result of *symmetria*, "a proper agreement of the work itself, and relation of the parts and the whole general scheme, in accordance with a certain part selected as standard."[23] As Vitruvius explains further, this "part selected as standard" is "the height of the capital, including its abacus," which is to "be equivalent to the thickness of the base of a column."[24] Thus, when Callimachus imitated the basket, roof tile, and acanthus plant as a *paradeigma*, he did so according to the rules of geometry and proportional *symmetria.* The composition was complete when it obtained *eurythmia*, "the quality of being well-shaped."[25] Once completed, the *paradeigma* was given to craftsmen tasked with making exact full-size copies. It is this role of *paradeigma* that Lothar Haselberger attributes to a Corinthian capital found at the Tholos of Epidauros (ca. 350 CE), which was designed by another person named Callimachus (figure 3.4).[26] Unlike the segment of the Tunnel of Eupalinos, this Corinthian capital at Epidauros was not incorporated into the structure but instead was carefully interred in the earth near it—a gesture that clearly indicates that the model was no longer needed in the service of the temple construction.

| 3.4 |
Corinthian capital found interred near the Tholos of Epidauros, ca. 350 BCE.

With the exception of municipal roof tiles, *paradeigmata* were unique works of an architect made for a single structure. For example, the simple, characteristic use of curved, scroll-like volutes sheltering egg-and-dart molding in Ionic column capitals produced anything but uniformity. Variations in this motif can be observed in the details of Ionic capitals created for two structures on the Athenian Acropolis: the Temple of Athena Nike (447 BCE) and the Erechtheum (421 BCE). Notwithstanding their proximity and the familiarity of the volutes in the Ionic architectural order, architects did not feel constrained from imposing their own artistic will on the design of the capitals. This individuality poses an explanation for the fate of the Corinthian capital found interred at Epidauros: it had fulfilled its usefulness, and burying it would prevent other architects from reusing it for their own temple designs.

Aside from the small models of a city wall and siege tower mentioned by Vitruvius in book 10 of his treatise on architecture, there is scant evidence for their use during Greek antiquity. By the first two centuries of the new millennium, however, a handful of examples from ancient Rome attest to a practice of constructing three-dimensional proportionally accurate models to study changes in and variations of proposed designs in miniature. These include a marble

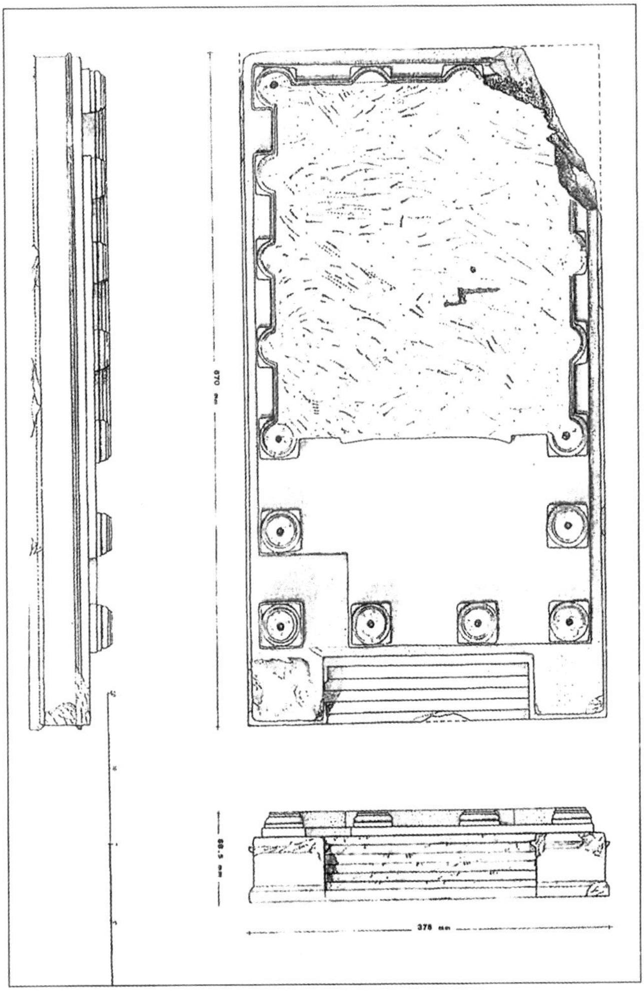

| 3.5 |

Drawing of marble model of tetrastyle on podium, found at Collegium of the Augustales, Ostia Antica, 1st century BCE.

model of a late Republican temple from Ostia and a soft limestone illustration of the adyton of the Great Temple at Niha (Beqaa). The first model, which depicts a conventional temple, was found in the Collegium of the Augustales at Ostia (figure 3.5).[27] The scale of the model is presumed to be 1:32 (one digit to 2 Roman feet) of a full-size construction; made out of marble, it depicts stairs, a stylobate, and column bases.[28] Although it is uncertain which temple the model represents, it is comparable to the Temple of Portunus and the Maison Carrée.[29] The presence of dowel holes on the top of some column bases suggests that the model was part of a larger structure into

which it would have been lowered so that variations to the treatment of the stylobate could be studied and compared. On the other hand, the markings on the model of the adyton for the Great Temple of Niha from the second century CE indicate the use of a measure and modifications to the design (figure 3.6). Featuring a staircase and platform, this model was found in the ruins of a small room adjoining the north side of the grand stairs leading to the temple.[30] It has been identified as a model of the adyton from an inscription on one of the edges: the Greek words προκεντεμα αδυ[τον], which translate as "plan of Ady[ton]."[31] The model is 1⁄24 the size of the completed structure and varies from it in minor details.[32] Incisions on the model in Greek describe measures in feet that indicate changes to the various stair depths.[33] A comparison between these scratches on the model with the remains of hexagonal bases at the site reveals correspondences in size and location, suggesting that the plans for this part

| 3.6 |
Limestone *prokentema* (design) of the *adyton*, found at Temple A, Niha, Lebanon, 2nd century CE.

of the adyton had been modified.[34] Aside from these examples, little evidence exists that architects regularly employed three-dimensional proportionally accurate models of proposed designs until the fourteenth century. Any use of scale models does not appear to have been important enough for architects to have made records of that use or to retain them for possible repairs.

At the beginning of the fourteenth century, however, the architectural model suddenly acquired a new significance among an administrative group of artisans and citizens acting as patrons for the reconstruction of the cathedral of Florence, Italy. The task of rebuilding the ninth-century cathedral of Santa Reparata was initially entrusted to Arnolfo di Cambio in 1294, and he worked on it till his death in 1302. A rededication of Santa Reparata to "Santa Maria del Fiore" during the laying of the new cornerstone in 1296 was an important self-referential act for the city of Florence, which the Romans had named Florentia or Fiorenza, the "city of the flower."[35] By naming the cathedral Santa Maria del Fiore, the citizens intended to broadcast the ideological premises upon which the new cathedral was to be constructed, not only "in honor and praise of God and of the blessed Virgin Mary" but also "in honor of the Florentine Commune and people."[36] Also during this time, the Opera del Duomo was established and put in charge of the construction, maintenance, and overall administration of the cathedral. When five years later the Arte della Lana (Wool Guild) was named to the role of patron of the Opera del Duomo, the appointment created a strong link between the *ecclesia maior* and the city's secular establishment.[37] This new administrative structure assigned the management of public funds to a secular organization accountable to the city government rather than to the ecclesiastical authorities. Because the cathedral project was entrusted to a committee of artisans and citizens acting as a "patron" representing the community, the architectural model quickly became an ideal, easily comprehensible tool for communicating and recording the size and shape of complex three-dimensional forms; in some instances it also offered a reduced-scale demonstration of their method of construction. In his account of Arnolfo's life, Vasari provides one of the earliest confirmations that architects were again using models, suggesting that Arnolfo left a model showing his conception of the dome and that it is pictured in the fresco painting known as *The Church*

Militant and Triumphant (ca. 1365), located in the Spanish Chapel of Santa Maria Novella near the Santa Maria del Fiore (figure 3.7).[38]

Of the models created during the fourteenth century for the erection of the Santa Maria del Fiore, only those made under the direction of Simone di Francesco Talenti can be confirmed: one for the campanile built in 1353 and a second, constructed two years later, for the choir chapels and part of the nave.[39] In 1366, hairline cracks appeared in the masonry supporting two of the recently completed nave vaults, inciting debates within the committee of artists and builders about the best way to construct Arnolfo's simple, buttressless semicircular cupola. To resolve this problem, the Opera del Duomo ordered designs for the completion of the cathedral's dome to be presented in drawings and models. This competition was held between Neri di Fioravanti, a principal master mason in Florence, who preferred the wide spaces and clear, sweeping lines of classical architecture and proposed a cupola that was structurally supported by inner tension rods (chains), and Talenti and Giovanni di Lapo Ghini, then *capomaestri*, who promoted a dome of Gothic design buttressed by vertical ribs of stone outside every vault, the tribune, and the cupola.[40] To describe their solution to the civic committee, Ghini used a masonry model of the cupola he had been working on since as early as 1360, while Neri produced a foundation plan and elevation. By the middle of August 1366, a decision had been made in favor of Neri's design, and Ghini was asked to produce a new masonry model in accordance with the winning scheme. However, the object that Ghini produced inaccurately represented Neri's design (presumably the measurements were

| 3.7 |

Andrea di Bonaiuto (Andrea da Firenze), *The Church Militant and Triumphant*, ca. 1365.

incorrect), and he used it to raise serious doubts about Neri's structural solution. After much debate Ghini's deception was discovered, and a few months later, on 19 November 1367, the decision to employ Neri's chains was finalized. To guide the continued work on the project, Ghini was paid to build a third large brick model in the aisle of the Dome, near the Campanile.[41] The drawings fell under "designum seu modellum," and the brick model of Neri's design referred to as "chiesa piccola" had to be both a copy and an exemplar: on the one hand, it had to be similar to the drawings, and on the other hand, the church had to be built to resemble the model.[42]

Ghini's misrepresentation of Neri's design demonstrates an important characteristic of an architectural model—the lasting influence it can have on the imagination of its users. Shortly after the model of Neri's design was completed, the Opera del Duomo issued a decree that all other models "si deba disfare" (must be dismantled).[43] This decision suggests that the Opera del Duomo was concerned about how the presence of Ghini's Gothic design might affect the future development of the project. The Opera del Duomo's fear was so great that until 1421, all masons were asked to periodically swear that they would abide by the design shown in the model of 1367. Yet despite these efforts, the construction of Neri's ambitious dome project, a double shell using no buttressing but only wooden or stone chains to prevent buckling, was never realized, for no one had the technical skill and knowledge to accomplish it.[44]

A handful of other examples from the fourteenth century demonstrate an increasing reliance on proportionally scaled physical models to represent the measures and masses of a proposed building in three dimensions. Among these is an important reference for the construction of a rood screen at Troyes Cathedral in 1382. As the French historian Jules Quicherat observes, because of the cathedral's good financial state, its canons wished to construct a rood screen; but since they could not adequately understand the drawings provided by the architects, Michelin and Jean Thierry, they asked that it be executed at full size. To this end, a raised earthen floor was prepared "in the roofs of the church."[45] Pierre du Colombier argues that because an earthen floor was used, this raised surface apparently was intended not merely to redraw the design but to model the roof *jubé* (screen) of the cathedral in relief.[46] Indeed, a single plaster fragment of a quasi-three-dimensional elevation found at Winchester Cathedral is considered by some to be material evidence for the existence of these practices.[47] In Italy there are additional examples of large-scale models emulating the mass and constructive techniques of stone. Perhaps because brick was being used to create models in nearby Florence, when the Fabbrica of the Bologna cathedral selected Antonio di Vicenzo as its chief architect on 26 February 1390, they instructed him to build what became a 59-foot- (or 18-meter-)long 1:12 scale model of his design in brick and plaster.[48] Concurrently, a number of architects from northern Europe were participating as *geometriae expertissimi* in discussions about the design of the cathedral of Milan.[49] These individuals included the German architect Heinrich Parler from Gmünd, who in 1392 created a partial wood model of a column for the experts and the faithful to study and appreciate.[50] Like the early models constructed for the Florence Duomo, these were not tools for the architect to use but descriptive illustrations of the architect's intentions for the client or builder to evaluate.

With the exception of ancient Greek *paradeigmata*, models created for clients and builders before the fourteenth century tended to emphasize a naïve simulation of a proposed structure's material and constructive characteristics in miniature. Notwithstanding the limestone Egyptian funerary apartment model mentioned at the beginning of this chapter, the diverse range of materials employed in ancient Egyptian funerary models demonstrates that miniature representations of architecture need not be created in carved stone. Similarly, Callias's wooden model crane and siege tower indicate that the use of stone to construct models, as in those found in Ostia and Niha, also was not a necessary practice. Rather, as the carved earthen or plaster models of Auxerre and Milan or stacked brick models of Bologna and Florence indicate, an architectural model could emulate the proposed building in a number of ways—not just in material but also in masses or method of construction. Naïve realism in architectural models corresponds to that in another kind of model in sympathetic magic whose use is based on an assumption that "like will produce like"; it has been applied, as Sir James George Frazer remarks, "by many peoples in many ages to injure or destroy an enemy by injuring or destroying an image of him."[51] In this light, the congruity between the construction of an architectural model and the construction of a building may be compared to the congruity between the method of harming an image of a person and the method of harming the actual person.

What the similarities between the construction of a magical object and a scale architectural model imply is that before the fifteenth century, a thing's veracity was dependent on the way it is made. This is also a primary argument put forward by the eighteenth-century Neapolitan philosopher Giambattista Vico in his own theory of human knowledge. Best known for his challenge to René Descartes, Vico set out to assert in his *New Science* (1725) that knowledge is true only if reason can ascertain its certainty by developing a new philosophy of knowledge based on the principle of "verum ipsum factum" (the true is the made).[52] The word *factum* "is essentially related to the word facture" in that both share the past participle of the Latin verb *facere*, meaning both "to make" and "to do."[53] That is to say that for Vico the *verum* of the *factum* resides in the unique method of human construction or "facture" of cultural artifacts, and human knowledge is founded on *homo faber* (man the maker). It is not the work as cultural artifact that is true but how the work is manufactured, as the value of the experiment in natural science demonstrates. Viewed from this angle, architecture is an *ars*, a productive skill that employs factures to convert made to true. Thus, for a prescientific mind, a model is a true representation of a building when it demonstrates the *ars* of the architect, albeit in miniature. But naïve realism contaminates the truth of the *factum* by undermining our assumption that a material will perform similarly at different scales, since, as Callias's model crane demonstrated, what can be built in a model is not the same as what can be constructed in a building. In architectural culture, the link between the architectural model and sympathetic magic was challenged by a new emphasis on form during the fifteenth century when Italian *legnaioli* (woodworkers) began to take up the practice of architecture.

BUILDING MODELS, MODELING BUILDINGS

We don't know the identities of individuals involved, but the Italian Renaissance biographer Giorgio Vasari tells us that one evening—probably during 1523—a number of Florentine artisans played a prank on one of their peers, the *legnaiolo* turned architect Baccio d'Agnolo, by adding "festoons of boughs" to the classical columns and pediments on the façade of his Palazzo Bartolini Salimbeni.[54] Reflecting on the formal exchanges between wooden micro-architecture and macro-architecture during this era, Vasari remarked in his biography of Baccio that because such individuals have labored in wood to execute with "true measurements the dimensions of their figures, which are columns, cornices, and bases, and all the ornaments," and because they are "continually handling such things," they "in course of time become architects."[55] Despite his praise of this *legnaiolo*'s achievements, Vasari did not hesitate to recount the prank of Baccio's peers, as well as the remark of Michelangelo Buonarroti on his return from Rome that the tambour which Baccio had completed by 1507 for the dome of Santa Maria del Fiore looked like a wooden "cage for crickets."[56] In the case of the prank, the decoration of Baccio's columns and pediments imitated the practice of decorating cathedral micro-architecture during holiday seasons and may also have been intended to evoke the wooden picture frame designs of the fifteenth-century Italian architect and sculptor Jacopo Sansovino. Known as "Sansovino frames," these diminutive architectonic structures are characterized by broken pediments, entablatures, overlapping scrolls, garlands of fruit, masks, and sometimes cherubs.[57] More likely, Baccio's peers were mocking his building's construction as taking on the character of fifteenth-century micro-architecture and architectural model construction in which pilasters, cornices, pediments, and even rusticated stones are similarly applied around openings and to the surface(s) of the model. These events in Baccio's career are important in the history of the architectural model, not least because they coincide with the sudden prominence of the model as a tool for making decisions and guiding work on a project, and also because they provide the reader with an insight into the model maker's lasting effect on future design practice.

Because of their skill in crafting buildings in miniature, *legnaioli* arguably took their first significant step into the practice of architecture at the beginning of the fifteenth century when seventeen models were entered into a competition for the construction of the cupola of the Florence Duomo.[58] Often overlooked by researchers is that fact that submissions came from *scarpellini* (stonecutters), *orafi* (goldsmiths), *pittori* (painters), and *legnaioli*.[59] That none of the individuals claimed the trade of "architect" is not surprising, since no architect's guild then existed in Florence or anywhere else in Italy. Rather, most architects, like Brunelleschi, were trained and also worked in the other arts. One can assume that *legnaioli* produced many if not all of the models submitted to the competition, including their own. To understand how the transition of the *legnaioli* to the roles of architect affected architectural practice during the fifteenth and sixteenth centuries, one must consider the events, types of models, and major figures surrounding the completion of the Duomo's cupola, in which they were so closely involved.

Although much of our knowledge comes from secondhand accounts, official records and payment receipts indicate that Brunelleschi had already utilized *legnaioli* to produce four wooden models before the cupola competition: two for the cupola itself and two for armatures of some kind.[60] At this time, Brunelleschi was officially engaged "in the making of designs and in labors for the Building Commission in cupola matters."[61] Also recorded is a loan of 10 soldi, received by Brunelleschi in 1410 for providing the Opera del Duomo with a bushel of model bricks for constructing the dome's tambour.[62] In 1415 the *capomaestro*, Antonio di Banco, died unexpectedly and Giovanni d'Ambrogio, who was called back from retirement, constructed a new model for the cupola's scaffolding. Other masters were at work on their own models of armatures, working platforms, hoists, and the cupola as a whole. According to Vasari, Brunelleschi was confident in his own ability and suggested that the Opera del Duomo hold a competition to find the best solution so that they might "serve to prove the greatness of his own intellect."[63] Thus, on 19 August 1418, the Arte della Lana in Florence announced a competition:

> Whoever desires to make any model or design for the vaulting of the main Dome of the Cathedral under construction by the *Opera del Duomo*—for armature, scaffold or other thing, or any lifting device pertaining to the construction and perfection of said cupola or vault—shall do so before the end of the month of September. If the model be used he shall be entitled to a payment of 200 gold Florins.[64]

For his part, Brunelleschi constructed a large 1:12 double-shell masonry model of the cupola—more than 2 meters wide and 3.5 meters tall—as four masons used standard-sized bricks to demonstrate his method for constructing the dome without centering. Brunelleschi's former competitor for the doors of the nearby Baptistery, Lorenzo Ghiberti, also used brick as a modelling material, and also with the help of masons and woodworkers, but his was of "mattoni picholini crudi" (little baked bricks).[65] Perhaps because of their models' size, but certainly also because of the high confidence they had in their schemes, Brunelleschi and Ghiberti constructed their models on the grounds of the *opera*, while the minor masters worked on their submissions elsewhere. Then, on 7 December 1418, the submissions were judged after a delay of two months (presumably to give Brunelleschi additional time to complete his model). It was during the judging process that Brunelleschi, once he had finished criticizing his competitors' submissions, famously refused to explain his solution and asserted his sole ability to construct the dome without centering. Clearly, the judges must not have been present on the grounds of the *opera* over the previous four months or Brunelleschi must have shielded his solution from prying eyes, since his model was assembled there. Nevertheless, in response to his refusal, Brunelleschi was also himself criticized, called a lunatic, and bodily removed from the judging process. It was shortly thereafter, as mentioned at the beginning of this chapter, that Brunelleschi challenged his competitors to stand an ordinary egg upright.

Brunelleschi's own contributions aside, the models submitted to the competition indicate a preference for the use of wood and, in the cases of Brunelleschi and Ghiberti, also brick to demonstrate in three dimensions the efficacy of their constructive solutions.[66] The competition of 1418 is also important for capturing one of the earliest uses of the Italian term *modello* to denote a three-dimensional model of architecture: the word appears in the Arte della Lana's payment receipts for the wood and brick models submitted to the competition.[67] One can observe from Brunelleschi's wooden model (figure 3.8), still on display in Florence's Museo del Duomo, that it was an ideal material for describing the external form of the cathedral, while brick came to play a role in demonstrating the method of construction by literally simulating it in miniature.

One must recall Brunelleschi's own penchant for constructing and having architectural models constructed as explanatory tools. The wax models that Brunelleschi and Ghiberti produced in 1402 to describe their designs of the Baptistery doors come immediately

| 3.8 |

Filippo Brunelleschi, wood model of Florence dome and side chapels, ca. 1418–1446.

to mind. But in his biography of Brunelleschi, Vasari portrayed him above all others as an avid model maker, creating proportionally scaled constructions to describe his ideas to builders and patrons for nearly every aspect of his work. Vasari noted how Brunelleschi on the building site would carefully examine the stones of the stonecutters "to see if they showed flaws and if they were hard, and he would give the men models in wood or wax, or made simply out of turnips."[68] Brunelleschi is also rumored to have created models of machinery for lifting blocks of stone, and his previously mentioned brick model in the great square in front of the cathedral was used to guide construction until 1431.[69]

What should not be overlooked in this context is a sudden emergence of *legnaioli* (woodworkers) not only as makers of architectural models but also as participants in competition for the Florence cathedral's dome, proposing not only designs but also solutions for its centering. This new role for *legnaioli* coincides with an increased artistry of wooden micro-architecture in Italian churches and especially in picture frames. Whether these frames were constructed for use around paintings, reliefs, or mirrors, they were typically designed as parts of an architectural interior and meant to harmonize with stonework surrounding doors and windows. One of the most famous *legnaioli* living in Florence during the turn of the fifteenth century was undoubtedly Manetto di Jacopo Ammanatini, a friend of Brunelleschi who was nicknamed *il grasso Legnaiolo*—literally, "the Fat Woodworker."[70] Ammanatini was known for his picture frames and intarsia work but gained his celebrity for a *beffe* (joke) Brunelleschi played on him in 1409, which was recounted by Antonio Manetti. Manetti claims Brunelleschi and their mutual friends made Ammanatini "believe that he has become someone else and that he's no longer Manetto the Fat ... that he had become someone called Matteo."[71] That Ammanatini was also familiar with the design and construction of architecture is verified by his accomplishments after emigrating to Hungary; there he gained wealth and esteem by completing a castle for the Scolari family in Ozora.[72] As already noted, some of the earliest evidence for the participation of *legnaioli* in the design of masonry structures during the fourteenth century is found in the payment receipts for models submitted to the competition for the Florence cathedral's dome. Of course, *scarpellini* and *legnaioli* were members of the same guild, Arte dei Maestri di Pietra e Legname, but *legnaioli* were the de facto experts in the construction of wooden vault centering or armatures, as in the case of the "modelo fe d'armadura a la Chupola magiore" submitted by the *legnaiolo* Niccolò di Guido.[73] That being said, from the descriptions of models submitted by two other *legnaioli*, Piero d'Antonio and Piero di Santa Maria al Monte, it appears that their proposals were not limited to armatures.

Perhaps the most significant change in the activities of *legnaioli* during the fifteenth century was signaled by another one of Brunelleschi's woodworkers, Antonio di Ciaccheri Manetti, who obtained the position of *capomaestro* for the completion of the Duomo after Brunelleschi's death in 1446. In 1432 Manetti had begun producing models for Brunelleschi, who Vasari claims had taught him the use of one-point perspective in his intarsia work for the Duomo's North Sacristy. In 1436 Antonio di Ciaccheri Manetti produced two very similar abundantly ornamented models of designs for a lantern to surmount the dome of Santa Maria del Fiore—one for himself and a second for Brunelleschi, which according to Antonio di Tuccio Manetti was almost identical with the one made by Brunelleschi himself.[74] Despite his loss in the competition, the Florentine government retained faith in Manetti's abilities and requested that he present Francesco Sforza, the Duke of Milan, with a design for a fortified stronghold at Pisa in 1459. By that time, he was *capomaestro* of the Florence Duomo, raised to that position after the dismissal of Michelozzo in 1452, and there he continued work on Brunelleschi's lantern.

Two events of the second half of the fifteenth century significantly affected the continued use of architectural models and the acceptance that their makers, the *legnaioli*, found among their Florentine peers in the design and construction of architecture. The first is the publication by the artist and architect Leon Battista Alberti of his first treatise on architecture in the same year that Manetti took over as *capomaestro* of the Duomo. In it Alberti strongly recommended the use of models as an aid to architects in designing and describing their designs but warned against those that are refined and highly decorated, demonstrating not the ingenuity of the architect's idea but the skill of the craftsman who made the model—almost certainly the *legnaiolo.* The second is Michelangelo's previously mentioned critique of Baccio d'Agnolo's tambour of the Florence Duomo and the prank that his peers played on his palazzo façade. In that instance Baccio's peers appear to claim that his façade is not integral with the macro-architecture but, like the micro-architecture of picture frames and cathedrals that Baccio was known to make, is simply applied to its surface. Although some have argued that Baccio was introducing a Roman architectural style to Florence, the memory of his training clearly still lingered in the minds of his peers. As we will see in chapter 4, the wooden architectural model remained an important tool for studying the lines and angles that define and enclose the surfaces of the building, but it was predominantly limited to plain, simple, and undecorated forms.

THE PREFERRED TOOL

The vast majority of models found in European archives and museums from 1400 up to the present demonstrate that these objects continue to be a valuable means for winning the approval of a patron, providing a guide during construction, and preserving a record for unforeseen repairs. From the client's point of view, the detailed model enabled a better understanding of the architect's design; once approved, it was both a guarantee binding the architect in their capacity as foreman to build the structure it described and also insurance that the design could be completed as commissioned. Throughout history one can find examples of structures left incomplete, abandoned, or destroyed because of an architect's death or a change in the patron's financial or political circumstances. In the former case, an architect must rely on a collaborator or the record of their intentions to ensure the work's completion. For their part, a client has little choice but to enlist the help of a second architect to discern the creative intelligence of the first's incomplete work. When a project does not meet the expectations of a client or is suddenly canceled, an architect's model can take on an independent role and can have the same impact on architectural culture as the building itself.

Already during the fifteenth century, architects were beginning to write about the utility of models as a tool for describing designs to patrons. As mentioned previously, the account given by Alberti in his treatise on architecture—noting how the scale model permitted the architect to "weigh up repeatedly and examine, with the advice of experts," their proposed design so that it may "demonstrate the ingenuity of him who conceived the idea"[75]—was one of the earliest. But not every architect during the Renaissance followed Alberti in recommending that a model should contain few details. Just over a century later, Vincenzo Scamozzi also advocated the construction of models for clients, but he preferred those that were "exceedingly well wrought" so that "all things were distinctly comprehended," including "the pedestalls, columns, and other ornaments, with all their severall parts plainely seen."[76] Despite these different approaches, in eastern Europe visual and textual sources attest to Ottoman architects' use of models during the sixteenth century as a tool for winning over patrons who may not have been able to visualize three-dimensional designs from a ground plan. Evidence of this is provided by a frequently cited miniature depicting several people carrying a large-scale model of the Süleymaniye Mosque in a ceremonial procession during 1582 (figure 3.9), as well as by an account of a wooden model erected in an emptied pool at the Topkapi Palace so that the sultan could understand the three-dimensional strategic layout of the Castle of Belgrade from above.[77] In 1774 Jacques-François Blondel

their effect on the entirety of the composition. In the context of modern fiction, one memorable example of a reworked model occurs in Ayn Rand's novel *The Fountainhead* (1943) when classical façades are added to the model created by the main character, Howard Roark, for his design of the Manhattan Bank Building. Like the modifications to the *modellone*, the façades put on Roark's design do not change the spatial arrangements or proportions of the overall building but alter only its external appearance, in the manner of the clothing draped on a mannequin. Of course, in many instances, the architect who constructs a model to obtain a commission never anticipates that the client would use it to plan later changes to that very design.

It was precisely because of the model's utility in making visible the formal and constructive characteristics of an architect's design that it became an ideal tool to ensure the completion of a project as they intended. For Scamozzi, contrary to Alberti, this was an argument for creating highly refined and well-crafted models; he argues, "[A]nd finallie in case the Architect should be absent, one may by the model shew, at least in general, what his will and intention was, that there need not anything after be removed, or defaced, as in such cases it sometimes happeneth, through the small understanding of others who come after, or their willfulnesse because they will be authors, and bringers up of innovations."[96] Florence's Opera del Duomo found itself in precisely this situation in 1366, when the project's custodians lacked knowledge about how to execute Arnolfo di Cambio's dome project, and again in 1374 after the death of Cambio's successor as the Duomo's *capomaestro*, Neri di Fiorvanti. In Rome, after the death of Sangallo in 1546, Michelangelo sought to forestall this problem when he inherited responsibility for St. Peter's Basilica: he made two clay models of the dome so that it could be finished after his death—one two weeks after his nomination as chief architect of the Fabbrica in late 1546 and a second in 1557.[97] In 1560 Michelangelo also had a large wooden model, standing over 5 meters tall, made by Maestro Giovanni Franzese, "fashioned with diligence in the model all the members" so that it might be completed as he foresaw.[98] North of the Alps, this approach is exemplified by two wooden models (now destroyed) from the sixteenth-century Italian architect and joiner Domenico da Cortona for his designs of the Château de Chambord and for the Hôtel de Ville in Paris. A document confirms that the

| 3.12 |

Joos Metsys, model façade of St. Peter's Church, Louvain, 1525–1530.

latter model was constructed "in order to avoid mistakes" in executing the approved design.[99] A similar purpose may be ascribed to the extant soft limestone model, over 8 meters high, of the tower façade of St. Peter's Church in Louvain, Belgium, that was carved by Joos Metsys between 1525 and 1530 (figure 3.12).[100] As the contract between Metsys and the city council of Louvain reveals, the model was commissioned to ensure that workmen would be able to complete the project in case of the architect's death. In the view of Franz Bischoff, this was the role played by a wooden scale model of a family museum in Stadhagen designed by Giovanni Maria Nosseni in 1608.[101] They are not full-scale models to be copied but rather reduced-scale descriptions of the overall architectural form(s) that might include the location of different openings, columns, and various ornaments, with specifications of their type, sizes, and materials.

The value that a model may acquire in the absence of the architect is made strikingly clear by two events from the twentieth century. The first occurred in Barcelona, when the models and plans of the Spanish architect Antoni Gaudí for the Sagrada Família church were destroyed during the Spanish Civil War and the city found itself with neither an architect nor a model to complete the project. Because Gaudí's architecture did not rely on regular or repeating forms, his models were invaluable tools for illustrating his intentions in three dimensions. The second occurred in Sydney in 1966, when the architect of the Sydney Opera House resigned and Jørn Utzon's former assistant Peter Hall was hired to complete the project, with no more to go on than some friendly advice from Utzon and measurements and clues given by the remaining models and drawings.[102] Hall's problem, like that faced by those architects who took on the completion of the Sagrada Família, was that many of the details were still unresolved. Whereas Michelangelo, Domenico da Cortona, and even Joos Metsys left models of their designs to ensure their completion, these examples demonstrate that a model has limits as a complete description of the architect's intentions, since, as any experienced architect will undoubtedly confirm, over time a design will always encounter unforeseen problems and changes that affect those intentions.

None of this means that a design which for some reason was never executed could not still make a significant contribution to architectural culture. Perhaps the most famous such design is Sir Christopher Wren's Great Model for St Paul's Cathedral. Built between 1673 and 1674 by a team of craftsmen, Wren's Great Model was made at a scale of 1:18, enabling the king and royal commissioners to walk inside its 5.5-meter-high interior (figure 3.13). Unfortunately, the very comprehensibility of Wren's Great Model opened it to criticism and requests for significant changes. Some enthusiasts today see Wren's model as the most beautiful cathedral in all of England. A number of

| 3.13 |

Sir Christopher Wren, the Great Model for St. Paul's Cathedral, 1673–1674.

failed competition designs also became as important as or even more important than the winning submissions. Among these is certainly Mies van der Rohe's entry for an office building on Friedrichstrasse in Berlin from 1921.[103] Even though there were 140 submissions to the competition, it is difficult to find one more familiar or well published than Mies's tripartite prism of glass sheathing twenty horizontal planes (floors). Although his design did not receive an official mention, much less win, it is viewed by some as a point of origin if not the beginning of the glass curtain wall dominating the twentieth-century skyscraper.[104] Another important unbuilt project made famous by its model is Vladimir Tatlin's Monument to the Third International from 1919. Envisaged as a towering symbol of modernity that would have dwarfed the Eiffel Tower, the project met its demise because of sudden changes in social, political and artistic policies. A similar end befell Giuseppe Terragni and Pietro Lingeri's homage to the great Italian poet Dante Alighieri, whose works had been appropriated by the Italian Fascist government.[105] Known as the Danteum, Terragni and Lingeri's design—an architectural translation of the *Divine Comedy*—was never begun because of political developments that led to Italy's entrance into the Second World War.

By the end of the twentieth century, the physical model's role as a preferred descriptive tool and record had been usurped by the digital model. So strong was the desire to give up the physical model (and drawing) that in 1992 Columbia University founded the paperless studio. Yet, less than a decade after the model's presumed demise, a handful of books appeared extolling the indispensability of physical models to "express an immediacy and a much more profound and exciting ... architectural language that cannot be readily experienced via drawing alone."[106] The model is undeniably present before the eyes in the same space as the user's body. The challenge that has faced architects since the early Renaissance is how to bring the user into the space of a structure that is too small to inhabit.

INHABITING MODELS

In a photograph taken for *Life* magazine in 1950, a scale model house is suspended above a desk to permit the mid-twentieth-century American designer Ray Eames to look inside and study the arrangement of its interior spaces.[107] The photo was probably staged for the magazine's article and the model was not intended for Mrs. Eames's use, since her diminutive size would permit her to look only at the model's ceiling. In retrospect, what the photo does indicate is a desire on the part of architects to position themselves in reference to the model in a way that allows them to imaginatively inhabit and study a proposed design.

Because the size, arrangement, and distribution of interior spaces cannot be seen from the outside of most miniature scale models, during the late fifteenth century architects began to experiment with different methods for removing and exchanging entire floors or parts of models. A notable early example of this practice is Giuliano da Sangallo's model of the Palazzo Strozzi (ca. 1489), whose three stories can

be detached from one another like a collection of stacked boxes. It didn't take long for this method to catch on, and it was even employed in one of the earliest extant models from north of the Alps—that for the Augsburg Rathaus from 1515/16 (figure 3.14). But Sangallo's model is also accompanied by two single-floor façade models. The first is half of a single board that is believed to be a rejected alternate for one of the two upper stories of the north façade. Here, seven biforate windows have rustication carved into the board above them, while the individual prismatic wood blocks below them are glued onto the board's surface (figure 3.15).[108] The second façade model is incomplete and shows three alternate solutions for either the first or second stories of the Palazzo's east façade: eight windows are surmounted by

| 3.14 |

Model of the Augsburg Rathaus, 1515/16.

| 3.15 |

Giuliano da Sangallo, north (below) and east (above) façade detail models of Palazzo Strozzi, ca. 1489.

| 3.16 |

Arduino degli Arriguzzi, model of the basilica of San Petronio, Bologna, 1514.

alternating triangular and segmental pediments—two of which are framed by pilasters—with an odd ninth arched window surrounded by rusticated stones, all glued onto the board. Dovetails at the ends of this board indicate the intention to insert it into the completed model, suggesting that it was used to work out alternate solutions and present them to the patron.[109] Such use is precisely what Alberti, Sangallo's contemporary, noted in his treatise on architecture: the model "will allow one to increase or decrease the size of those elements freely, to exchange them and to make new proposals and alterations until everything fits together well and meets with approval."[110]

The approach is different when the interior is a single multistoried space rather than a multifloor structure. Thus, for the basilica of San Petronio in Bologna, Arduino degli Arriguzzi's 1514 model is constructed in two halves so that it may be pulled apart in section along the center of the nave (figure 3.16).[111] Arriguzzi's design was never completed as the model presents it, but the model remains important today as one of the earliest extant experiments with the separation or sectioning. To fully comprehend its significance during this period, it is necessary to unpack the meaning of the inscription *Noli me tangere* (Do not touch me) on its base.

Noli me tangere is the translation in the Latin Vulgate Bible of the words from John 20:17, spoken by Jesus to Mary Magdalene when she recognized him after his resurrection from death; her faith, he believed, needed no confirmation. By contrast, when Jesus later appeared before his disciples (John 20:19–29), he invited the doubting Thomas to physically touch his five crucifixion wounds (four from nails in each hand and foot, and one from a Roman soldier's lance in his side). Thomas's doubt of Jesus' resurrection is reflected in the aphorism "Seeing's believing, but feeling's the truth." The story of Christ's resurrection is central to the Christian mass, but his wounds were particularly important in Italy between the fourteenth and sixteenth centuries, when masses and prayers were dedicated to their religious significance. During the fifteenth century, some prints of Christ's wound would contain an actual physical wound, a cut in the drawing surface, so that some worshippers could imitate St. Thomas's touching of the space of the divine interior by inserting their own fingers through the simulation.[112] This association of touch with verification also emerges in Arriguzzi's cutting of his model for the basilica of San Petronio.

From an architectural point of view, Arriguzzi's sectioning of the model for San Petronio in two parts can, as Jesus did for doubting Thomas, abate the faith required by the client in the efficacy of the proposed design by providing them with direct formal and spatial perception of it. Thomas, who needed to touch in order to understand, is sometimes portrayed as having an architect's square in his hand, suggesting a reluctance to trust in visual perception alone as a guide for constant, invariable knowledge.[113] Thomas must use his first instrument, his hand, to inspect the truth of Jesus' resurrection. Those who doubt the veracity of Arriguzzi's design may open the model. Arriguzzi's cut, like the wound in Jesus' side, provides this opportunity. Unfortunately, Arriguzzi's challenge was met nearly a century later by Carlo Carazzi, a local tailor who argued that the proportional scheme being carried out by the cathedral's architect at that time, Francesco Morandi, was incorrect. Two sectional models of the nave of the basilica of San Petronio were executed in 1590 or 1591 by the local architect Floriano Ambrosinsi to help the Bolognese senate make a decision between the two competing schemes.[114] In the end, neither scheme was chosen for completing the nave of the basilica, and their models remain with the cathedral.

Throughout the next four centuries, architects experimented with a variety of techniques to separate or remove a model's mass in order to make the interior spaces visible from the outside. Alessandro Dori's 1745 constructed model of the Biblioteca Marucelliana in Florence (figure 3.17) deserves particular attention, because it demonstrates how the method of model construction resulted from the conditions of the design. Although the Biblioteca Marucelliana was a single space, like Ariguzzi's San Petronio, it was not a single freestanding structure but occupied the space between two existing buildings; the façade and interior space of the library were therefore difficult to study without removing one or the other building. If we accept that a drawing of Michelangelo's now lost model of the church of San Giovanni dei Fiorentini in Rome from 1607 is an accurate depiction of the model as Michelangelo constructed it, we can assume that he also explored a sectioning of the model similar to Arriguzzi's but only as a single half section on top of a relief ground plan of the entire structure (figure 3.18). This partial construction of the model enables the viewer to discern the entire configuration of spaces from the entrance to the

| 3.17 |

Alessandro Dori, Biblioteca Marucelliana, 1745.

| 3.18 |

Tiberio Calcagni, drawing of Michelangelo's model of the church of San Giovanni dei Fiorentini, 1607.

| 3.19 |

Carl Martin Frantz, model of the Kreuzkirche, 1743.

| 3.20 |

Pier Francesco Silvani, model for the church of San Firenze, ca. 1667.

altar and floor to the dome in two and three dimensions. Carl Martin Frantz's 1743 model of the Kreuzkirche (figure 3.19) and a second one from 1762 by Traugott Nicolai for the Peterskirche utilized a different approach to the study of a large single space structure, removing the roof to provide the user an angel's-eye view. Certainly, there were still more ways to dismember a model. In England during the second half of the seventeenth century, the gentleman architect Sir Roger Pratt recommended that although "the inward parts may so clearly appear to us, the sides of the model are so to be ordered, that the four corners of it remaining always firm, as to the rest they may be pulled up as occasion shall require."[115] In Pratt's method the exterior walls are separate from the individual floors, resembling a box containing a stack of plates. The drawback to this approach is that the model's user is limited to examining only those floors still remaining in the container, the model's exterior walls. A similar approach was employed by Tommaso Giusti for his 1713 model of St. Clemens Basilica in Hannover, which "can be dismantled into twenty-four parts so that the interior wall decorations can be easily seen."[116] In its partial recomposition, the model would have the appearance of a ruin rather like the complex irregular sectional model of Pier Francesco Silvani's church of San Firenze from ca. 1667 (figure 3.20).

Silvani's model is an important development that demonstrates a unique interchange between sectional drawings, models, and buildings during the sixteenth and seventeenth centuries. The son of Gherardo Silvani, an architect who produced a design and model for the façade of the Florence cathedral in 1635–1636, Pier Francesco Silvani was certainly familiar with the use of orthographic sectional drawings by his father's peers, including Giovanni Antonio Dosio, who drew composite sectional and elevation drawings. Jacques Guillerme and Hélène Vérin argue that orthographic sectional drawings like Dosio's have their beginnings in those created to study "natural" breaks in ancient ruins.[117] As a composite, Dosio's drawing of a centralized single-space structure is comparable to Michelangelo's model for San Giovanni dei Fiorentini mentioned previously, as it attempted to juxtapose multiple views of a structure in a single representation. By contrast Silvani's method of cutting the model is closer to sectional drawings of the Roman Pantheon's interior and exterior structure such as those created over a century earlier by an anonymous

La Gallerie triumphalle des Florentins,
a veoir par dedens & dehors.

La largeur .L. piedz.
La haulteur .lx piedz.
Longeur .C.xxx. piedz

artist in the Chlumczansky Codex (ca. 1500) and by Antonio Lafreri in 1553, to name only two examples. Because the Pantheon had come down through the centuries nearly intact, its method of construction remained hidden and provoked a range of conjectures expressed by partially breaking up the external surface to show its structural or inner workings.[118] Silvani's approach to the model of San Firenze is more complex, however, because the structure he is attempting to describe in three dimensions is not a simple centralized space but an oblong cruciform basilica church. As C. Schriver did in the sectional perspective/elevation drawing "Triumphalis Florentinorum Porticus ..." from 1550 (figure 3.21), Silvani constructs a model depicting only parts of the cupola, nave, aisle, and transept. Rather than being a simple longitudinal cut between two halves or a set of stacked floors that may be pulled apart one by one, Silvani's model is instead a static, complex, wandering sectional cut through the major spaces of the dome, nave, and side aisles, demonstrating the real need for a method to simultaneously show the entire design and also its interior spaces.

An engraving from Johann Friedrich Penther's 1764 *Zweyter Theil der ausführlichen Anleitung zur Bürgerlichen Baukunst* indicates that there had been few advances in model sectioning since Silvani's project for the church of San Firenze. Penther's engraving shows four *putti* sitting on the floor of a room; a young man is lifting the roof off a model on a table while a second model of similar size and proportion stands in the background with its façade removed, placed on a footstool (figure 3.22). By the eighteenth century demountable models took on the appearance of architecturally decorated chests or cabinets, hinged so that the roof or top floor of the represented structure could be lifted open and the model's user could see the proposed arrangement of spaces inside.[119] However, this approach appears to be unsatisfactory, as the second model in Penther's image is freshly cut and a saw is resting against the wall behind it. Obviously, the teeth of the saw are too large to have been used to cut the internal members of the model without damaging them, but the saw is a particularly telling metaphor: it underscores that a multistoried model is limited in its ability to describe the vertical distribution of interior spaces, their heights, the quality of sunlight, and relationships to the street.

Alternatively, architects sought to explore ways of bringing clients and builders bodily into the space of their proposed designs

| 3.21 |

C. Schriver, sectional perspective/elevation drawing, "Triumphalis Florentinorum Porticus ... ," in *La très admirable, très magnifique et triomphante entrée ...* , 1550.

| 3.23 |

Model of a *Landhauses Bauer* on Mühlenberger Weg 33, 1860.

"to convey the appearance."[128] One technique mentioned in this article was echoed nearly a century later, in 1922, by Columbia University's Professor Alciphron Boring, who advised the reader to attach a card to their model with a hole at the prescribed level, thereby encouraging the model's user to view it "in such corresponding positions as the originals might be seen from."[129] A similar method is reiterated by Edward W. Hobbs, an engineer and author of an assortment of instructional books for domestic use, who recommended in *Pictorial House Modelling* (1926) that a model be studied at true eye level to permit users to connect its miniature scale with their own and thus make the proposal seem real.[130] Today it is a common practice for an architect to include a miniature human figure, from which the user can ascertain the size of the model and its parts in relation to their own body. An early example of this technique is evident in a house model from 1860 in which miniature human figures of an entire family were placed on the garden, steps, windows, and balcony of a *Landhaus* (country house) near Hamburg to help the model's user—presumably a client—understand the scale of the proposed design (figure 3.23).[131] Whatever the method, the aim of these techniques is the same: to enable the model's user to experience the proposed design.

However, when the client or patron is still not convinced of the efficacy of a proposed structure's forms or materials, architects have resorted to the construction of full-size building elements in situ. One frequently cited example is Michelangelo's 1547 competition entry for the cornice of the Palazzo Farnese in Rome. Standing more than 3 meters tall, a wooden section of Michelangelo's design was placed in situ over a corner of the palazzo under construction to judge its effect from the ground.[132] This was not an unusual practice for Michelangelo, who built a full-size architectural model of the wall tomb for the Medici chapel in 1524 and adorned it with models of his proposed sculptures.[133] In Rome during the middle of the seventeenth century, full-scale models continued to be made and were "carefully crafted to imitate the form and substance of the intended material."[134] For example, Francesco Borromini, like Michelangelo, also placed an in situ model of "perishable materials" for his design of the lantern of the Sant'Agnese in Piazza Navona, while Gian Lorenzo Bernini had full-scale models of his piazza design for St. Peter's created at "every stage of the design, from planning to the execution of details."[135] In his *Cours d'architecture* (1771–1777), Blondel attests to the "usefulness" of these practices, advocating that constructing models "of the same size" may "ensure the perfection of their work"; to exemplify this practice he thus pointed to Bernini's colonnades of St. Peter's Square alongside French examples constructed by Pierre Lescot, Claude Perrault, and François Mansart.[136] It is hard to imagine, however, that Borromini and Bernini bore the high expense of constructing full-size models for their own benefit; these must have been used as descriptive tools to obtain approval of a client or to show the methods of construction to a builder. Such appears to have been the intention of Jacques-Germain Soufflot, who constructed several full-size models of M. de Marigny's house in Faubourg du Roule and most famously an elaborate full-size representation of the Sainte-Geneviève Church for the laying of the foundation stone on 6 September 1764—a low plaster and gravel wall defining the plan, together with a canvas and screen façade, so that the king could judge the proportions and size of the elements at one look.[137]

The construction of elaborate models of architecture at full size for clients became somewhat less frequent during the nineteenth and early twentieth centuries, but the practice certainly did not die out. In 1910 Sir Edwin Lutyens constructed a full-size timber and tarpaulin

mock-up of his barbican design for Castle Drogo, which was never realized (figure 3.24). Using similar materials, in 1912 Peter Behrens and his assistant at the time, Mies van der Rohe, created two full-scale models of their separate designs for Helene and Anton Kröller-Müller's house-museum on the Ellenwoude Estate outside The Hague (figure 3.25). Both architects had their balsa and canvas constructions fitted with wheels so the models could be rolled around the grounds on rails to test out different locations for their designs.[138] Despite these efforts, neither project came to fruition, and the Kröller-Müllers sold their estate later that same year. Today many architects continue to make large models of proposed buildings and building parts to persuade a client or builder; these include Steven Holl's half-size model made for the Helsinki Museum of Contemporary Art, constructed to win over the engineers and to "demonstrate the quality of light and the economy of surfaces and textures."[139]

In the dialog between architect and builder, the full-size model or mock-up remains an important tool for confirming the construction method to be employed by a builder in executing the building. Several partial full-size constructions are recorded in Germany, England, and the United States from the nineteenth century, including a partial

| 3.24 |

Sir Edwin Lutyens, full-size timber and tarpaulin model of the barbican for Castel Drogo, 1910.

| 3.25 |

Ludwig Mies van der Rohe, full-scale wood and canvas model of Kröller-Müller house project, erected on actual site on the Ellenwoude meadow in Wassenaar, The Hague, Netherlands, December 1912.

| 3.26 |

Mock-up model of the Opera House in Frankfurt am Main, 1874.

front façade of the first floor of the Opera House in Frankfurt am Main from 1874 (figure 3.26), a cornice of Charles McKim's Boston Public Library from 1889, and one and a half bays of Rankin, Kellogg, and Crane's 1908 Department of Agriculture Building in Washington, DC. These were not constructed by the architect to win over the client with a design proposal but were created by the builder as *paradeigmata* for the approval of the architect. The American architect Egerton Swartwout confirmed in an article from 1911 the existence of full-size models that, because of their expense, are limited to details or ornament. Swartwout noted how difficult it is to judge their effect in an entire composition, since at "the modeler's [workshop] it is huge, massive, and rich in beautiful detail; [but in its intended location on the building] thirty or forty feet in the air it is thin, flat and characterless."[140] For Swartwout, a preferred approach was that employed in the design and building of the Denver Post Office, for which models of various parts of the building were executed at one-quarter of the full size. Once these were approved, "full size profiles and models were made, from which were cut full size zinc templates for the marble work."[141] By 1920, a handful of publications on the use of models promoted the use of cardboard at ¹⁄₁₆" or ⅛" = 1' 0" to study and gain approval of a building's general massing and appearance. As the American architect Frederic C. Hirons points out, once approved these were studied in Plasticine modeling clay at "¼ inch or ½ inch scale and later the detail and ornament may be developed to 1½ inch scale" by an architectural sculptor "to guide the stone cutters or terracotta men."[142] Yet, when technical questions arise concerning the efficacy of a proposed design, a full-size model can also be employed to demonstrate its structural soundness. This was certainly the case for Frank Lloyd Wright, whose tapering, thin steel mesh–reinforced concrete columns for the "Great Workroom" of his S. C. Johnson Wax Administration Building in Racine, Wisconsin, were rejected by the building inspector in 1936. To prove the stability and strength of his column designs, Wright had one constructed and loaded with sandbags on top until it collapsed (figure 3.27).[143] Wright's full-scale model became more than a tool for presenting designs to clients or to approve as a *paradeigma*, serving as a conversation between the architect's design and the engineering of that design—the testing and configuration of materials in relation to their performance.

| 3.27 |

Frank Lloyd Wright, testing of the structural column for the S. C. Johnson Wax Administration building, Racine, Wisconsin, 1937.

For a client or builder, a physical model is a demonstration of an architect's idea before their eyes. It is what Johann Gottfried Herder referred to as "physically present, tangible truth."[144] In his famous essay "The Work of Art in the Age of Mechanical Reproduction" (1935–1938), Walter Benjamin described this effect of the model as its "aura."[145] For Benjamin, all original, unique art has an invisible aura—something not transcendental but felt in the presence of its actual material, its making and aging over time. The physical model is for this reason approached with a degree of respect until it is accompanied by an alternate proposition. Because a three-dimensional model is not the actual building but a miniature, partial, or imperfect rendition of it, architects have sought to develop different methods for bringing their clients both physically and imaginatively inside such models to display the efficacy of their ideas.

....

AS A TOOL FOR DESCRIBING a proposed design to a patron or craftsmen, the scale architectural model continues to undergo subtle changes and developments in its use and methods of construction. For those architectural models whose use can be associated with the planning of an identifiable structure before the fourteenth century, there is evidence that congruency between the material and method of constructing the model and the building was expected. In part because of a diversity of artisans participating in the design and construction of wooden micro-architecture in Italy during the fifteenth and sixteenth centuries, this correspondence gave way to questions about how the use of wood as a modeling material affected how stone and brick architecture was imagined. At the same time, architects began to prefer to use larger scale models to win over uncertain clients who had questions about the visual effect or structural integrity of a proposed solution. The continued construction today of full-scale prototypes on building sites or in classrooms attests to the architectural model's popularity as an ideal tool for both architect and patron to judge how well a design performs in its material, form, and construction.

4
IN PLAIN AND SIMPLE FORM

> *Better then that the models are not accurately finished, refined and highly decorated, but plain and simple, so that they demonstrate the ingenuity of him who conceived the idea, and not the skill of the one that fabricated the model.*[1]

ARGUABLY NO STATEMENT in architectural history had a more profound effect on the use of architectural models than the one quoted above from the fifteenth-century artist and architect Leon Battista Alberti. It is central to his claim about architectural design in his treatise *De re aedificatoria* (On the art of building) that plain and simple scale models are a tool to aid the visualization of architectural ideas in three dimensions.[2] To preface his argument, Alberti introduced a concept of architectural design as the unity of invisible and visible elements: lineaments (*lineamenta*) and matter (also structure).[3] By "lineaments," Alberti is referring to a kind of imaginary or ideal structure of lines that make up the physical forms and masses of existing and proposed structures. Or in his own words, "All the intent and purpose of lineaments lies in finding the correct, infallible way of joining and fitting together those lines and angles which define and enclose the surfaces of a building."[4] For Alberti, these lineaments are independent of material and remain in the mind of the architect as abstract Euclidean lines with neither substance nor thickness. But these lineaments are not created ex nihilo: they can be recognized in different buildings that share the same form.[5] Since, as Alberti reasons, even the most experienced architects will know that in the course of construction, unforeseen problems will occur, forcing them to make costly changes, he recommends the construction of physical models as a tool to study and give definition to architectural ideas in three dimensions. He notes simply, "Having constructed these models, it will be possible to examine clearly and consider thoroughly the relationship between the site and the surrounding district, the shape of the area, the number and order of the parts of a building, the appearance of the walls, the strength of the covering, and in short, the design and construction of all the elements."[6] But Alberti is careful to warn that these models should not be "colored and lewdly dressed with the allurement of painting ... to attract and seduce the eye of the beholder." This is important for Alberti, since the aim of design is aid the architect in finding its lineaments.[7] Decorations would distract the model's user from concentrating on the lines and angles that define and enclose the surfaces of the building in physical three-dimensional form.

Alberti's method provides an important insight into a role played by modeling materials in the process by which architects give mental concepts form in nature. In distinguishing between "lineaments" and "matter," Alberti viewed matter not as irrelevant to architectural form but in dialogue with it. The elucidation of this idea had already occurred in Aristotle, who, in a discussion about causation, uses the example of an architect to explain the relationship between idea and matter as two different kinds of cause or explanation (*aition*). In his *Physics* Aristotle claims that there are four kinds of answers when one asks "why" something is: its material, formal (*eidos*), and efficient causes and its end or purpose (*telos*).[8] Using the example of a house, Aristotle reasons that a house could not exist unless material has received the idea (*eidos*) of "house" from the architect.[9] For Aristotle this *eidos* is an invisible form or idea that exists only when it is instantiated in a thing. This does not mean, however, that Aristotle's eidos is eternal and unchanging such that architects always create the same buildings. As a *nous poiētikos* (making mind), each architect generates their own mental representation of the house according to its *eidos*.[10] Alberti's pupil, Marsilio Ficino, similarly describes the architect as the one who "develops a Reason or Idea, as it were, of a building in his soul. Then he builds, as nearly as possible, the kind of house he has conceived."[11] It is these mental representations that Alberti believed the architect brings forth by transforming materials into a building, and indeed into a model of architecture.

The plain and simple physical scale model promoted by Alberti finds itself between the architect's idea and contingent realities. It would be wrong, though, to think that the architectural model results from a vision of something absent, a to-be-constructed building. Rather, the model fosters insight by allowing the idea of the architect to saturate the visible, without claiming to reduce the invisible to the forms and spaces of the model. The corporeality of the model makes architectural form, space, and structure immediately accessible to perception, and therefore the model is particularly useful as an anticipatory entity for study and speculation.

Given the long-standing use of architectural models as funerary, religious, dedicatory, didactic, and descriptive tools, it is strange that the familiar practice of an architect constructing small three-dimensional scale models to study or work out designs became normative only during the second half of the fifteenth century CE. If the activity did exist previously, it was considered either not worthy of mention or secondary to a conventional use of drawings and written descriptions. As evidenced by records and payment receipts from the Renaissance, assistants in an architect's workshop prepared models and then dismantled them when they had outlived their usefulness as a working tool or item of historical significance.[12] As a result, few of these design models remain today in municipal or museum archives demonstrating their use in architectural practice. What we do know from the extant materials and recommendations of architectural handbooks and treatises is it that until the twentieth century, plain and simple models were preferred over elaborately decorated ones for the study of architectural ideas in physical form.

If we want to know something about how an architect gives visible form to their first imaginings, we can certainly trace a line from Alberti to contemporary practice; doing so will show the real need for models to enable the architect to study and experience the space and forms of their designs in physical form. Following the repeated references to Alberti's modeling method, it will show how the introduction of new materials changed the emphasis of these models from a study of form and volume to surface and mass. This chapter, therefore, tracks the historical trajectory of using plain and simple models as a design tool to convey a sense of the way in which architects give mental concepts physical form. It thereby aims to illuminate the utility provided by these models in the process of translating an architect's idea into a sought-after building.

To begin with Alberti himself, we can find only a few examples of his proposed use of the model as a design tool during the fifteenth century CE. By his own account, Alberti had a wood model for the Tempio Malatestiano constructed before work began on site. Although the model is now missing, a letter from Giovanni di maestro Alvise from 21 December 1454 confirms that it became a useful point of reference for making decisions about the roof construction when Alberti was absent from the building site.[13] Of course, there is also Brunelleschi's wood model of the cupola and apses for the Florence Duomo. Alberti certainly knew Filippo Brunelleschi, to whom in 1435 he dedicated his treatise on the laws of perspective, *De pictura*.[14] It is difficult to date Brunelleschi's 1:50 cupola model, but specific characteristics including the width of the splays and diameter of the oculi correspond to the project of 1420.[15] Alberti would have seen the model during this time and observed its simplicity, as did Brunelleschi's biographer, Antonio Manetti, who claimed that Brunelleschi intentionally kept his models as simple, formal descriptions of his projects so that the woodworker who made the model "should not discover his every secret"[16]—a quality that resonated with Alberti's own thoughts about the model.

Perhaps the best demonstration in practice of the modeling method promoted by Alberti is a 1519 wooden model for the church of San Giuseppe in Florence, attributed to Baccio d'Agnolo, that was mentioned in the previous chapter. Although Giorgio Vasari claimed that Baccio made a wooden model for the church, scholars have debated its provenance, since the extant model bears a stronger resemblance to his design for the reconstruction of San Marco in Florence.[17] Some argue that these inconsistences are due to the model's having been constructed at an early stage in the planning of the church of San Giuseppe, when the client was seeking to acquire land and determine the costs.[18] Whatever its original intention, the simplicity is consistent with Alberti's recommendation: it is not painted; there is no hint of surface treatment but just a few pilasters, cornices, incisions, and markings in red chalk suggesting various features not actually built in the model (figure 4.1). Rather, the model primarily shows the disposition and relation of the parts of the building, their dimensioning, and the scheme of lighting. In this way, it would

enable Baccio to study and make changes to the design as, for example, Michelangelo would do with his model of a vault in the south hemicycle of St. Peter's in 1557.[19]

Also from this period is documentary evidence that models were regularly used in the cooperative work of stonemasons and goldsmiths as a medium to design and present architectural ideas north of the Alps in Augsburg, Germany. This evidence includes the 1503 wood model by the Augsburg goldsmith Jörg Seld, depicting his proposal for the Perlach Tower.[20] Seld's model is a relatively simple box but clearly indicates its relationship to the site (the city wall) and shows substantially more ornamentation than is displayed by Baccio's model for the church of San Giuseppe. Of particular relevance for our discussion is the date of Seld's model and its label as a *Visier*. This term is found in the payment receipt from the community of Augsburg, which refers to Seld's model not by the German word "Modell" but as "um ein Visier des Perlachturms."[21] The use of a similar term, *Vysierunge*, to denote a model to be copied in building construction occurs as early as 1459 at the Regensburg meeting of stone masons.[22] By the beginning of the sixteenth century, the term *Visierung* apparently

| 4.1 |
Baccio d'Agnolo, model of church of San Giuseppe, Florence, Italy, 1519.

was regularly used by masons and goldsmiths of a building model. The records for the construction of the cathedral of Bern contain a request from Bernhard Engelberg, a stonemason in Augsburg with whom Seld was known to collaborate, for the return of "ainer hultzin Visierung" (a wood model) illustrating his proposal for the completion of the cathedral tower.[23] The word, which derives from the Latin *videre* (to see), is an outdated term referring to a schematic outline or design sketch that shows the principal lineaments of a proposed work of art or architecture. The contemporary German word *Visier*, which refers to a gunsight through which one looks at one's target, retains some of this sixteenth-century meaning. In their *Deutsches Wörterbuch* Jacob and Wilhelm Grimm note the introduction of the word *Modell* into the German language in Nuremburg, Augsburg, and Strasbourg, where it was first used by goldsmiths as a replacement for *Visierung* and referred to lead and plaster jeweler casts or *modelli* coming from Italy.[24] For a long time, molds, forms, and models were commonly used in the art of goldsmithery.[25] Although the German word *Modell* was not yet applied to architectural models during this time, the Grimm brothers' account does connect it with an introduction of Italian modeling methods north of the Alps.

In accordance with the recommendations of Alberti in Italy, extant examples from Germany during the sixteenth through the eighteenth centuries show that plain and simple preliminary design models were used to study and visualize buildings in three dimensions. Because the majority of these were collected in only a handful of municipal archives or in princely *Kunstkammern* in Munich and Dresden during the mid-sixteenth century, they do not give us an adequate sense of the frequency and geographical reach of their use. Nevertheless, particular attention should be paid to the preliminary and second wooden models from the woodworker Adolf Daucher the Elder for the restoration of the eight-story *Lueginslandturm*—literally, "look into the countryside tower"—in the imperial city of Augsburg. Destroyed by fire in 1498, the *Lueginslandturm* was located at the city's northeastern corner, where it functioned as both a military observation post and a symbol of defensive readiness.[26] With the exception of windows and cornice-like bands marked on the surface, Daucher's 1523/24 preliminary model for the reconstruction of the *Lueginslandturm* is a simple, tall hexagonal mass with cylindrical turrets on each of its six sides surmounted by

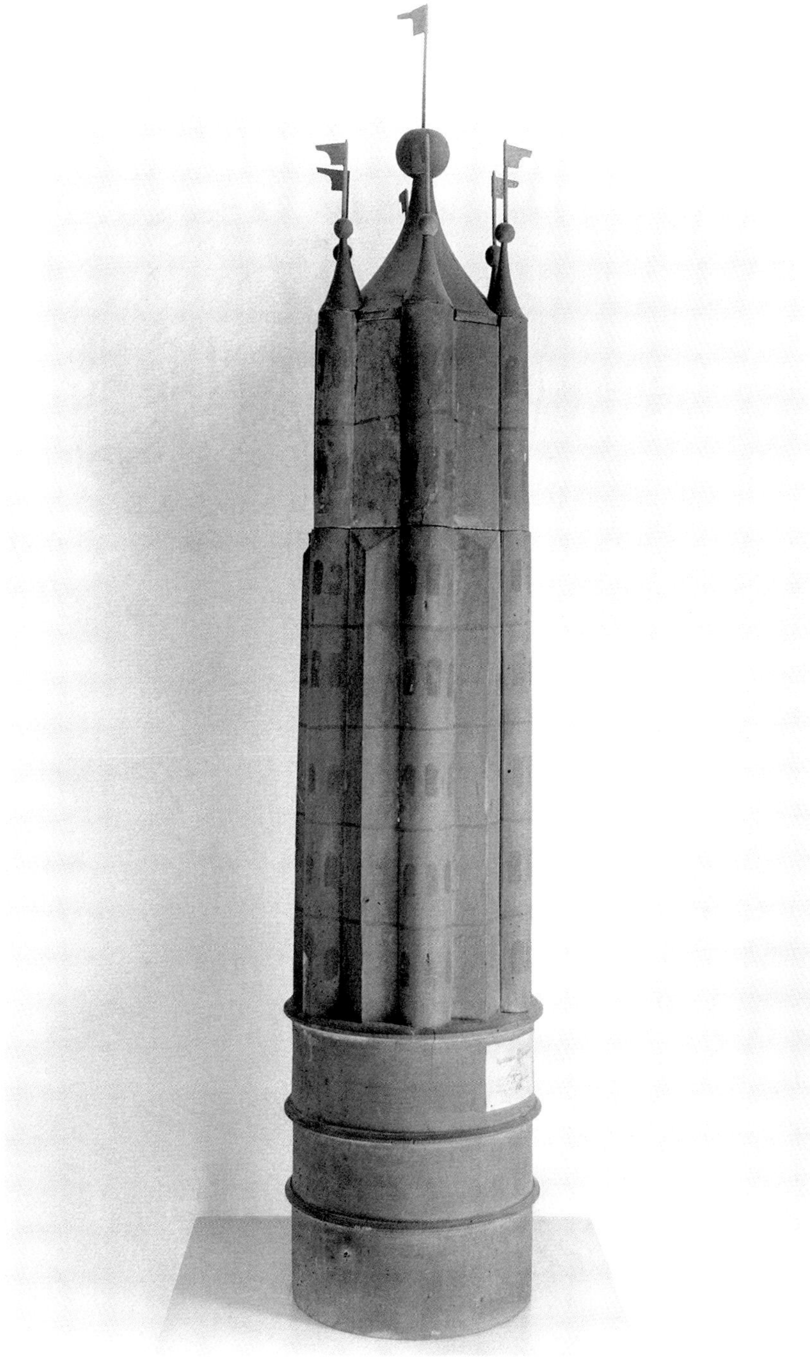

| 4.2 |

Adolf Daucher the Elder, preliminary model of the *Lueginslandturm*, 1523/24.

a curved bell-shaped spire (figure 4.2). In contrast, Daucher's second model is more complex; it includes windows, horizontal banding, and cornices that project from the surface of the tower shaft; it also shows adjustments to the heights of the tower turrets.

A handful of other *Entwurfmodelle* (preliminary models) from the same archive demonstrate how the architect's idea is given simple form in three dimensions so that its primary size, shape, and organization of spaces may be studied and compared with other designs.[27] Most notable among these are Elias Holl's three preliminary wooden models of the Augsburg *Rathaus* from 1614/15.[28] Compared to the final model from the same year, Holl's *Entwurfmodelle* are, with the exception of the painted windows on the so-called *Venezianisches Modell* (Venetian model), mainly unadorned, stacked wooden boxes perforated by holes (windows), thereby restricting the consideration of variations to the overall building plan, window treatment, size, and especially the configuration of the roof gables in either a cross or parallel format (figure 4.3).[29] These examples demonstrate that the model

| 4.3 |

Elias Holl, first preliminary cross roof gable model of the Augsburg City Hall, 1614/15.

filled a real need in helping the architect to make decisions by comparing alternative schemes simultaneously or sequentially.

As in Germany, the use of architectural models in France during the sixteenth century was greatly influenced by Italian practices. A vestige of this cultural exchange is the contemporary French word *modelle*, which, like the German *Modell*, derives from the Italian word *modello*; it was used for the first time during the sixteenth century in connection with the designs of the visiting Italian architect Domenico da Cortona (1465–1549) for the Château de Chambord and the Hôtel de Ville in Paris. Models were also recommended by the French architect Philibert de l'Orme (1514–1570), who, after spending three years in Rome measuring and excavating its ancient structures, returned to his hometown of Lyon in 1536. He inevitably found his way into the French royal court, first as conductor general of buildings and fortifications in Brittany for Francis I during 1545 and then, two years later, as first architect to Henry II. Unlike Elias Holl in Germany, de l'Orme left no known models exemplifying his use of them in practice; but after being replaced as royal architect by Francesco Primaticcio, an Italian artist with no specific training in architecture, he penned two insightful essays in which he reflected on their use. In the first, a memoir written in the first person and titled "Instruction de Monsieur d'Ivry" (1560), de l'Orme remarked on their importance in his own practice: he claimed that of "all the models I had made … they did not pay me a penny and if I did so, it cost two or three hundred crowns."[30] Seven years later, in two chapters of his *Le Premier tome de l'architecture*, de l'Orme advised architects to make models of building parts (staircases, vestibules, colonnades, windows, etc.) and a general model of the entire building as a way of prethinking architecture.[31] As in his memoir, he invoked his own personal experience to justify his claim, arguing, "I have conducted many great buildings[;] … what I have done, I have truly realized that everywhere there is nothing more necessary than a good model."[32] In the same spirit as Alberti, he warned that "a good architect who wants to represent a natural building must never produce a model which is 'made-up' or adorned with painting, gold plating, or colors. This is the manner of those who want to deceive."[33] Despite de l'Orme's advocacy, there is little evidence that architects were using models in France like those in Germany during the same period.

Though archives in France preserved few models, drawings created for handbooks on architecture and perspective during the sixteenth century suggest that models were constructed on a small scale in fragile, perhaps even perishable, materials and that they were immediately destroyed or recycled once they had fulfilled their purpose. These include drawings of model-like, siteless domestic structures by Jacques I Androuet du Cerceau for his *Troisième livre d'architecture* (1582), drawn from above at a variety of angles in both perspective and paraline form—that is, constructed from lines that remain parallel and do not converge at any point (figure 4.4).[34] Here du Cerceau was producing not renderings of existing structures but "invention drawings" for which perspectival views could not have been drawn from life. Du Cerceau probably created his drawings according to the rules of perspective he set down in *Leçons de perspective* (1579).[35] It is possible but unlikely that he would have created a detailed model for his drawings, since it would have been far cheaper to rely on a simple, unadorned physical scale description of the overall form and distribution of spaces and openings to obtain the proportion and scale of the entire structure in perspective and then add to it his own embellishments, including windows, door frames, cornices, and columns. This was certainly the approach of Jacques Perret, who attests to the use of small cardboard models as a tool for drawing his perspectives of fortification designs for his treatise *Des fortifications et artifices* (1601).[36] Like those of du Cerceau, Perret's drawings depict aerial views of siteless structures in perspective or paraline form. In many instances, the drawing of the entire structure is accompanied by a plan and a three-dimensional representation of the ground floor, enabling one to see the arrangement of spaces, openings, and architectural ornamentation inside—as if looking into a model from above (figure 4.5).

Following the establishment of the Académie Royale d'Architecture and later the École des Beaux-Arts, the use of architectural models in France greatly diminished. Founded in 1671 by Louis XIV, on the urging of Jean-Baptiste Colbert,[37] the Académie was the response to a crisis provoked by Gian Lorenzo Bernini's temporary commission for the design of the Louvre's east façade,[38] when designs submitted by French architects for the same east façade were perceived to lack of a comparable degree of "magnificence." Three models constructed under the guidance of Bernini's pupil and assistant Mattia de Rossi

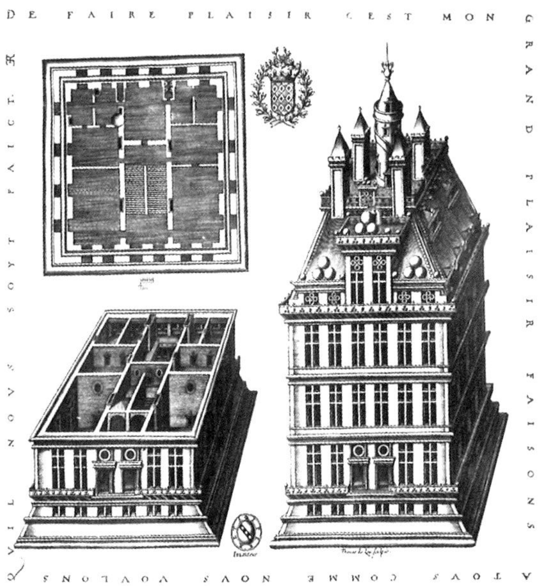

| 4.4 |

Jacques I Androuet du Cerceau, representation of a model in *Troisième livre d'architecture*, Project XX, 1582.

| 4.5 |

Jacques Perret, drawing of a model in *Des fortifications et artifices*, 1601.

in March 1666 attest to their use as an important tool for studying questions of design and construction. Although Bernini seems to have relied primarily on two-dimensional graphics in working on this project, a model of a staircase preoccupied de Rossi, causing him "much doubt as to the position to be given to their columns because they ... appeared to me very fine in relation to the vault which they must bear."[39] As a tool for visualizing a design in three dimensions, the model thus enabled de Rossi to continue the development of an aspect of the project that his master was content to represent in a small-scale drawing. Despite the Italian's efforts, his proposals failed to satisfy local norms and his project was dismissed. Nevertheless, they drove Colbert to propose the Académie to create an architectural culture that would institutionalize a distinctly French way of building—one especially suitable for royal buildings tied to the monarchy and its ambitions. It was replaced in 1795, a little more than 100 years later, by the École des Beaux-Arts, but the aims of these two institutions differed little: both sought to direct the arts toward glorifying France, as represented by the king and by the state, respectively. This did not mean that architectural models were irrelevant, but they were seen as an unnecessary expense for the education of a young architect. As the Académie noted early in its development, "After considerable deliberation concerning the difficulty, indeed the occasional impossibility of hitting upon everything with drawings and doing all that is necessary for the construction of a large building, this society has reached the conclusion that for the complete realization of the project, drawings as well as models cannot be dispensed with."[40] By the late eighteenth century, the physical scale architectural model was constructed for most significant building projects in France and came to be included among the tools (a pair of compasses, rulers, and a roll of drawing paper) that in a portrait identified an individual as an architect.[41]

| 4.6 |

Robert Maude, pasteboard model of preliminary design of the main quadrangle of University College, Oxford, early 1630s.

Similar to the situation in France, only scant evidence exists for the use of architectural models as a design tool in England during the sixteenth and seventeenth centuries. Arguably, the most familiar of these is given by the English architect Sir Henry Wotton. Referencing "Philippe" de l'Orme and the "Italian Architects" (presumably Alberti's *De re aedificatoria*), he endorsed the construction of study models made of "Pastboord or Wood" in his *Elements of Architecture*

(1624).[42] As Wotton advised, these models should "bee as plaine as may be, without colours or other beautifying, lest the pleasure of the Eye preoccupate the Judgement." The value of models—and, he says, "the bigger that this Type be, it is still the better"—is that they make it possible to see the entire project clearly, since "a little misery in the Premises, may easily breed some absurdity of greater charge, in the Conclusion."[43] An extant contemporary model from England is a pasteboard depiction of the perimeter walls of Richard Maude's design for the main quadrangle of Oxford's University College (figure 4.6).[44] Building accounts indicate that a number of models were constructed, including one of the building made out of wood by the Oxford joiner David Woodfield on 1 June 1632, as well as several pasteboard models created in connection with the westward extension of the Bodleian Library in the 1630s.[45] The extant pasteboard model consists of elevation drawings affixed to pasteboard and sewn together with thread at the corners. By assembling the drawings into such a model, its user is able to quickly and easily study not just the vertical distribution of the walls, rooms, and openings on the different floors but also their relation to one another and the masses defining the volume of the quadrangle. A similar approach is employed by Notaio Giuliano De Ferrari, who constructed a small paper model on top of the drawing of a proposed building in Genoa, Italy, in order to give a

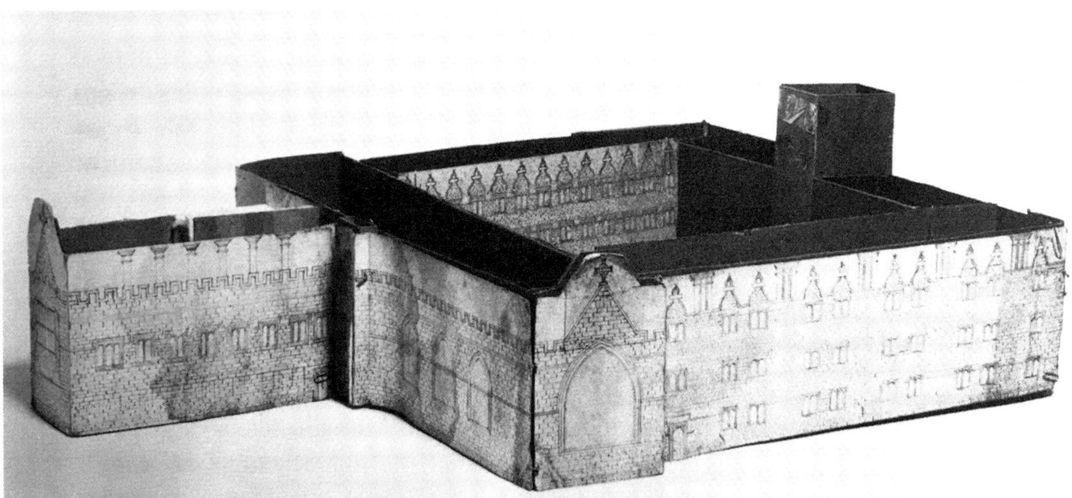

Goethe scholar, and occultist Rudolf Steiner was similarly inspired by nature in the design of his first Goetheanum at Dornach, Switzerland, in 1914, which he saw not as a kind of decoration but "just like a living organism that allows elevations and depressions to grow harmoniously out of itself."[65] In one of his lectures given during its construction, Steiner described how the activities that will occur in the internal space of the building should correspond with the architecture: "What is enclosed here in the spatial forms, what is spoken and done in them, should adapt to them, as the cake dough adapts to the negative form of the mold."[66] A sectional model of the Goetheanum in Plasticine, wood, and card demonstrates this sculpting of the interior with Plasticine in the hemispherical "mold" of the two domes. After the destruction of the Goetheanum by fire on New Year's Eve in 1922, Steiner developed a Plasticine model of a new design for the construction of a second Goetheanum in 1924 (figure 4.9). Unlike his models of the first Goetheanum, this one depicts only the exterior form of the structure, marked less by the sculptor's hands kneading and forming the Plasticine than by the flat surfaces of a knife. In its completed state, the interior and exterior of the second Goetheanum are created from the same material—reinforced concrete—as if formed by nature into a single organic entity. This organicism that Steiner found in the use of Plasticine resonated

| 4.9 |

Rudolf Steiner, Plasticine model of the second Goetheanum, 1924.

with the experimental ethos of his contemporaries in the German avant-garde.

A significant change in the use of architectural models occurred at the end of the First World War. After the abdication of Kaiser Wilhelm II in 1918, many German artists and architects, emboldened by a faith in a better future, joined together to speculate about the creation of a new postwar architecture: they created drawings and above all models that came to epitomize their search for new form. Initially formed as the Novembergruppe (November Group) and later the Arbeitsrat für Kunst (Working Council for Art), they published a manifesto that echoed the architect Bruno Taut's earlier call from 1914 for his peers to experiment and challenge the conventions dominating German architectural practice.[67] A handful of these individuals also questioned a normative use of physical models to create illustrations of preconceived architectural designs. Their plastic, unconventional, and seemingly irrational experiments in molding Plasticine and carving plaster designs of architecture were later given the label "expressionist." In his 1920 essay "Über Apollinisches und Dionysisches in der Baukunst" (On the Apollonian and Dionysian in architecture), the architectural historian Paul Klopfer speaks of the new architecture as if it were modeled in clay. For Klopfer this architecture is like an "entirely different, frameless, nontectonic style of building that as if with giant hands hollows out a walled block and creates space by hollowing."[68] What is remarkable about Klopfer's observation is that it demonstrates the profound effect that the modeling material—Plasticine—came to have on those imagining this new expressionist architecture.

Perhaps no individual better epitomizes this experimental spirit of German architecture during the postwar period than Hermann Finsterlin. Although Finsterlin did not train as an architect, he first came to the notice of his contemporaries in the Arbeitsrat für Kunst when its second director, Walter Gropius, invited him to exhibit a number of architectural sketches in their 1919 *Ausstellung für unbekannte Architekten* (Exhibition for unknown architects) in Berlin.[69] The models Finsterlin produced during the decade following the First World War are plastic, biomorphic formal compositions that are molded in clay, cast in plaster, carved, and painted a variety of primary and naturalistic colors (figure 4.10). A building as envisioned by Finsterlin was a natural living organism whose interior and exterior would be

experienced as one unity in the same way that nature has, over millions of years, created its own forms and monuments by growth and erosion. In a statement that could also be an explanation of Steiner's second Goetheanum design, Finsterlin likened the occupant of his house projects to "a privileged inhabitant of an organism, wandering from organ to organ, a giving and receiving symbiont of a gigantic fossilized parent body."[70] When the models are compared to the drawings of his houses it is clear that the one is not a faithful rendition of the other in all its materials and measures; rather, the model is a step in the process of making visible the architect's idea in three dimensions.

| 4.10 |

Hermann Finsterlin, study for a House of Sociability, project, ca. 1920.

By kneading clay, according to Finsterlin's contemporary Wassili Luckhardt, the architect could discover and imaginatively contemplate new ideas in the process of modeling their designs. As Wassili Luckhardt put it in "Vom Entwerfen" (On design) in 1921:

> One lays pencil and ruler aside, takes clay or Plasticine, and starts to knead right from the beginning, immediately and uninfluenced, and one will be astonished by the unformed clumps that are seen on the modeling table, and that have none of the nice proportions from the

> drawing table. But one will notice to one's astonishment that the light plays in these forms and that an air space surrounds this form. One will see by continuing the work, how these forms grow into the air space and, on the other hand, surround and enclose it.[71]

The Plasticine in Wassili Luckhardt's *Formphantasie* (form fantasy) model from 1920 and in his brother Hans's model of a *Volkstheater* (public theater) from 1921 (figure 4.11) is formed into mountain-like masses with wide bases that become narrower and more angular at their peaks. In Hans's *Volkstheater* model, the Plasticine mass has been drawn out into roofs while niches impressed into the surface describe arcades. The advantage of using Plasticine to test designs is that one can quickly and easily cut, divide, or add to the mass(es). Unlike work done with plaster or paper, changes and additions to the Plasticine do not leave tears, and marks may be quickly forgotten once the surfaces are smoothed out.

Luckhardt's effort aside, discussions about the use of architectural models in the design process were relatively scarce in Germany during this time. One striking exception that is relevant to this history comes from the German architect Fritz Schumacher in the multivolume *Handbuch der Architektur*, published between 1880 and 1943. In his contribution to the fourth volume of the handbook, "Das Entstehen des baulichen Kunstwerks" (The generation of the architectural work), Schumacher names the physical model as an important tool.[72] As he reasons, the aim of designing is the visible realization of the architect's idea, which he compares to a cloud that has a definite being but can transform into different shapes.[73] Schumacher claims that at the early stage of designing complex structures of cubic masses, the architect prefers "anspruchslose Linienzüge" (inelegant

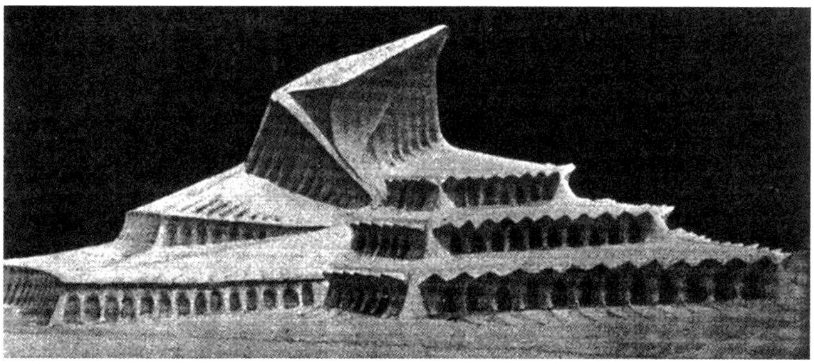

| 4.11 |

Hans Luckhardt, public theater, 1921.

| 4.12 |

Ludwig Mies van der Rohe, view of clay model (lost), preliminary scheme of Weissenhof Housing Colony master plan, *Die Wohnung* exhibition, Stuttgart, 1925–1927.

sketches) and a "plastische Modell" (malleable model),[74] not unlike the one employed by Mies van der Rohe for the planning of the Weissenhof Siedlung (Weissenhof Housing Colony) in 1925–1926.

Because it was necessary to determine the setbacks and overall layout of the masses for the Weissenhof Siedlung before the architects began working on their designs, clay became an ideal material for Mies van der Rohe to use in creating his a 1:200 scale model of the master plan (figure 4.12). Organized by Mies van der Rohe, the Werkbund's 1927 exhibition *Die Wohnung* (The Dwelling) aimed to display housing prototypes for middle- and lower-class people using various strands of modern architecture that had been developed during the first half of the decade.[75] Mies's task was to develop the urban plan, select the architects, and determine the sizes and budgets of the colony's twenty-one structures.[76] Without knowing the appearance of the future projects, the architect could study and control the sizes and formal relationships of the different building masses on the topography of the site by adding to, and cutting from, the clay of the model.[77]

In the Soviet Union of the 1920s, this compositional addition and subtraction of material from a clay mass became an important modeling exercise at the Soviet architecture school, Vkhutemas, intended to develop students' expressive perception of form and space during their first year of study. Nikolai Ladovskij was the school's founder and leader, along with Vladimir Krinsky and Nikolai Dokuchaev, of a movement of so-called rationalist architects who saw the design of architecture as reliant on timeless and scientifically verifiable properties, which they sought to define and articulate. They viewed rational architecture as the application of objective criteria, derived from scientific research, to questions of art in architectural design.[78] Receiving training frequently compared to the Bauhaus's *Vorkurs* (preliminary course),[79] students enrolled at Vkhutemas completed an introductory year of study in the "Basic Division," where lectures and seminars introduced fundamental theoretical concepts from physics, mathematics, art history, social science, and other specialties while studio and shop exercises taught practical knowledge of representation and composition (drafting, drawing, painting, modeling, and composition).[80] During this first year, students were assigned four increasingly complex space/volume compositional exercises, with each solution representing a step toward the creation of a complex three-dimensional final model made of clay or cardboard at a scale determined by the teacher.[81] Then, progressing from two to three dimensions, they employed clay to study the mass of a volume that emphasized a demonstration of weight, not as the illustration of physical forces but as a spatial solution to a spatial task. To that end, the models created by students in Ladovskij's course were simple cubic and at times cylindrical masses of clay that, following a similar process of design during the second year, were thereafter drawn in perspective as a building with windows, doorways, steps, and a roof (figure 4.13).

Unlike in Russia and central Europe, it was not until the 1930s that clay and Plasticine emerged as a popular material for modeling preliminary designs in England and the United States. The idea of including model making in architectural training was first mooted in 1914, when Berthold Audsley argued that "[i]t is very desirable that

| 4.13 |

Exhibition of student works, preliminary course, "space" discipline, Vkhutemas, mid-1920s.

all students in the architectural schools all over the country should be taught architectural miniature work in the elementary stages at least."[82] Around 1921 the Columbia University School of Architecture was one of the first institutions to introduce model making to the curriculum, and thereafter models increasingly became an integral part of architectural education.[83] By 1942 another writer observed that this practice had also extended to England, where "most schools of architecture now regard scale model making as an essential part of training."[84] This new status of the model occurred at a time when architectural education began to change its emphasis from a Beaux-Arts approach to the composition of the "elements" of architecture—orders, windows, walls, columns, stairs, pediments, and the like—to a "primary concern of architecture with the grouping and proportioning of enclosed spaces for human need."[85] The American architect and pedagogue Ernest Pickering published an academic handbook, *Architectural Design* (1933), that advocated developing an architectural scheme for the totality of architecture. Following Pickering's

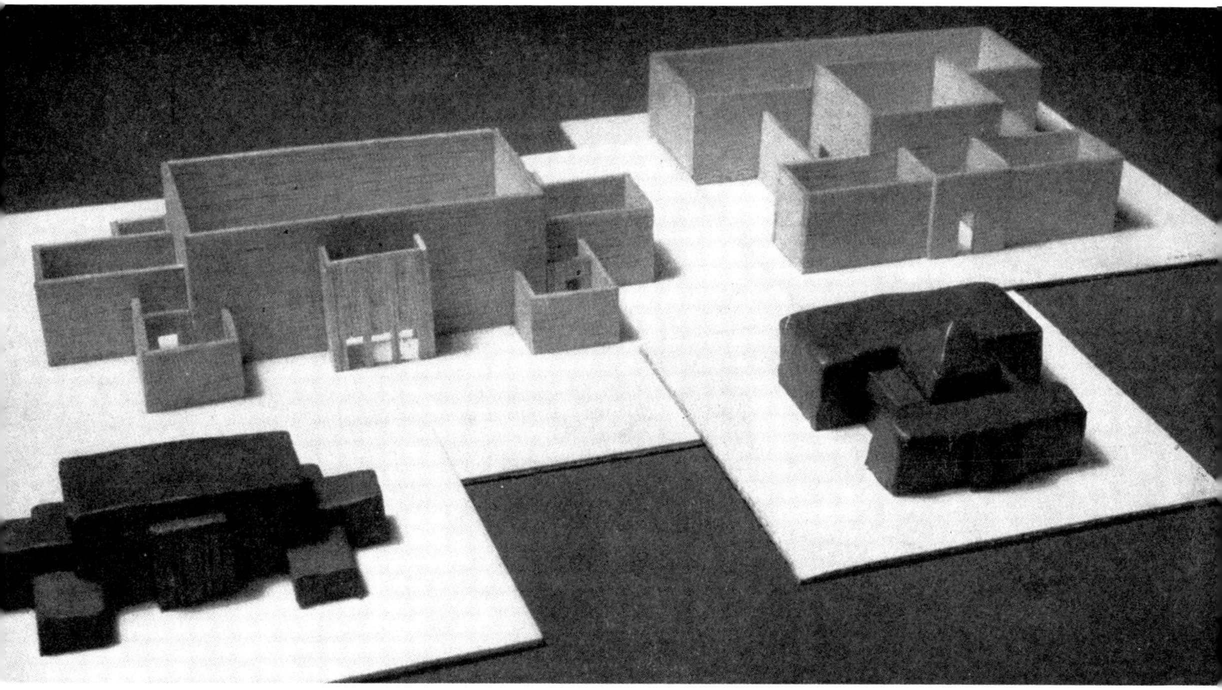

recommendation, a student or member of an atelier would begin by making small-scale freehand studies on tracing paper during the first or second week to establish a conceptual approach, an *esquisse*, toward the general relations and proportions of the masses and spaces before attempting to develop the design to a plan or section at a prescribed scale.[86] Eight years later, when Pickering published the second edition of *Architectural Design* (1941), the model gained more prominence in the design process and he included the use of models in the preliminary development of a design solution. In a chapter of his book dedicated to the design process, Pickering advised designers not only to cultivate an *esquisse* in plan and section but also, with the aid of small clay massing and balsa wood "space models," to study the different aspects of the proposed design and their relationship to each other (figure 4.14).[87] For Pickering, "These models, together with small clay models to show mass, give a quality of realism to architectural design which is lacking in two-dimensional drawings."[88] The distinction between the cardboard and the clay model had already

| 4.14 |

Ernest Pickering, mass and space models, 1941.

been made by LeRoy Grumbine, who, anticipating the observation of Fritz Schumacher cited above, wrote in 1925: "Clay is useful where the draftsman draws freehand: cardboard where he uses T-square and triangle. To make a scale model of a building in clay is like drawing an elevation freehand."[89]

In part because of this increasing use of architectural models in academia, but also because of a changing economic landscape in the United States during the 1930s and '40s, a new profession of model maker emerged in the mid-twentieth century to assist architects in their designs. The number of people studying architecture rose during the first two decades of the twentieth century, but many found themselves unemployed when the Great Depression hit the United States during the 1930s. Thanks to the installation of model shops in architecture schools during this time, some found work as professional architectural model makers, preparing models for exhibitions, fairs, and architectural practices. In a 1936 article from *Architect's Journal*, Kenneth McCutchon noted that early modern architects in England were actively creating "sketch models ... very early into the conception of a building," adding, "In this way faults and weaknesses that never reveal themselves on paper become instantly apparent, and these can be rapidly studied by altering the model or by adding and taking away pieces as desired, until the best solution is found."[90] An article from 1942 similarly explained, "In modern processes the necessity for the model arises at an early stage in design. The initial idea may be formulated on paper, but immediately the model directs mass relationships of parts and their proportions, shows the necessities of light, shade and color and the deference of building to environment."[91] We should note, however, that these preliminary study models, crafted by a professional model maker, differ considerably from the Plasticine or clay models that Pickering argued could, like those employed by Luckhardt or Mies in Germany, be freely altered as their maker discovered new ideas in the process of molding them.

Nevertheless, by the middle of the century, the architectural model attained an important role in the design process of larger firms such as Ludwig Mies van der Rohe (set up by Edward Duckett as early as 1946)[92] and I. M. Pei and Partners (since 1959), which installed model shops in their own offices. As can be seen in photographs of Mies explaining his

| 4.15 |

Mies van der Rohe and the real estate developer Herbert Greenwald discussing a model, 1956.

| 4.16 |

Theodore Conrad, preliminary cardboard model for the Metropolitan Life North Building (design by Harvey Wiley Corbett), 1928.

design for the ITT campus plan or discussing a housing project with the Chicago developer Herbert Greenwald (figure 4.15), Mies was fond of simple preliminary models. By the 1950s, for the first time in history individuals could specialize completely in architectural model making without having to supplement their income in some other way.[93] One of Skidmore, Owings & Merrill's favorite model makers was Theodore Conrad, the "dean of the model makers," who was among the first independent architectural model makers to create a range of model types for architects, including construction models, details, mock-ups, sections, and even simple mass models that marked the space a building or buildings would occupy (figure 4.16).[94]

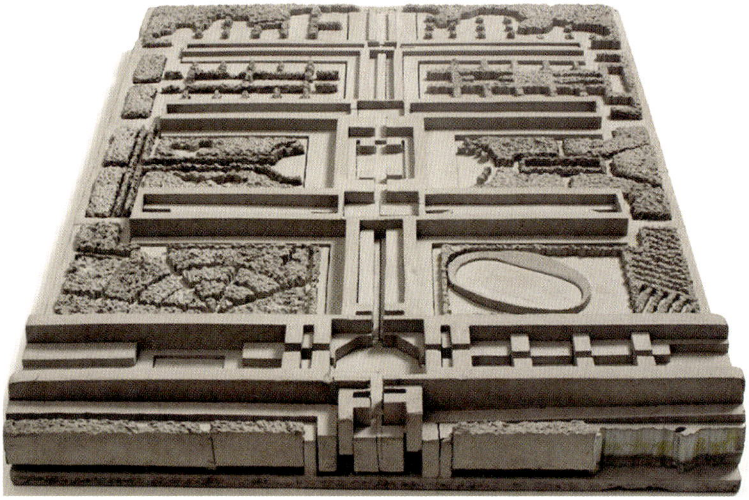

Unlike in the first three decades of the twentieth century, most publications about architectural models during the 1950s focused on the practice of professional model makers rather than on their use by architects as a design tool. In Germany, though, two architects from the early 1960s are worth a mention.[95] The first is Oswald Mathias Ungers, an architect and architectural theorist; during his early career he became known for the use of unornamented solid wood blocks to represent the formal mass of his designs in three dimensions, as demonstrated by the models he created of his 1960–1961 Bauer House design (figure 4.17) or the Neue Stadt housing project near Cologne from 1961 to 1964. In April 1964, Ungers became a professor at the Technische Universität Berlin, where his teaching began to include so-called weekly assignments that explored the spatial program of a conventional single-family house.[96] Students in Ungers's seminar displayed a marked preference for preparing extremely abstract models, usually without windows or doors, and often even without roofs. More important to them than to realistically depict the proposed design was to concisely encapsulate the formal concept.[97] The second architect is Rob Krier, who constructed a number of 1:850 scale painted Styrofoam models of ideal urban designs between 1964 and 1973 (figure 4.18). Although extruded polystyrene foam was originally conceived by the Swedish inventor Carl Georg Munters, its patent rights were purchased in 1947 by Dow Chemical, which began selling Styrofoam as insulation for buildings because of its good thermal insulating properties and moisture resistance. No one knows who first employed Styrofoam as a modeling material, but the US Navy used it during the Second World War for constructing swimming floats and in the 1950s it found new applications in everything from furniture to the floral arts. Already in 1957, it was common practice to cut Styrofoam with a hot wire or a knife heated in a flame.[98] Krier used a wire to cut and assemble both hard and rough-edged blocks to represent ideal urban configurations of building masses surrounding green spaces. These designs, which Krier referred to as "construction kits," were used as modules; he assembled them side by side to create a proposal for Stuttgart as a new 12-kilometer-long linear city. Despite the differences between the materials and scales of Ungers's and Krier's models, both are significant because they demonstrate a change in the use of a plain and simple model from serving as a preliminary

| 4.17 |

Oswald Mathias Ungers, Bauer House, 1960–1961.

| 4.18 |

Robert Krier, reconstructing devastated urban space with examples from the city of Stuttgart, 1973.

Over the past few decades, a number of digital tools previously relegated to the factory have found their way into architectural design schools and practices.[108] As was done in models made of hand-molded clay or wire-cut foam, computer numerically controlled (CNC) additive and subtractive technologies construct physical representations of digital architectural models in a single material. Here, the movements of the tool to remove or add material (with a router or extruder, respectively) are controlled by a digital file generated by the architect. In the subtractive process, equipment takes away material by cutting or milling it in sections. Conversely, the additive manufacture (AM) of architectural models—often called "3D printing" or "rapid prototyping"—employs an automated fabrication technology to make a three-dimensional physical object directly from digital data by adding material to a mass, layer by layer.[109] Although molding and cutting clay or Styrofoam by hand can also enable the architect to visualize a variety of three-dimensional forms and textures, using a computer to numerically cut or print a 3D model gives the model maker more control over the scale and complexity of the model's curved surfaces. One benefit of 3D-printed models in particular is that multiple interlocking (and at times movable) parts can be printed as a single mass without any need for assembly. Like those who drew on cast plaster or folded paper models at the beginning of the twentieth century, today's architect who employs a CNC device to print, cut, or rout a model in three dimensions must already have a clear understanding of the architectural idea before the model is begun. This technique is hardly useful for an architect whose ideas are still undefined, however, and it leaves little room for the designer to continue making changes and discoveries during the modeling process.

The enduring employment of simple, unadorned models attests to their utility for making designs visible in three dimensions. Whether constructed as a mass of Plasticine, as folded paper, or as an assembly of stiff wood planes, these models retain their value in the design practice by giving their user the ability to interact with the actual forms and space(s) of the proposed architecture. The French philosopher Maurice Merleau-Ponty called this preobjective, kinaesthetic awareness "être-au-monde" (being-toward-the-world): he argued that it is made possible by a preconscious system of bodily movements and spatial equivalences or "body schema" that involves a dialectic between the present body and the habit body (the sedimentations of past activities that are unnamed and independent in character).[110] In this position, as "being-toward-the-world," the architect uses the same awareness to inhabit the model in order to contemplate the efficacy of lived goals that are both spatial and structural.[111] This doesn't mean that preliminary models are limited to designs that primarily emphasize form, like those of early European modernism; rather, because of their simplicity, they enable the architect to quickly and easily study changes to the primary configuration of spaces, volumes, and the masses that define those spaces and volumes while a project is being developed. As Scamozzi warned, "Yet models are like young birds, amongst which one can not discerne the males from ye females but being growen bigger are knowen whither they be Eagles or Ravens: and therefore the owners of the workes may sometimes easily be deceaved by Modells."[112] When the use of a model is limited to describing a proposed design's formal and spatial attributes, the architect's imagination is free to speculate on building materials and structural possibilities. This equally important role played by modeling materials themselves—as informant, guide, and source of inspiration for an architect's designs—is the subject of the next chapter.

5
MODELING MATERIAL AS MEDIUM

WHEN MAKING A MODEL of architecture, a designer has a wealth of different materials to choose from. Almost immediately, though, the model maker will discover that not all materials are the same, nor can they be used to create a three-dimensional description of every architectural form, space, or structure. Rather, modeling materials such as bent card, cut balsa, and even clay have individual qualities that can be manipulated in only a limited number of ways. It is not that the materials employed will restrain the architect's imagination, but that they are endowed with a vital propensity which invites the architect to think about their designs in particular ways.

We saw in the previous chapter that this function of the model to inform thinking was not a primary concern of pre-nineteenth-century architects, who preferred to study and develop planned designs using plain and simple models. In these instances, models were frequently constructed of single materials such as wood, paper (pasteboard), plaster, or clay so that they could evaluate the primary effect of the form and organization of spaces. But this is only one history of the architectural model. There is evidence that since antiquity, architects have also relied upon their architectural modeling materials to act as an informant and source of inspiration for new design ideas in miniature. The term "medium" itself comes directly from the Latin adjective *medium* (middle), and during the sixteenth century it referred to an intermediate agent or instrument, whether person or thing, used as a means of communication or expression. It is this sense of the term, as applied to modeling materials, that will be the focus of this chapter.

The first half of this chapter explores the appropriateness ascribed by architects to one modeling material over another for studying modeling material for another became an important factor in how they evolved. One notices that the preliminary models of both projects were constructed as hollow cardboard masses, but the employment of a new modeling material—string in the case of the de Young Museum, and wire mesh for the Prada Aoyama—engendered a significant change in the project's development.[3] Once the model maker began to experiment with string as a modeling material for the de Young Museum's observation tower design, the faceted cardboard mass of its surfaces was transformed into a smooth twisting hyperbolic surface, along whose edges visitors would slowly turn 360 degrees as they ascend to a panoramic view of San Francisco. Similarly, by following the iterative development of models for the Prada Aoyama design, one can observe how the introduction of wire mesh became a motivating force for the conception of the glass façade's cellular grid. As demonstrations of the compelling force of the modeling material in an architect's work, these models in Herzog & de Meuron's work testify to the importance of a specific modeling material as an appropriate medium for both the conception and also the description of architectural ideas.

This role that modeling materials can play as informant in the development of an architectural design is not confined to contemporary practice but can in fact be observed in examples from antiquity. For example, we saw in chapter 3 that the limestone employed in making the miniature column capitals from early Egypt enabled the model maker to fashion sharper edges and angles than would have been possible using the sandstone of the full-size temple. In contrast, Vitruvius's story about the architect Callias's use of a model crane to deceive the citizens of Rhodes, told in chapter 2, demonstrates an awareness of how a modeling material can provide both information and disinformation about the performance of building materials in a larger structure.[4] A few centuries before Vitruvius, in *Physics* 2.3 Aristotle formulated an understanding of materials as one of the essential causes of created things. In terms of architectural modeling, even a miniature depiction of a completed design may be expected to represent not only its visible characteristics but, as the citizens of Rhodes assumed in Vitruvius's example, also its structural limitations. Despite Vitruvius's warning, modeling materials did not receive the same consideration from early Italian Renaissance treatises on architecture, which tended to echo the preference for "plain and simple" models expressed by the fifteenth-century architect Leon Battista Alberti.[5] With the exception of a few architects and the specific uses to which they put architectural models, in only a handful of cases over the next four and a half centuries were modeling materials employed as a medium for thinking about the building materials.

One exception is the sixteenth-century Italian sculptor, painter, and architect Michelangelo di Lodovico Buonarroti, whose design of the Laurentian Library Vestibule Stairs demonstrates an awareness of the informative role of modeling materials. Michelangelo began the Laurentian Library project in 1525 but left for Rome in 1534 when he fell out of favor with the young Alessandro de' Medici. At the time of Michelangelo's departure, only the walls of the reading room had been erected and completion of the project was entrusted to Niccolò Tribolo, Giorgio Vasari, and Bartolomeo Ammannati, using plans and instructions from Michelangelo. The plans for the staircase were incomplete, however, frustrating Tribolo's attempts to lay out the treads. In 1549 Tribolo abandoned the project, and Vasari begged Michelangelo several times during the 1550s to return to Florence to help guide its completion; each time the master refused, citing existing obligations in Rome. The staircase thus remained unresolved until 1559, when Michelangelo sent Vasari a clay model of a tripartite stair, together with a letter in which he explained that it was intended to do no "more than give you [Ammannati] an idea, remembering that what I formerly proposed was freestanding and only abutted on to the door of the Library."[6] Constructed in stone rather than the walnut specified by Michelangelo, the vestibule staircase that Ammannati constructed leads up to the reading room in three flights—the treads of the outer flights are straight while those of the center are convex, resting on top of three elliptical steps and giving the entirety the character of a stream flowing down to three pools of water.[7] The length of time that it took for Michelangelo to produce a design for the completion of the stairs was due in part to his preoccupation with other projects but also in part, as his letter suggests, to his not yet having formulated the final scheme.[8] Michelangelo's method of working, which was open to changes and alterations throughout a project's development, lends support to this inference.[9] Although the majority of Michelangelo's extant architectural models are constructed out of wood, for his sculptures he was known to create three-dimensional clay and wax sketch models called *bozzetto*, while a more finished scale model was known as a *modello*.[10] Similar to a *bozzetto*, the clay employed by Michelangelo in constructing his architectural model was an ideal material for sculpting the curves and angles of the stairs, serving not as a receptacle of the architect's design but as the means through which he could search and think about how people moved down the steps like water over stones in a stream.

One of the earliest discussions about the proper selection and employment of materials for constructing models appeared in 1615 in Vicenzo Scamozzi's *Idea della architettura universale* (*Idea of a Universal Architecture*). As Scamozzi observes, architectural models can be made of "diverse materials, as wood, stucco, & pasteboard or the like according to euerie man's mind or fancie," and he made numerous suggestions for the kinds of woods to be used to represent the visual qualities of the materials employed in constructing the "ornaments."[11] For Scamozzi, though, a model should "show the worth and estimation of what it represents," and to this end he cautioned against the use of a "flimsy material" like pasteboard, because "such thinness cannot rightly represent the thickness of the walls."[12] By criticizing a particular modeling material as inappropriate for emulating the building material, Scamozzi is departing from Alberti's primary focus on using a model to describe the form of the building. Though the model is still an important tool for impressing a client, in Scamozzi's view to make such an impression the modeling material must also adhere to the characteristics of the building materials, not merely for the architect's benefit but also to demonstrate the "worth and estimation" of the proposed design. As we will see, Scamozzi's approach to his modeling materials is not unique in the history of architecture, but it was practiced by only a handful of architects before the twentieth century.

Among them was one of Scamozzi's contemporaries, Francesco Borromini, who employed red wax as a medium for making visible its complex spatial formations. Unfortunately, during the last few days of Borromini's life, he destroyed most of his wax and clay models as well as many drawings when he was "afflicted by a fever which gave signs of some violence and malignance."[13] Judging by the inventory of goods at his death, one can observe that Borromini created models of clay, wood, and above all red wax for a number of projects, including Sant'Agnese in Agone, San Carlo alle Quattro Fontane, and the Oratory of the Chiesa Nuova.[14] Compared to clay, red wax is stiffer and makes sharper edges; its pliability is increased when one rubs it beneath one's fingers or, as Vasari observes, adds "a little tallow or turpentine and black pitch; of which tallow renders it more manageable; turpentine, holding itself together, and pitch gives it a black color, and gives it a certain hardness after which it is worked into a finished state."[15] This workability of red wax must have appealed to Borromini, for he could push and pull the models' masses to study the spatial fluidity of the sculptural, convex, and concave walls or the sharp pilaster and cornice edges in the same space of the to-be-constructed building. Borromini used these wax forms in tandem with graphite drawings. Once a form was made manifest in the model, it was then geometrized in the drawings according to the numerical-metric language of the orders: one method enabled the architect to visualize the complex transformation of the forms across the x, y, and z axes; the other, the orthogonal distribution of the measures.[16] But the two media were also similar in that the red wax, like the graphite of his drawings, could be altered, erased, reinterpreted, and corrected.

Despite the advantages identified by Borromini in employing red wax to model complex forms, it seems to have fallen out of use by architects when, during the mid-eighteenth century, architecture experienced a decisive turn to classical and especially Vitruvian principles. The most significant modeling materials to emerge at that time were cork and plaster for representing extant and idealized depictions of antiquity. Cork models were originally used for creating models of *presepe* (Christian nativity scenes),[17] but during the 1760s the English painter and art dealer Thomas Jenkins and the English collector Charles Townley commissioned the fabrication of two cork models of important antique structures: the round temple at Tivoli and the temples of Paestum, respectively.[18] Because of its soft, porous, cellular nature, cork lends itself easily to being cut with a knife to model smooth surfaces and straight edges. But it can also be broken with one's hands or a blunt instrument, giving the surface a rough and uneven edge. These characteristics of cork were taken advantage of in its use as the background structure for a *presepe*, and they made it a popular material during the eighteenth century for modeling faithful depictions of the partially decomposed surfaces and edges of

| 5.8 |

Ludwig Mies van der Rohe with a model of Crown Hall, Illinois Institute of Technology, 1956.

architects and their clients exceedingly realistic and accurate models, in some cases providing a map that was better than the territory.

What emerged from the increased level of detail available to the model maker were constructions that were no longer simply miniature imitations of buildings but structures with their own complex engineering and construction problems. As Jacobs observed in her article, some of these models required their own roof cables, tension rods, and air-conditioning systems.[41] The argument for making such detailed and complete models was that the client and architect could see the entire structure and study its appearance, the interrelationship of its parts, and its context to avoid what would become full-size mistakes. Some materials, however, did not always achieve the effect of reality. For example, if one compares the model of Mies's Crown Hall at the Illinois Institute of Technology (figure 5.8) with the completed structure, the acrylic used in the model is far more transparent than glass is in the reflective light of the sun. The challenge facing architects after the miniature boom continues to be to find materials and methods for representing architectural ideas in ways that communicate their intended effect. Certainly many examples of architects who introduced a new modeling material or devised an innovative use of an existing one could be named, yet any discussion about such advances over the last four decades of the twentieth century would be incomplete without mentioning Friedrich Kiesler, Paolo Soleri, and Frank Gehry.

The renowned architect, set designer, artist, and philosopher Friedrich Kiesler is an important model maker because of his innovative use of wire mesh and concrete as appropriate media to study the complex forms of his 1958 Endless House project. The Endless House is notable as an early exploration of unifying the disconnected vertical and horizontal surfaces of the wall, floor, and ceiling popular in late twentieth-century avant-garde architecture. In designing his Endless House, Kiesler sought to develop spaces based on the concepts of "connectivity," "correality," and "biotechnique" that would be in direct opposition to what he perceived as the static, rectilinear rooms of the glass boxes dominating the modern architecture of his era.[42] Continually revised over a sixteen-year period, Kiesler's drawings and models attest to his search for a continuous three-dimensional surface that he desired to be "endless like the human body—there is no beginning and no end."[43] In 1950, for his first model of the house, Kiesler produced an eight-piece egg-shaped ceramic mass in collaboration with the sculptor David Hare.[44] Almost immediately after the completion of the model, Kiesler produced drawings in which the walls and grouping of cellular rooms became increasingly fragmented into shells. When Kiesler was invited to participate in the Museum of Modern Art's *Visionary Architecture* exhibition in 1958, he turned to another material to model his house, wire mesh—a porous, pliant metal frame that would permit him to bend and fold the surfaces of his house around each other (figure 5.9). The resulting 2.5-meter-long model was covered with cement to fix the organic arrangement of overlapping shell-like surfaces that slope up to form walls, which in turn bend inward to create the ceiling and then down again to the floor. His project is one of the first since Borromini's to demonstrate reliance to his most preliminary imaginings about his building volumes. In a frequently quoted remark, Gehry declared: "Paper is structure. If I can make it out of paper I know I can build it."[46] In truth, he is relying on a separate structure to keep his paper-thin walls standing up; this was made possible by CATIA, a computer program from the aerospace industry that he used for the first time in 1992 to develop the steel framing for his Barcelona Fish project and used again for the Guggenheim Bilbao, completed in 1997.[47] Once the *x*-, *y*-, and *z*-coordinate points of Gehry's paper models were digitized, the design team edited the 3D model in the computer, which was used to smooth out surfaces and create better transitions from surface to surface (figure 5.11).[48] When the 3D model was complete in the computer, CATIA was able to add structure (steel I beams) to the model in real scale.[49] The program can give the designer exact dimensions of steel beams, columns, and sheets of material needed to build Gehry's paper and card models at full scale.

While these developments might suggest that architects would continue to search for tools for translating their physical models into buildings, in fact almost the opposite has happened, as building materials are being influenced by modeling materials. This has largely resulted from the advent of new digital tools to cut, print, and assemble digital models in physical three-dimensional form. Some of these are tools that cut planar materials such as wood, plastic, and some metals along two or three axes using computer numerically controlled (CNC) lasers, routers, or water jets; others enable the architect to "print" physical three-dimensional renditions of digital models, numerically depositing 3D powder or plastic layer by layer onto a surface as a mono-material mass. Because the CNC lasers, routers, and jets used by architects to create the planar elements of models emulate tools used for cutting and assembling building materials, questions have arisen today regarding whether it is possible to develop new materials and methods for printing buildings that emulate those used for printing models.

What the examples mentioned thus far attest to is the unique role of the modeling material as an aid to imagining architecture in three dimensions. Bachelard observes that this "material cause" of imaginative activity has been neglected by philosophical discourse, proposing in his *Water and Dreams* (1942) a distinction between the formal and

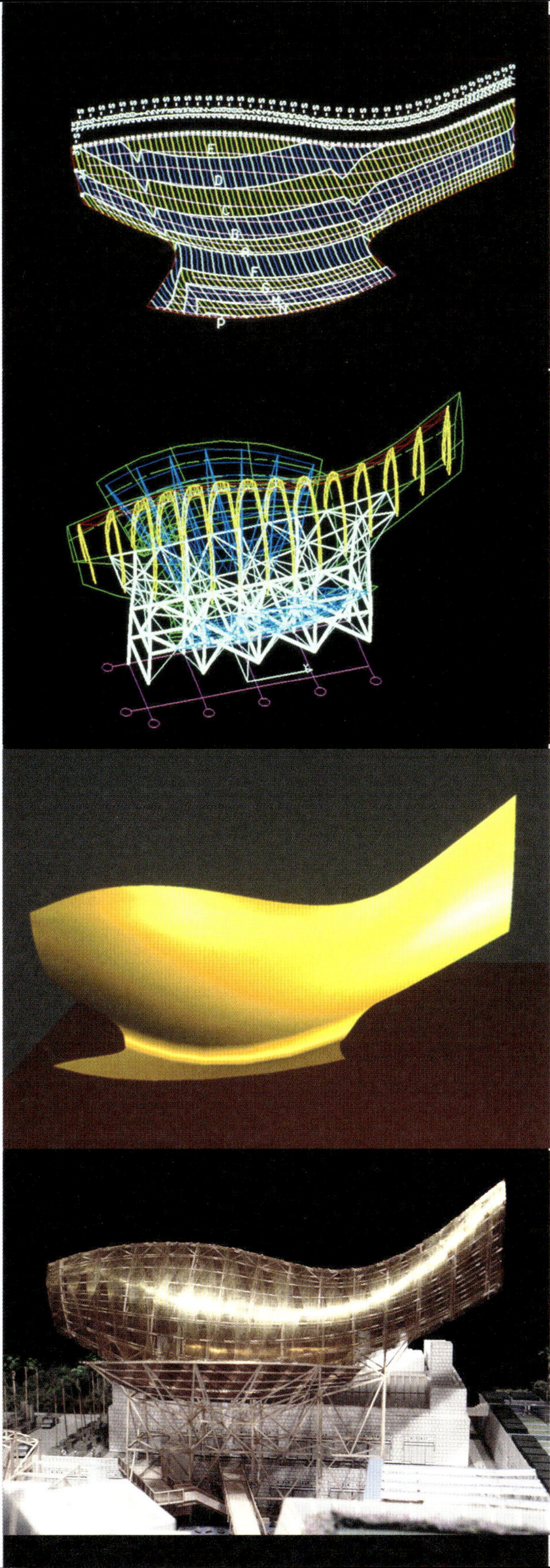

| 5.11 |

Frank Gehry, computer and built models for Gehry's fish sculpture for the Olympic Village in Barcelona, 1992.

material imagination by considering how images arising from matter tend to project deeper and more profound experiences than those arising from form.[50] As we witnessed in the previous chapter, the privileging of form over matter has been deeply imbedded in the modeling practices of architects since as early as Alberti, who promoted design as a formal process to find the "lines and angles which define and enclose the surfaces of the building."[51] Yet the split between form and matter goes back even further in the philosophical tradition, as seen in Aristotle's concept of *hylomorphism*, or that substance is made up by *hylē* (matter) and *morphē* (form).[52] Aristotle endowed his architect, as the one giving form to buildings, with a faculty that forms images, an imagination that resides between sensible and rational experience.[53] By considering the propriety of modeling materials, the architect is encouraged to speculate on the efficacy of the building material not as secondary to architectural form and structure but as essential to its raison d'être.

FORM-FINDING

While the physical model is uniquely positioned as a tool for informing architects about the efficacy of their building materials, experienced designers also know that their modeling materials have inherent tendencies and propensities that can aid them in generating unexpected formal and structural solutions. In *The Nature and Art of Workmanship* (1968), the craftsman and professor of furniture David Pye describes these unexpected discoveries in the arts and crafts as "the workmanship of risk."[54] According to Pye, there are risks involved in the creation and production of any artifact crafted by hand. In handmade work, unlike those works that are manufactured by a machine, "the quality of the result is not predetermined, but depends on the judgement, dexterity, and care which the maker exercises as he works."[55] What is interesting about Pye's thesis is that it challenges the notion that the model maker's approach toward their modeling architecture is *hylomorphic*—that is, the assumption that physical objects result from the combination of matter and form—and that their modeling material is therefore selected because of its ability to depict the form or, as mentioned above, to emulate a proposed structure's material characteristics. But for an architect who wishes to explore how extrinsic forces may be a source of inspiration for new formal and structural solutions, the modeling material is no longer a passive receiver of form but rather an important player in a process of morphogenesis. The French philosopher Gilbert Simondon explicates this role of matter in his theory of individuation, arguing that form is really emergent in the form-taking activity rather than given in advance.[56] As Simondon concludes, the hylomorphic model corresponds to the perspective of someone who, like an architect's client, stands outside the work and sees what goes in and what comes out but nothing of the actual processes whereby materials take their ultimate forms.[57]

The problem with Pye's and Simondon's theses is that few architects are free to generate architectural forms at will; instead, they are tasked with the design of a structure for specific purposes. This doesn't mean that inspiration comes ex nihilo, because the act of modeling is in many ways dependent upon memory: an architect's previous thoughts, images, and experiences strongly influence which modeling materials they choose to inspire their designs. This is a matter not of predetermining the architectural form and all the steps needed to get there, but of opening up a path to find an analogical relationship between the model construction and the building construction. As the design theorist Lars Spuybroek observes, "If the mind wants to be involved in the process of making, it must not only be open but forward-thinking, in the direction of as-yet-unknown creation."[58]

Perhaps one of the best-known uses of a modeling material to help the architect find the form of an architectural surface is the hanging chain or rope known as a "catenary curve." These curves are generated by chains or ropes supported only at their ends and hanging under their own weight, which exerts a uniform force over their length. Because ropes were used to determine the location and shape of walls, openings, or larger architectural elements of structures throughout antiquity, one must be cautious not to confuse an accidental catenary curve like that found on a granite obelisk from Luxor with a curve intentionally used as a model for building construction.[59] Some argue—the point is highly debated—that this model was used to determine the domed shape of a Greek temple platform by what Vitruvius referred to as *scamilli impares* (uneven steps).[60] An early proponent of this theory is Oscar Broneer, who proposed in 1949 that the curve on the fourth-century BCE South Stoa of Corinth could be obtained by imitating a hanging rope.[61] Ten years later Roland Martin argued that a similar method had been employed at the somewhat older Northwest Stoa of Thasos, and Dieter Mertens put forward the most notable application of the hanging rope theory in 1974 when he used it to explain the use of cross marks incised at equal measures along the faces of the *euthynteria* at the late fifth-century BCE Temple of Segesta.[62] Mertens's study is significant less for its own merits than for the critical response it drew in 1999 from Lothar Haselberger, who claimed that the curvature of the stylobate was determined not by a hanging rope or chain but by the arc of a circle whose measures were then transferred to the larger structure.[63] A handful of other unconfirmed examples from antiquity that appear to take the catenary form are more likely the result of an emergent design process; these include the so-called Archway of Ctesiphon (sixth century CE) in modern Iraq, the exit gate for the city of Labna in the Yucatán Peninsula in Mexico, the Musgum clay huts in Cameroon, and even the dry-stacked stone beehive homes used by Irish monks in the Skellig Islands.

This catenary curve is worth exploring a little further for the light it sheds on the evolution of models used as a medium for generating architectural form and structure. Between the sixteenth and eighteenth centuries, artists, engineers, and mathematicians sought to understand the mathematical principles of the catenary curve. The earliest of these is Leonardo da Vinci, who sketched a few hanging chains in his notebooks.[64] Over a century later, Galileo Galilei wrote about the strength of materials and used a parabola to describe the bending moment of cantilevered beams in his *Discorsi e dimostrazioni matematiche intorno a due nuove scienze* (Discourses and mathematical demonstrations relating to two new sciences, 1638). After instructing the reader how to draw such a curve via projectile motion, Galileo then explained: "The other method of drawing the desired curve … is the following: Drive two nails into a wall at a convenient height and at the same level. … Over these two nails hang a light chain. … This chain will assume the form of a parabola."[65] The resulting curve certainly looks like it could be a parabola, but the Dutch physicist, astronomer, and mathematician Christiaan Huygens was the first person to prove that such a chain did not hang as a parabola and referred to it instead as a "catenary."[66] The seventeenth-century scientist Robert

Hooke argued that when inverted, this curvature represented "[t]he true mathematical and mechanical form of all manner of arches for buildings"; he expressed this as an anagram that has been unscrambled as "Ut pendet continuum flexile, sic stabit contiguum rigidum inversum" (As hangs a flexible line, so but inverted will stand the rigid arch).[67] On the basis of his observations, Hooke advised Sir Christopher Wren, the architect of St. Paul's Cathedral in London, to match the form of the cathedral's dome to this curvature. For a 1930 paper presented to the Royal Institute of British Architects (RIBA) concerning the preservation of St. Paul's Cathedral, W. Godfrey Allen and Captain C. Stanley Peach studied drawings of Wren's dome and confirmed that he did use an inverted catenary to determine its shape during an intermediate stage of the design's development.[68] In 1742 Giovanni Poleni adopted Hooke's analogy between the hanging chain and the rigid arch to complete his analysis of the dome of St. Peter's in Rome, which had developed severe cracks.[69] Using hanging chains weighted proportionally to the gravitational forces acting on the vault, Poleni argued for the stability of the structure so long as the thrust line of the chain did not extend outside the section of the dome's masonry. Poleni's use of the hanging chain, like the examples before him, attest to a familiarity with, and a need for, a verifiable simple method to determine the optimal curve of arched structures.

It didn't take long for architects and engineers to begin applying Hooke's simple hanging chain method to design and calculate arches and domes around central Europe. The most notable of these early accounts came from the English engineers John Robison and Thomas Young in 1801 and 1807, respectively,[70] and from its mention in influential French treatises by Bernard Forest de Belidor in 1729 and Amédée-François Frézier in 1737.[71] At the turn of the century, a German architect by the name of Wilhelm Tappe promoted a catenary-shaped loam construction as a new architectural style.[72] While Tappe preferred the pointed arch or ellipse over the catenary, which he deemed archaic and primitive, his contemporary the German engineer Heinrich Hübsch designed and built structures utilizing the catenary hanging model, including the St. Cyriakus church of Bulach near Karlsruhe, Germany, between 1828 and 1837.[73] By trial and error Hübsch drew the section of a vaulted structure, using as a guide a suspended string loaded with weights at regular distances.[74] To verify his own method he built a half-scale, over 9-meter-tall stone model of the nave of his design for the church of Bulach, confirming its loading under several weight conditions.[75] Two French architects, Jacques Germain Soufflot and Jean-Baptiste Rondelet, also employed the catenary form in 1837 for some designs of the dome of the Pantheon in Paris.[76] In Spain, the catenary arches and vaults of gunpowder magazines and the Carlón wine cellars in Benicarló, Spain, also illustrate the widespread application of Hooke's chain method in central Europe.

Arguably, the most familiar use of a hanging chain to model structural form was made by the Barcelona architect Antoni Gaudí, who developed a unique approach to the design of architecture using hanging rope and chains to model his church of Colònia Güell near Barcelona, Spain. Born the son of a coppersmith in Reus, Spain, in 1852, Gaudí studied at the Escola Superior d'Arquitectura in Barcelona and designed his first major commission for the Casa Vicens using a Gothic style that he came to believe was, in the words of a later critic, "an art of formulas that cannot in any way solve the problem of very high naves"; instead, "his aim was to give [architecture] the life that calculations with a compass cannot achieve."[77] Using a hanging chain to find the form of a catenary curve, Gaudí developed two models that generated domed and vaulted spaces by incorporating additional chains around the central axis of the arches, thereby enabling the architect to see the entire structure in three dimensions. Both models

| 5.12 |

Antoni Gaudí, preliminary 1:100 scale hanging model for the church of Colònia Güell, ca. 1898.

| 5.13 |

Antoni Gaudí, hanging model for the church of Colònia Güell, ca. 1898.

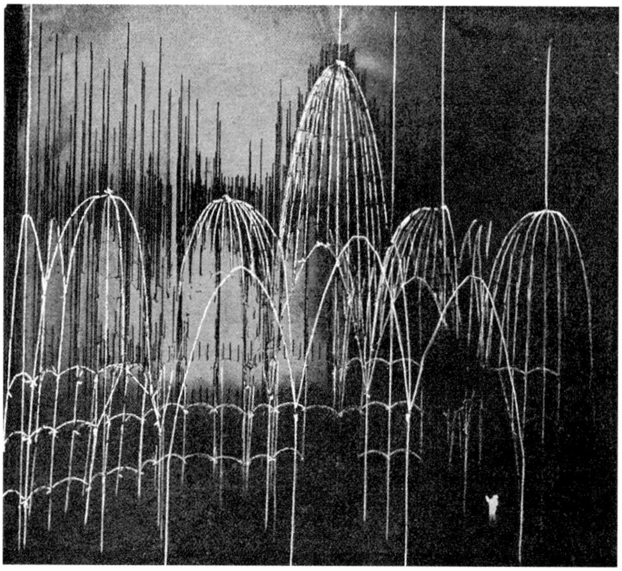

were lost during the Spanish Civil War and are known today only by photographs and reconstructions (figures 5.12–5.13). The smaller of these two models is presumed to represent half of a preliminary design for the church at a scale of 1:100. Completely symmetrical along its longitudinal axis, the model has spaces defined by hanging catenary threads to which have been attached chains to simulate the deadweight of the individual building components. The second, larger model is said to have been produced in a hut next to the building site between 1898 and 1908 at a scale of 1:10.[78] Hanging 4 meters from the ceiling with a width of 6 meters, this model represented a significantly more complex design and incorporated a netlike formation of chains, fabric sheets, and textile threads loaded with small weighted sacks. Like the chains attached to the preliminary model, these sacks correspond to the loads of the various parts of the building; Gaudí would move them and, by adding proportionally accurate loads, alter the polygonal shape of the arch in a way that remained true to the principles of the hanging model. Only the crypt of the church was completed by 1914, when the project was abandoned and never finished. Today Gaudí's models are known by reconstructions created in 1983 by the Institut für Leichte Flächentragwerke (Institute for Lightweight Structures) at the University of Stuttgart, which are now on display in the crypt of the Sagrada Família cathedral in Barcelona.

Not only did Gaudí apply hanging models more generally and extensively than had been seen before, he also experimented with modeling his vaults as ruled surfaces—hyperbolic paraboloids and revolving hyperboloids—by using two sets of mutually skewed straight lines or strings. The beams of the Sagrada Família School (1909) near the basilica attest to the use of a ruled surface to design and construct its roof, while the vaults surrounding the crypt of the basilica are the shape of a revolving hyperbolic paraboloid.[79] An account from Gaudí himself confirms his use of these figures: he explained, "Paraboloids, hyperboloids, and helicoids constantly varying the incidence of light, they have a richness of nuances of their own."[80] One can see in a photograph of his workshop the model of a revolving hyperbola constructed of strings standing behind a desk, which confirms an account given by Joan Matamala i Flotats, a former apprentice of the Sagrada Família workshop, that Gaudí studied hyperbolic paraboloids and used them to explain their principles to others.[81] As he did with his hanging catenary models, Gaudí used ruled surfaces to generate, study, and alter complex structural forms until he found a satisfactory design without resorting to complex formulas. The model is not the visualization of a prior idea but a tool with which Gaudí worked to find the size and shape of the vaults according to the needs of the spaces beneath them. Structure, form, and dimension are determined simultaneously.

In Germany, Mies van der Rohe came up with a method for modeling the architectural form of his 1922 Friedrichstrasse Glass Skyscraper Project that used another natural phenomenon: sunlight whose play of reflectivity on glass surfaces was used as a criterion for modeling its form. An early version of Mies's project was developed in response to a call for German architects to design Berlin's first skyscraper on a triangular site alongside the busy shopping street of Friedrichstrasse near the S-Bahn (city rapid transit railway) station. Designed during the autumn of 1921, Mies's competition entry was a steel-and-glass structure with a crystal-shaped plan he named the *Wabe* (Honeycomb) for its cellular interior.[82] Mies's scheme was summarily dismissed by the jury, who favored a dumpy fifteen-story block clad in brick.[83] Despite losing, Mies developed a second version of his high-rise building project with a curved glass surface and published photographs of the model alongside an explanation of its design in the spring 1922 issue of Bruno Taut's architectural journal *Frühlicht* (figure 5.14). There he sought to justify his extensive use of glass: "Skyscrapers reveal their bold structural pattern during construction. Only then does the gigantic steel web seem impressive. When the outer walls are put in place, the structural system which is the basis of all artistic design, is hidden by a chaos of meaningless and trivial forms."[84] However, compared to the *Wabe* project, which conformed closely to the angles of the trapezoidal plot of land, the curving plan of Mies's 1922 design seems to move arbitrarily within the site's borders. As Mies explained, the configuration of the plan was not random but the result of working with the model in accordance with the demands of the site and use of the spaces:

> I placed the glass walls at slight angles to each other to avoid the monotony of over-large glass surfaces. I discovered by working with actual glass models that the important thing is the play of reflections and not the effect of light and shadow as in ordinary buildings. ... At first glance

> the curved outline of the plan seems arbitrary. These curves, however, were determined by three factors: sufficient illumination of the interior, the massing of the building viewed from the street, and lastly the play of reflections.[85]

Like Gaudí, Mies used a natural phenomenon—here the reflection of sunlight—acting on his modeling material as a medium for finding an architectural form to accommodate the needs of the project.

It was during these early years of the twentieth century that new scientific theories about the origination of form in nature came to inspire a generation of architects and designers seeking to produce new architecture. The earliest theory was proposed by the Scottish-born mathematician and biologist D'Arcy Wentworth Thompson, whose book *On Growth and Form* (1917) sought to challenge Darwin's concept of evolution: he argued that physical laws and mechanics were the fundamental determinants of the form and structure of living organisms. But it was the concept of *Biotechnik*, a melding of technological and biological form described by the Hungarian microbiologist Raoul Francé, that caught the attention of architects and designers in Germany. In his book *Die Pflanze als Erfinder* (*Plants as Inventors*, 1920), Francé postulated that the forms of nature and their technologies are inherently a *Funktionsgesetz* (functional law) and argued: "All must have its best form, its 'optimum' which is also its nature at the same time. … There is for everything, be it a concrete thing or a thought, only one form that corresponds to the nature of that thing."[86] In Germany a key chapter of Francé's book explaining his concept of *Biotechnik* was published in the January 1923 issue of *Das Kunstblatt*,[87] and it was picked up by an emergent group of International Constructivists in Berlin. They included the Russian El Lissitzky, who in 1924 coedited a special issue of the Dada-Merz artist Kurt Schwitters's journal *Merz* titled *Nasci*, from the Latin word for "becoming," or "coming into being." Like Francé, Lissitzky set up a number of analogies between works of art and natural technologies, including that between Mies's Glass Skyscraper and the drawing of a human femur—an analogy that Mies would also make in comparing his design's use of concrete, steel, and glass with structures of skin and bone.

| 5.14 |
Ludwig Mies van der Rohe, Glass Skyscraper project, view of lost model, 1922.

By the 1950s, many European modern architects rediscovered a fascination with the use of complex mathematically derived architectural surfaces that could, like Gaudí's, also be developed using simple models of string and wire. The popular proponent of these surfaces was the Spanish-born Mexican architect Felix Candela, whose graceful thin-shell structures were just becoming known in Europe. Candela began building his shells not for clients but as full-scale experiments; he worked intensely with hyperbolic paraboloids (also called "hypars"), a type of ruled surface whose stresses could be determined with simple equations. For Le Corbusier and his employee Iannis Xenakis, the use of strings was less attractive as an approach for calculating complex shell structures than as a modeling method: it was used to determine the architectural form of his Palace Assembly Hall at Chandigarh during the early 1950s and the Philips Pavilion in 1956. While the strings used in modeling Corbusier's Assembly Hall more closely correspond to a simple revolving hyperboloid, the model Xenakis constructed with strings and piano wire for the Philips Pavilion is a complex assemblage of hyperbolic paraboloids.

At the outset of the pavilion project, Le Corbusier conceived a symmetrical plan in which a central space he referred to as the "stomach" was accessed by two narrow corridors, the entry and the exit.[88] Xenakis's task was to give the plan a three-dimensional form in a model using piano wire for the ribs anchored in a wooden base, while the surfaces were produced by spanning strings at even intervals between them (figure 5.15).[89] In making the model Xenakis proceeded by trial and error, varying all the angles and the shape of the ribs to a create satisfactory result.[90] This design method contrasted strongly with that of Candela, who dismissed all surfaces except the

| 5.15 |

Iannis Xenakis, preliminary model of the Philips Pavilion (designed by Le Corbusier), 1958.

hyperbolic paraboloid as stylistic sensationalism: in 1958, the same year that Corbusier's Philips Pavilion was completed, he argued that the hyperbolic paraboloid was the only compound surface that could be easily calculated and that "[t]his is its real justification and a far more valid one than the beauty of its form."[91] For Xenakis, though, it was the straight-line generatrices of the hyperbolic paraboloid that enabled him to find a form that would meet the needs of the space in accordance with Le Corbusier's plan while at the same time facilitating the static calculation. The resulting design was a cluster of nine hyperbolic paraboloids, and the strings used by Xenakis to define the form of the model became in the pavilion steel cables that were clad with prefabricated concrete panels.

Late in his career, the Finnish American architect Eero Saarinen undertook challenging structural projects in which models played an important role in the form-finding process. One of these is St. Louis's Gateway Arch, a 192-meter-tall arch completed in 1965 that was designed using a hanging chain. A photograph of Eero Saarinen crouching below models of the project shows in the background a dark catenary-shaped ribbon or mass suspended from the ceiling (figure 5.16). In 1959, Saarinen confirmed that "[t]he arch is not a true parabola, as is often stated. Instead it is a catenary curve—the curve of a hanging chain—a curve in which the forces of thrust are continuously kept within the center of the legs of the arch."[92] Saarinen studied models ranging in size from a few centimeters to 2.5 meters high, but found that they were either too flat on top, too pointed, or too heavy. Using a chain provided by the architect, the engineer Hannskarl Bandel replaced some of the links with others of a different size; in this way, by changing the weight and its distribution, he created a variety of weighted, flattened catenary curves and their accompanying formulas for Saarinen's office to model and select. Like Le Corbusier's Philips Pavilion model, the engineer's formula proves the model's constructive principles, but it is the selecting hand and eye of the architect that ultimately must determine the efficacy of the form in relation to the architectural idea.

While the Gateway Arch was waiting to begin construction, Saarinen undertook the design of TWA's terminal for New York International Airport (now John F. Kennedy International Airport), for which he again made extensive use of models from which drawings

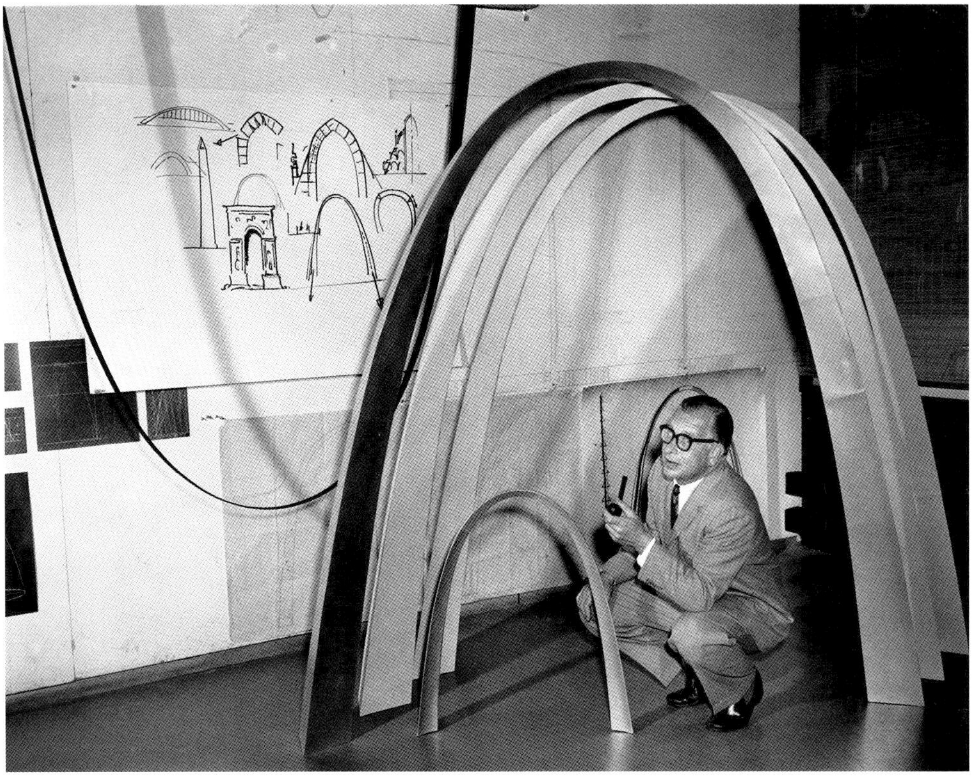

| 5.16 |

Eero Saarinen with model and sketches of St. Louis's Gateway Arch, ca. 1958.

were then derived. At the outset Saarinen and the codesigner Kevin Roche aimed to shelter the movement between ground transportation and the planes under a saddle-shaped, concrete shell supported on four points located close to the center of the building. But the façade did not follow the curve of the entry road, the beams that would support the wide cantilevers were cumbersome, and Saarinen decided that the building looked "pigeon-toed."[93] Roche recalls that while the architects were trying to find the right shape, "Eero was eating breakfast one morning and using the rind of his grapefruit to describe the terminal shell. He pushed down on its center to mimic the depression that he desired, and the grapefruit bulged. That was the seed for the bulges in the shell."[94] However, once the rest of the building had been worked out, the design of the columns on each side of the entrance still remained unresolved. The shape of the columns was found by using heavy wire to express the forces of gravity, wind, and snow loading on the columns.[95] Around these elements were

| 5.17 |

Eero Saarinen, wire model of a column for TWA Terminal, ca. 1958.

wrapped lighter gauge wire and a skin of cardboard defined by the area needed for concrete and steel reinforcing (figure 5.17). To convert these three-dimensional models into two-dimensional drawings for the purpose of construction, the architects photographed their models but also used techniques and mathematics familiar only to molders, pattern makers, and contour surveyors.[96] Unlike Gaudí's hanging chains, Saarinen's columns are not the result of forces acting on the modeling material; instead, like a ruled surface, they are determined by the direction of the forces that the building material needs to accommodate.

Known for his thin concrete shells, the Swiss structural engineer Heinz Isler gained renown for his experimental physical methods of form-finding that employed hanging sheets of fabric. After graduating from the Eidgenössische Technische Hochschule (ETH, Federal Institute of Technology) in Zurich in 1950 with a degree in civil engineering, Isler worked as a teaching assistant for the Swiss civil engineer and professor Pierre Lardy; in that position, he encountered the use of model tests as a method of exploring the behavior of structures. His first project as a shell builder was a free-form concert hall roof for the Hotel Kreuz in Langenthal, Switzerland, completed in 1955, whose shape was loosely inspired by a plumped-up pillow on his bed. By combining the natural domed shape of the pillow with the principles of a hanging chain, Isler began experimenting with different methods for designing thin-shell concrete structures using hanging fabric.[97] Isler presented his findings in a paper titled "New Shapes for Shells" at the first conference of the International Association for Shell and Spatial Structures, in Madrid, in September 1959

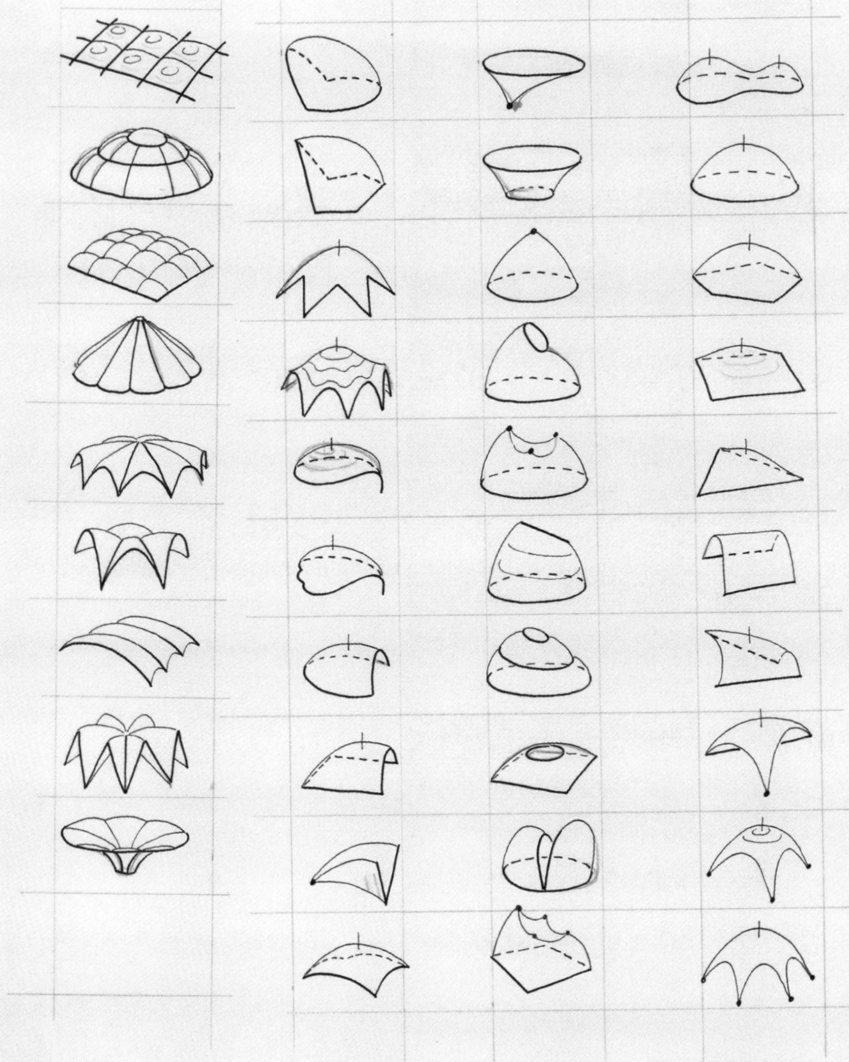

217 - Natural Hills

(figure 5.18). In it Isler introduced three unconventional form-finding methods for shells, including "the freely shaped hill, the membrane under pressure and the hanging cloth reversed," viewing the last (i.e., fabric-forming) as the most satisfactory.[98] In these instances, Isler first tried loading fabric with a plaster of his own formula to maintain a constant thickness on its surface but soon replaced the fabric with a high-quality latex rubber membrane, because the orientation of fabric weave would affect the boundaries.[99] Because of their uniformity, Isler's shells are not well suited to specific uses and are often relegated to the role of structural art.

Widely regarded as a pioneer of tension structures, Frei Otto was a great innovator in the ww3use of natural morphology to construct models for his designs. After graduating as an architect in 1952, Otto was awarded a ten-month grant to complete his doctoral study on lightweight tent structures; in 1954 he published his thesis, *Das Hangende Dach* (The suspended roof).[100] Beginning in the following year, Otto received a considerable amount of attention for his relatively small hypar- or saddle-shaped stressed canvas tents created for the 1955 and 1957 *Bundesgartenschauen* (Federal Garden Exhibitions) in Kassel and Cologne, Germany, respectively.[101] In 1964, when Otto was appointed full professor at the University of Stuttgart, he became director of the newly founded Institut für Leichte Flächentragwerke and experimented with a wide range of what he termed "form-finding" methods with various material systems, ranging from soap bubbles to sand, and from grid shells to cable nets. Otto's primary aim was to study their inherent capacity to physically compute the form that could achieve an equilibrium between system-intrinsic material behavior and extrinsic forces. During these early years, the main challenge facing Otto was how to undertake the design of a large tensile surface structure when conventional structural calculations were too complex to solve conveniently and the designs he could obtain from small models were virtually impossible to scale up to full size. His breakthrough came when he used a mesh of cables to support a woven polyester fabric, both of which could be arrived at on the basis of simple "soap bubble" saddle forms with minimal surfaces. The earliest examples of Otto's work that relied on this design and constructive process were prototypes for the pavilion of the Federal Republic of Germany at the 1967 Montreal World Expo (figure 5.19), which

| 5.18 |

Heinz Isler, illustration 9 from the paper "New Shapes for Shells," 1959.

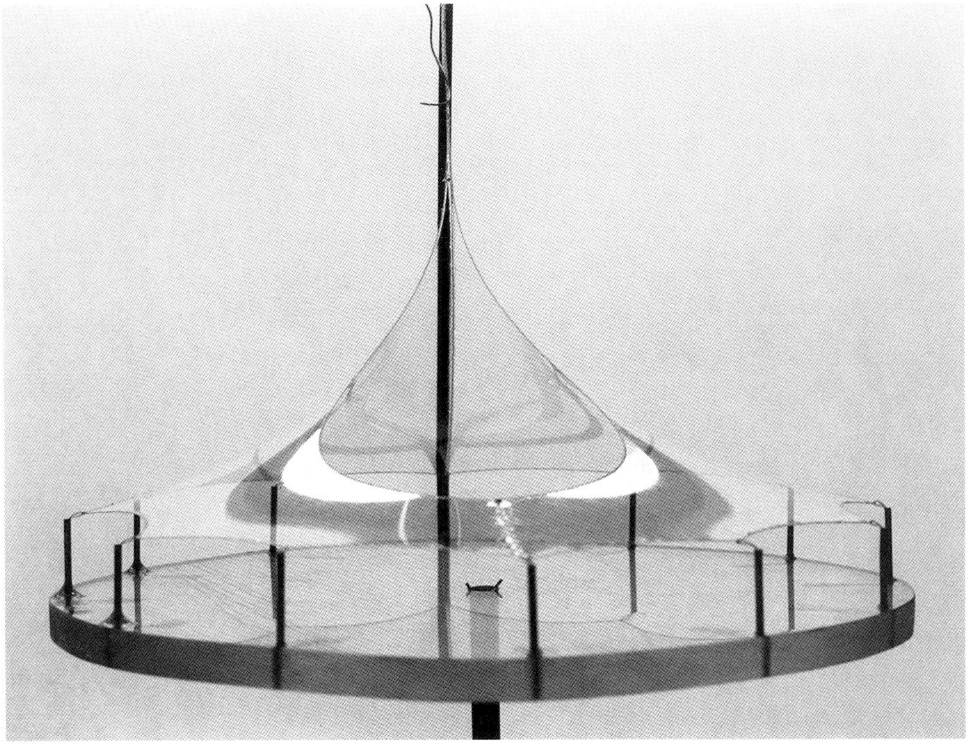

| 5.19 |

Frei Otto, soap film model of German Pavilion, Montreal, 1967.

was constructed at the home of the Institut für Leichte Flächentragwerke in 1965, and for roofs of the stadia at the 1972 Munich Olympics. These models remain today important demonstrations of possible points of departure for developing architectural designs by examining materials' behavior, rather than by making a top-down determination of form and space.

Like Otto, the Italian engineer Sergio Musmeci was a pioneer in the use of form-finding techniques for structural surfaces. Musmeci's best-known project exemplifying this approach to architectural design is his bridge over the Basento River near Rome; in it, he sought to create a structure that minimized material by optimizing form. Musmeci's initial concept was to create an isotropic shell membrane carrying only tensile stress, which he could then translate into a structural surface carrying compression. Beginning in 1967, Musmeci engaged in a search for a form to define the bridge's structural surface via an iterative use of physical models, starting with soap film to define the three-dimensional geometry of the

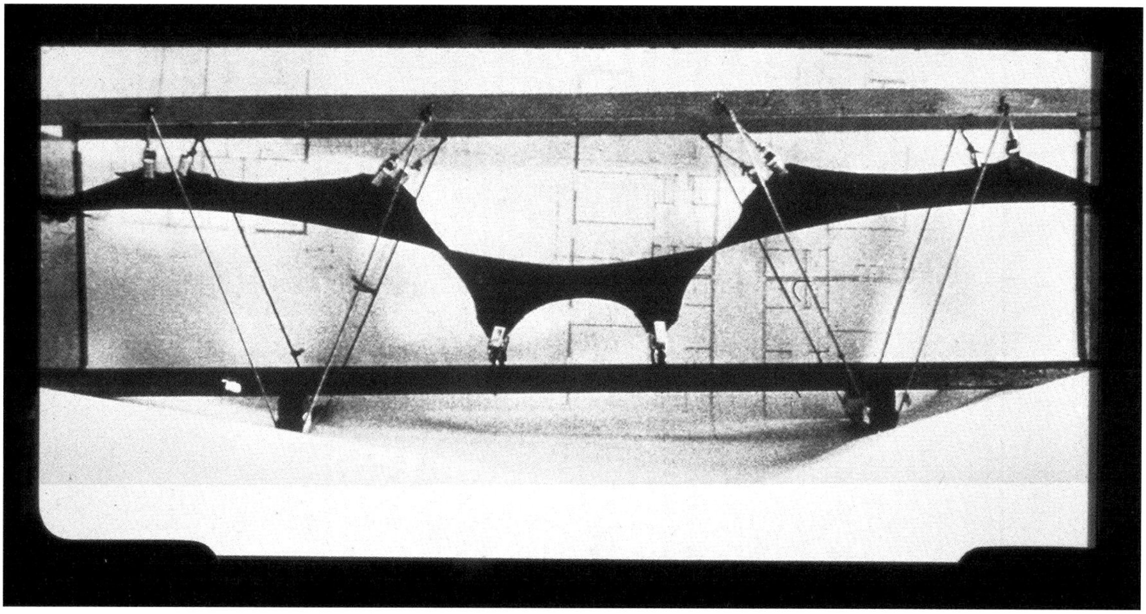

lower section of the bridge, which connects to the foundations.[102] When his efforts were compared with work being conducted at the Institut für Leichte Flächentragwerke, Musmeci claimed, "I didn't know that Frei Otto was embarking on similar experiences with tensile structures in the same years. Le Ricolais had also experimented with soap films, although Antoni Gaudí was perhaps the first to replace compression with traction in models made using taut wires."[103] Despite the comparisons, Musmeci deemed the curved soap film models too small for his needs and wanted to explore the point of contact between the deck and the structure using a force-modeled surface. He therefore created a second physical model of 0.8mm thick neoprene rubber scaled at 1:100 of the actual bridge (figure 5.20).[104] To achieve the desired curvatures, the prestresses applied in the longitudinal direction were three times larger than those in the transverse direction of the bridge.[105] It was by using this model that Musmeci was able to form, test, and transfer the nascent

| 5.20 |

Sergio Musmeci, 1:100 scale neoprene mechanically prestressed form-finding model, 1977.

structural principles of his materials to a new vocabulary of forms in the Basento Bridge.

During this period of exploration in modeling minimal surface structures, the Spanish architect Emilio Pérez Piñero began to experiment with the geometrical and mechanical formal possibilities created by scissor hinges. In 1962, while completing his fourth year of architectural studies at the Escuela Técnica Superior de Arquitectura Madrid (ETSAM, Superior Technical School of Architecture of Madrid), Pérez Piñero participated in a student competition for the design of a mobile traveling theater pavilion that could hold five hundred spectators. Designed and presented in model, Pérez Piñero's proposed "teatro ambulante" (traveling theater) was a collapsible three-dimensional reticular structure that could unfold in every direction, with a dome that became rigid when the ends of the rods were connected to cables to complete its triangulation and limit its movement (figure 5.21).[106] The most important features of the structural systems Pérez Piñero developed over the ten years of his brief career are the joints that permit structural members to turn within their plane.[107] What Pérez Piñero discovered was that if the central joints are located at the midpoint of members, flat spatial meshes are obtained, while moving these joints to the ends of the members would create curved spatial meshes.[108]

Also relevant to this discussion is the manipulation of surfaces into fixed and deployable plate structures. Such systems in nature include the hornbeam leaf and the corrugated scallop shell, whose folded surfaces give the material its rigidity and strength to withstand buckling from external forces. An early example of the use of a folded plate structure in architecture was the Orly Dirigible Hangars constructed between 1916 and 1924 (demolished 1944), which were designed by the French structural engineer Eugène Freyssinet. Because of the height and size required, Freyssinet employed a parabolic cross section to accommodate the dead load of the structure and, after much trial and error, came upon the shape of a folded longitudinal section to resist buckling.[109] Reflecting on his career and working method, Freyssinet attributed great importance to everyday experience and intuition in his design process as "the soundest basis of his technical training," going so far as to question his calculations if they were contradicted by his intuition.[110] This was

|5.21|

Emilio Pérez Piñero and his "teatro ambulante" (traveling theater) model, 1961.

|5.22|

Ron Resch, folded single-sheet dome, 1961–1963.

certainly also the attitude of the Bauhaus pedagogue Josef Albers, who introduced folding paper as an exercise for young designers so that they might have an efficient means for thinking about how to solve packaging and structural problems. It was undoubtedly a method that Jean Prouvé embraced in his use of metal to construct his furniture and architectural prototypes.[111] The artist, mathematician, and designer Ron Resch developed a folded paper tessellation that he presented in a computer-animated film in 1970. He obtained a patent for his designs and intended to use the tesselation as a model for a structural system, since it offered both positive and negative double curvature (figure 5.22).[112] Some of its mechanical properties were investigated, and variations of the pattern were suggested by an assistant professor at the University of Tokyo, Tomohiro Tachi, who has developed special software that would allow companies to employ "origami engineering."[113]

In recent years the computer has acquired an important role in the design process of architects as a tool for generating architectural form by digitally simulating the performance of their building materials. An important difference between these digital methods of form-finding and those of Gaudí, Mies, Isler, or Otto is that in the latter, the model maker's hands and eyes are directly engaged in a sensory experience with materials in which accidents with surprising results may occur during the forming process. By contrast, digital modeling software will typically control the modeling environment to predetermined parameters, but it has the advantage of enabling its user to explore the formal and spatial implications of a structural or material system that are otherwise inaccessible. We can see this use of a parameter-driven design process in William Massie's 2002 MoMA/P.S.1 project, Playa Urbana/Urban Beach. Using PVC piping, Massie bent the material to its point of failure and then digitized this curvature, assigning it as a parameter for the digital pipes in his modeling program. From this data set, the digital pipes were multiplied and steel brackets could then be defined to support these white PVC pipes as screens.[114] In 2010, Fabio Gramazio and Matthias Kohler employed a similar process for their ICD/ITKE Research Pavilion. Like Massie, Gramazio and Kohler began their project with intensive laboratory testing of the material limits of their building material—in their case, plywood (figure 5.23).[115] The results from these tests

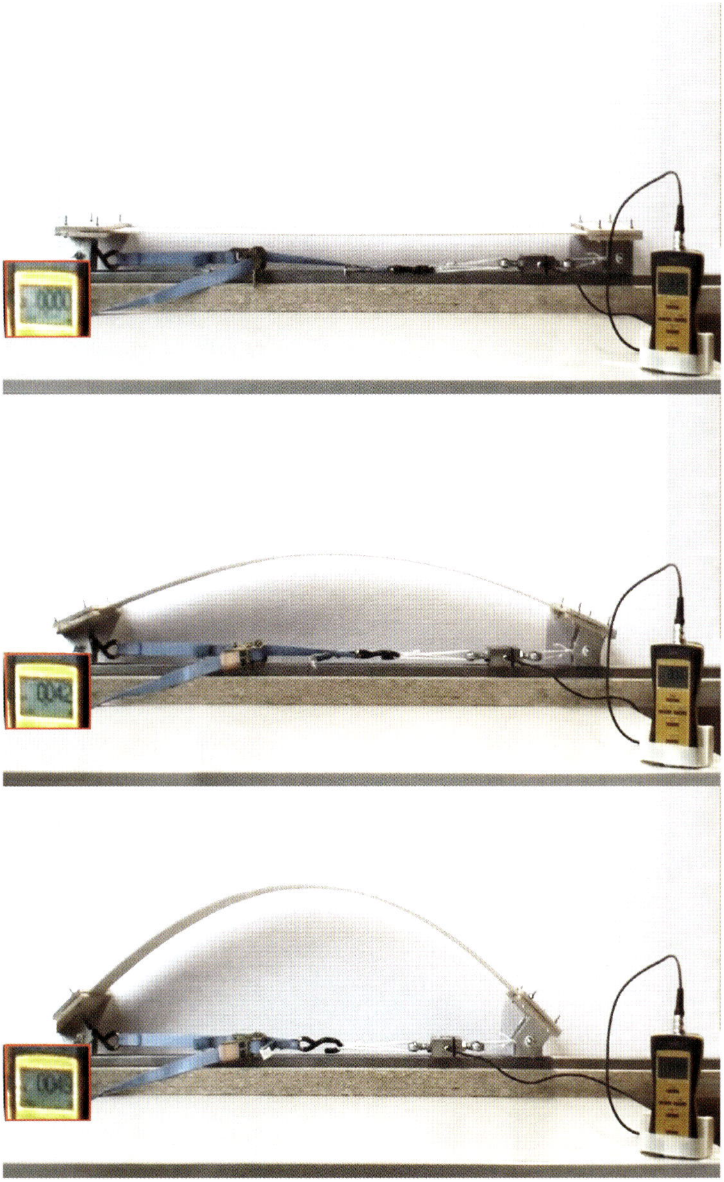

| 5.23 |

Gramazio Kohler, bending plywood elements: experimental and digital studies, ICD/ITKE Research Pavilion, 2010.

were employed as constraints in digital parametric design tools and used to calibrate finite-element simulations. By synchronizing the physical studies with the digital model, the designer could develop a form that would work with the actual material behavior of the plywood while at the same time providing more feedback on the resulting geometry of the structure (figure 5.24). The advantage of the methods of Massie, Gramazio, and Kohler is that the forms in the digital model simulate the actual building material, enabling them to find inspiration in everyday materials and to design *with* them before engaging in the building process.

....

WHEN ARCHITECTS CUT, bend, score, or cast their modeling materials, the activity becomes vividly lodged in their memories. Furthermore, as they work with card, balsa, or even plaster, their will to fabricate a thing must accommodate the materials' properties. The architect and European theorist of modern architecture Adolf Loos made up a story about a stonemason's failed attempt to craft a salamander in stone, emphasizing that he himself had developed an eye for which materials resisted the imposition of form and that the stonemason should have thought *with* his materials rather than *about* them.[116] We can see this approach to modeling materials operating across the examples of material propriety and form-finding above. But as the examples of Rietveld, Gropius, and even Wright made clear, there is also a persistent cultural assumption about the use of modeling materials that is not easily overcome in representing new ideas about architecture. This dimension is demonstrated most aptly by Kiesler, whose search for a new architectural form demanded his use of new materials—wire mesh and cement—not commonly employed in architectural practice or in the model shops of his time. Here, consideration of the appropriateness of a material for representing an architect's design led to the idea of using the model as a medium for also generating architectural form and structure. It is precisely through such considerations that the model became a medium for generating form-finding techniques. As the model takes this role, a model maker will perceive a direct haptic connection between the object, its representation, and

| 5.24 |
Gramazio Kohler, ICD/ITKE Research Pavilion, 2010.

the designer's concept. Similarly, as architects model the form of an object, they touch and feel its surface and internalize its character. In this gap between the model and building, the propensity of the assembled or formed materials that are, at times held in the palm of the hand depends upon how closely they match how the architect imagined the building's material or structural form. It is here that the architect's imagination resides—in a gap between matter and form, where the appropriate modeling materials become a medium that inspires architectural images.

6
MODELING ARCHITECTURAL CONCEPTS

AT THE BEGINNING of an architectural project, a design is not always known and the architect must formulate a strategy to organize building materials and their assembly into structures. That a model may play an important role in this compositional scheme is made particularly evident by the "spherical solution" produced in 1961 by Jørn Utzon to resolve the geometry of the shell-like roofs in his Sydney Opera House project (figure 6.1). Utzon's winning design was a collection of interconnected thin shells, without walls or supports, housing a large and a small performance hall.[1] Thin-shell structures were popular among architects and engineers of the 1950s, but Utzon's proposed application had no precedent.[2] To build the shells, the engineers at Arup & Partners needed to express their shapes mathematically, and Utzon spent four years working with parabolic geometries to accommodate the structural forces acting on them. However, because the design of each shell was unique, it lacked a defining geometry that would make it possible for the builders to reuse formwork and thereby reduce the building's costs. Then, in 1961, while stacking pieces of a large model of the opera house in his office, Utzon noticed their similarities and observed that the shells could be derived from the surface of a sphere; he went on to produce a wooden model to demonstrate the efficacy of the scheme for determining the building's form and its exterior tiles, using repetitive geometry.[3] Utzon's accidental discovery of the sphere as a model for the shape of his shells demonstrates the value that a physical or intellectual strategy can have for providing answers to an entire series of formal, spatial, and structural questions about an architectural design. A similar reliance on an organizational scheme to complete creative works is found in a branch of philosophy

| 6.1 |

Jørn Utzon, model illustrating the origin of the roof geometry of the Sydney Opera House (the so-called spherical solution), 1961.

known as "'Pataphysics," which sought to exploit precisely these sorts of constraints—both accidental and intentional—in the processes of creation.

Here it is useful to recount some observations I have made elsewhere about the congruency between the use of models in architecture and the pataphysical use of structures or patterns in literature to inspire creative work.[4] Invented by the French Symbolist writer Alfred Jarry, 'Pataphysics is the science of imaginary solutions, and it was employed as a method for creative inspiration by members of a subcommittee of the College of Pataphysicians: the French literary group Ouvroir de la Littérature Potentielle (Workshop for Potential Literature), better known simply as the Oulipo. As the founder of the Oulipo, Raymond Queneau, argues, 'Pataphysics behaves as a philosophy of the *as if*, being simply the imaginary solution to the question "*what if?*" For 'Pataphysics, however, the exploration of the "what if?" does not imply "blind obedience to every impulse."[5] The Italian writer Italo Calvino—who became a member of the Oulipo in 1973, the same year as the Sydney Opera House's completion—gives insight into Queneau's argument, observing, "What Romantic terminology called genius or talent or inspiration or intuition is nothing other than finding the right road empirically."[6] This "right road" is dependent on the imposition of a structure or pattern, often based upon mathematical equations, and thus Oulipians, as Queneau suggested, are comparable to "rats who build the labyrinth from which they plan to escape."[7] We see a preexisting arrangement or framework used to guide the development of a creative literary work in Italo Calvino's *The Castle of Crossed Destinies* (1973), in which a tarot deck is a prop that two groups of travelers employ to tell the stories of their lives.[8] Like Utzon's sphere, Calvino's tarot deck establishes a set of parameters; here they are a finite set of images, about which he weaves the narratives of his characters.

This chapter explores the different ways in which architects use models as guides in designing and constructing new architecture. In such cases, materials not only are transformed but also are found, assembled, and imagined as what contemporary books on architecture refer to as a "concept" or "conceptual" model. The term derives from the Latin verb *concipere*, meaning "to take in," "to derive/draw from," or "to catch." In architectural modeling, the concept is an idea or notion about the spatial, structural, or formal design of architecture that is taken in or derived from a specific configuration or assembly of materials—a concept model. Because even a miniature model relies upon an act of interpretation about its scale or material, this chapter argues that architectural concepts associated with these physical objects have a long history of being "taken in"—allegorically, analogically, and anagogically. In these instances, an object or assemblage of materials is not interpreted as a visual depiction of architecture but is employed to describe the design, construction, or experience of a structure figuratively, as an exemplar or definition of its final cause. In other words, when a model is being made and then later presented to an associate or client, the architect will instruct the viewer that the model before them is not to be understood as a proportionally accurate depiction of a proposed structure at a specified scale. Rather, it is an invitation to consider how the materials or methods of the model's construction are an analogical, allegorical, or anagogical description of that structure. This is the model working as an exemplar: a demonstration of an idea about architecture or a guide for user's decisions about the design of an architectural form, its organization of spaces, or its structure.

Whereas the previous two chapters considered the use of the model to inform and generate architectural form or construction, the models discussed here are, like the structures or patterns developed by the literary members of the Oulipo, employed as a set of visual, material, and intellectual parameters to aid the designer in defining the organization of materials and their assembly into structures. The sections of this chapter follow a hierarchical progression from visible to invisible by first exploring the figurative use of modeling materials and their assembly to describe allegorical ideas about architecture and its use or construction. The discussion then moves on to examine the imitation of an actual or imagined thing's formal, material, or compositional principles as an analogical model for designing similar attributes in a proposed structure. These descriptions of architecture or the exemplary ways it should made anticipate the anagogical models, which give direction to and describe an architect's ideas about the final cause of a structure's organization of forms, spaces, materials, and structure. These discussions will show that far from being a mere mirror of reality, the architectural model is also a lamp that illuminates an architect's understanding about the experience and design of existing and to-be-constructed architecture.

ALLEGORICAL MODELS

During the late 1960s, the American architect Peter Eisenman experimented with an innovative approach to the use of a cardboard model as an allegorical prototype for a series of house designs. The primary hypothesis propelling his work was that there has been no change to the notion of architecture as provider of shelter, and Eisenman proposed the concepts of "physic" and "metaphysic."[9] Where man's first shelter was the cave, he set forth a notion of the physic in architecture. In addition, Eisenman claimed that architecture also arose as an idea or metaphysic in the mind of the caveman, and it was shelter that was found.[10] For Eisenman, a dislocation of this metaphysic of architecture occurred when the caveman left the cave and found materials—sticks, straw, stones, and mud—with which to build. However, he argued,

| 6.2 |

Peter Eisenman, model of House I, 1967.

stylistic innovations in architecture—including modernism—need not dislocate the metaphysic of architecture. As he reasoned, because buildings must also support, shelter, enclose, and allow access, in order to create architecture there must be an intentional act.[11] By redefining the notion of a wall, column, beam, or house in general, Eisenman sought to make the elements autonomous and signify that intent. To this end, Eisenman embraced the notion of "Cardboard Architecture" less as an aesthetic than as a general idea. To replace our previous assumptions about the role of a column, brick, or wall, Eisenman used the material and structural possibilities of their doppelgangers in a cardboard model as an ideal for generating a new metaphysic of architecture (figure 6.2). "Cardboard Architecture," he wrote, "is a term which attempts to shift the focus of the existing conceptions of form to a consideration of form as a signal or a notation which can provide a range of formal information; 'Cardboard' is a means for an exploration into the nature of architectural form itself, in both its actual and conceptual states."[12] By using the scale cardboard model as an ideal for his new architecture, Eisenman aimed to free the house of acculturated

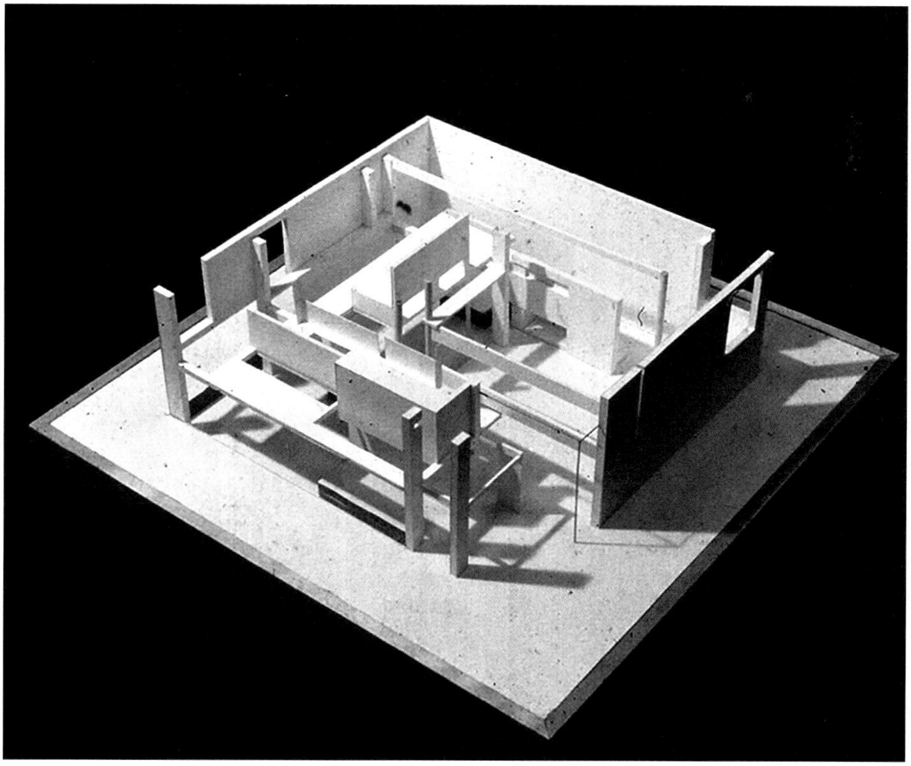

meaning, whether traditional or modern. Lack of specificity of scale and material was achieved by emulating characteristics of Eisenman's cardboard models in the completed houses: they were built of uniform, thin, mass-produced materials like plywood, and they were painted and constructed without the traditional details of mullions, flashings, and copings conventionally associated with an "actual" house. As in a cardboard model in which the rigidity of the material can support itself, some of Eisenman's columns do not connect to the ceiling and some beams support nothing at all, thereby raising the following question: what if they were not there?[13] Eisenman thus used the cardboard model to develop an allegorical critique of cultured meanings associated with domestic inhabitation—for example, by constructing a stair that is too low to descend in the Frank House (1972), or adding a split in the floor of the master bedroom of House VI (1975) to separate the client's bed into two beds.

For Eisenman, the scale cardboard model could therefore represent not only a depiction of a to-be-constructed house but also an idea about the intentional acts that define architecture in general. By emulating cardboard models, the houses built from them are encoded, as Angus Fletcher said of allegorical texts, to say one thing and mean another.[14] Not only do Eisenman's houses emulate the uniform surfaces and structural performance of a cardboard model, but they are also used to speculate about architecture, its construction or use. In terms of architectural modeling, Eisenman's houses demonstrate that beyond the literal meaning of the architectural model as a miniature representation of a structure, it may also express an allegorical sense when the user finds a continuous series of associations between it and the object of its representation—as, for example, "the house is like a cardboard model."

At the turn of the sixteenth century a new generation of treatises on architecture appeared that included not only illustrations of architectural elements, construction details, building sections, and plans but also memorable allegorical images relating to the architect's practice. The aim of these allegories is didactic: to provide the reader with a memorable image of the treatise's practical or ethical recommendations for the architect's education, approach to the design of buildings, or relationship with the client or builder. To understand the use of allegory in making models of architecture, it is useful to

| 6.3 |

Philibert de l'Orme, *The Prudent Architect*, from *Le premier tome de l'architecture*, fol. 51v, 1567.

take a closer look at how these images employ identifiable objects as a trope in order to describe ideas about the construction, use, or practice of architecture.

One important example is Philibert de l'Orme's depiction of the architect included in the preface of the third book of his 1567 *Le premier tome de l'architecture* (figure 6.3), a work discussed in chapter 4.[15] In de l'Orme's drawing, the architect is shown crouched over as he walks a large compass out of a cave toward a palm, signifying glory and honor in design. The path upon which the architect walks is strewn with spikes, and a serpent is wrapped around the compass much as two asps are coiled around Hermes' (Mercury's) caduceus at the top of the frame. De l'Orme explains that this snake is not dangerous to the architect but instead signifies the prudent and mature use of the compass to "measure and compare all things and all works and constructions" so that he might see with certainty the path he must tread through the traps and thorns of "envy, hatred, disappointments, insults, barriers and impediments."[16] Plato also uses a cave in his *Republic* to describe the philosopher's escape from its shadows and echoes of the divine archetypes to true knowledge under the light of the sun.[17] In contrast, de l'Orme's cave is not a prison for the architect but "a place of meditation, solitude, and study in order to arrive at true knowledge and perfection in his art."[18] For de l'Orme, those who practice architecture should be guided by the prudent use of a compass and construct simple unadorned models to visualize the three-dimensional application of geometry as an aid in prethinking architecture.[19]

A contemporary of de l'Orme, the German mathematician, physician, and author of popular scientific works Walther Hermann Ryff, also developed a didactic image of the architect's practice to convey his view of the conception of architecture. However, unlike de l'Orme's, Ryff's architect is not a man but a young boy, or putto, standing on a pedestal, surrounded by the tools of the architect: the image was used as the frontispiece of his 1547 *Der fürnembsten notwendigsten der gantzen Architectur*—republished in 1548 under the title *Der Architectur*—and also for his German translation of Vitruvius, *Vitruvius Teutsch*. In Ryff's image the putto is gazing upward toward his raised right hand, which is holding a pair of wings, while a stone tied to his left hand is weighing it down (figure 6.4).[20] Surrounding the figure and filling the rest of the page is a collection of tools, including instruments for drawing and those for translating drawings into buildings. Paul Emmons unpacks the allegorical associations in Ryff's frontispiece, arguing that this figure represents the spirit of architecture, who stands on a pedestal crafted according to the medieval mason's rule of proportional geometry: the rotated square.[21] The immediate source of Ryff's cherubic figure is an emblem in Andrea Alciato's 1531 *Book of Emblems* that is often called the "Allegory of Genius held back by poverty," or "Constrained Genius" for short.[22] The poverty in Alciato's emblem refers less to the putto's lack of monetary wealth than to the human condition, as genius is viewed as bound to a body constrained by the poverty of materials. Contrary to the Platonic assumption that the idea precedes its material manifestation, the spirit of architecture is here situated between the metaphysical and the physical. Ryff's architect, whose "subtle skillfulness" is to "put forth and pre-figure" designs as "ingenious inventions,"[23] is not burdened by materials but stands on the rules of proportional geometry as an agent between idea and matter—each a necessary condition for the other in modeling forth architectural constructions.

| 6.4 |

Gualtherus Hermenius Rivius, frontispiece, verso of title page, *Der furnembsten notwendigsten der gantzen Architectur*, 1547.

Ryff's image, like that by de l'Orme, is an early example of a tradition which developed over the next half a millennium of using drawings and sculptures to depict the so-called allegory of architecture—typically

Viuitur ingenio, cætera mortis erunt.

Aurum probatur igni, ingenium uero Mathematicis.

personifying architecture and the architect as an elegant woman (often in ancient Greek dress) and a young boy (putto), respectively. Perhaps because of the physical model's traditional role as a utilitarian device for proportionally describing the space and form of a design to clients or builders, there are few examples of its use allegorically until the beginning of the twentieth century, when architects began to experiment with the conflation of the materials and methods for making art and architecture.

In my doctoral dissertation and the publications that emerged from it, I sought to explicate the applications which the German Dada artist and amateur architect Kurt Schwitters intended for two architectural models he created during the early twentieth century, including one constructed as an allegorical description of architecture.[24] The model Schwitters created in 1920, called *Haus Merz* (House Merz), had the appearance of a miniature cathedral: a children's building block was used to create a tower upon which he placed a trouser button for a clock face and a spinning top for a spire, while a set of gears occupied the nave (figure 6.5). As I reasoned, that Schwitters created *Haus Merz* as a cathedral makes sense in the context of his times. After the end of the First World War, his peers set aside their divisions and formed the Arbeitsrat für Kunst (Workers Council for Art) to work with the new socialist German government in order to reform art education and project a new German architecture.[25] Holding up the Gothic cathedral as the favored prototype, the second director of the Arbeitsrat für Kunst, Walter Gropius, claimed that this

| 6.5 |

Kurt Schwitters, *Haus Merz* (House Merz), 1920.

new architecture would find its "crystalline expression" as a *Gesamtkunstwerk* (total work of art) and metaphorically "shine its light into the smallest things of everyday life."[26] Following closely on the heels of the Arbeitsrat für Kunst, Schwitters hailed his new Merz art as the creation of a "*Merzgesamtkunstwerk.*"[27] Schwitters made this claim in the same article in which he introduced *Haus Merz* and "his first piece of Merz architecture."[28] Clearly, because of its diminutive size, *Haus Merz* could not itself be a *Gesamtkunstwerk*, but it was a model describing how his Merz method of making art could achieve comparable aims in making architecture. Like the snake wrapped around the compass of de l'Orme's prudent architect or the wings in the hands of Ryff's putto, the gears assembled in *Haus Merz* are out of place in a cathedral nave, which is normally occupied by people. This comparison between and exchange of people for gears in *Haus Merz*'s nave was an important trope in Schwitters's oeuvre, which described the specific manner in which he proposed that a new German architecture could be constructed.

For an exhibition at the expressionist Sturm Gallery in 1919, Schwitters explained that "Merz" denoted his artistic transformation and reassemblage of discarded man-made and found materials into new matrixes. For Schwitters, each object in a Merz work began as a unique combination of material form and immaterial idea that had been corrupted with an *Eigengift* (literally, "own poison")—an identity or purpose.[29] In order for an object to become useful as material for his Merz art or architecture, this *Eigengift* had to be *entmaterialisiert* (dematerialized) or lost through a mental process he compared allegorically to the milling of grain into flour.[30] *Haus Merz* demonstrates this approach to constructing architecture by reusing materials that have been found already transformed into the products of everyday life—a set of gears, a trouser button, and a spinning top. In the same way that wheat is milled into flour to bake bread, so the *Eigengift* of a found object is "dematerialized" in the architect's imagination so that it can be used as material to make Merz art or architecture. Contrary to Gropius's employment of a crystal to describe the effect that the *Zukunftskathedrale* (cathedral of the future) would have on making a new German architecture, Schwitters sought to use *Haus Merz* as an allegorical model for the projection of new architectural designs through the imaginative transformation of found materials.

Indebted to Schwitters, and certainly inspired by many of the sixteenth-century themes and imagery of Ryff and de l'Orme's cultural world, the contemporary architect Daniel Libeskind developed three allegorical machines as didactic illustrations of architectural theory for a show at the 1985 Venice Biennale titled *Three Lessons on Architecture*.[31] Libeskind's machines, which he presents as a demonstration of reading, memory, and writing architecture, are manifestations of the idea that architecture must be read in the same way as a written text whose structural features of language, grammar, and syntax organize how words are put together into a coherent, meaningful ensemble. Like many of his peers, Libeskind is indebted in his approach to language to Jacques Derrida's critique of structuralism,[32] which assumes that written texts have a fixed meaning given by the author and that readers will interpret it for themselves by using various cultural codes and references. Following the example of Agostino Ramelli's design for a multibook "Reading Wheel," Libeskind sought with his Reading Machine to demonstrate that the reading of architecture is like a text whose meaning is different for each reader, each time they encounter it. To reinforce this idea, the books of Libeskind's machine each contain one word or phrase—idea, spirit, subject, power, will to power, *energia*, being, created being—repeated anagrammatically to describe a poststructuralist idea about the encounter with architecture. In making his Memory Machine (figure 6.6), Libeskind took inspiration from another sixteenth-century structure, Giulio Camillo's "Memory Theatre"; once inside that theater, the user occupies a stage looking out toward the auditorium, where images have been placed among seven pillars or steps and provide so much information that the individual is able "to discourse on any subject no less fluently than Cicero."[33] Libeskind claimed, however, that his Memory Machine consisted of only the backstage "[a]s a mechanism for projection, concealment, and illusion," which, "[a]s a ghost of humanism's cosmic hubris, … seeks to disengage the sites from the Earth in order to return them to their original, destined locus."[34] The Writing Machine, in contrast, was conceived to describe the making of architecture, which "processes both memory and reading material," including "all places written into the book of culture."[35] Although the Writing Machine is commonly associated with Raymond Roussel, since it was intended to print only his *Impressions of Africa* (1910), Libeskind's design is actually based on

a satirical automated writing engine described in Jonathan Swift's *Gulliver's Travels* (1726). According to Libeskind, the Writing Machine "teaches the artless and science-less making of architecture."[36] As K. Michael Hays observes, technique is here presented as a process, a combinatorial system in which the architect is relieved of their duty as the definer of architectural meaning to now merely set in motion the processes of assembling already-formed codes.[37] For Libeskind, the three machines are a mirror of contemporary architectural practice. They coexist as a kind of triplet, each "form[ing] a starting point for the understanding and functioning of the others" as "a cycle in which projects are seen, explicated, and overcome."[38] As allegorical

| 6.6 |

Daniel Libeskind, Memory Machine, 1985.

equipment, Libeskind's machines construct a narrative about the actual and metaphorical production of humanist architecture that in Libeskind's opinion is ending. Compared to Schwitters's mill, which proposes a method for using found materials to construct buildings, Libeskind's machines are not a design strategy but rather a critique of the making and reception of architecture in general.

Between 1986 and 1990, the American designer Ben Nicholson, a friend and former student of Libeskind, conceived and constructed a study of domesticity in the mass-produced American suburban home: he named it the Appliance House. The house was not intended to function as a real suburban dwelling; instead, it was meant to be an allegorical critique of its occupants and of the nature of collecting that occurs within the consumerist society with which the home is associated.[39] In Nicholson's design, the Appliance House is made up of six rooms connected to the main hall. Each room is conceived and constructed according to a social disorder associated with the activities in that particular domestic space: thus, a study/trophy room, lounge, kitchen, and bedroom were imagined as a Kleptoman Cell, Pyroman Chamber, Bulimia Chamber, and Narco-room, respectively. The walls of the Kleptoman Cell were a framework made to accommodate the objects that Nicholson collected from his forages in the city (figure 6.7).[40] These objects form the skin and threshold between the interior and exterior; the appearance of the house, like that of the inhabitant who acquires their own identity from these objects, is in constant transition. Similarly, the living space of the Pyroman Chamber, like a home's lounge, was arranged around a hearth. But instead of offering a cozy nook and warming fireplace, it contained an inferno fit for pyromaniacs to indulge their fantasies.[41] By exaggerating and displacing the objects and activities that take place in the rooms of the suburban house, Nicholson aims to draw attention to them and have them take on the role of figurative gestures. In this way, the house is compared to an appliance—an armature for the objects and activities of consumption that are collected and make up the suburban home.

| 6.7 |

Ben Nicholson, Tealmon Cupboard and Kleptoman Cell, 1990.

Two years later, in 1992, the American architect and pedagogue Dan Hoffman developed his own reflection on the built environment with an installation titled *Recording Wall*.[42] The completed work consisted of an approximately 2.5- by 5-meter concrete block wall assembled using no mortar. As Hoffman set each block into place, a remote

shutter release activated two cameras positioned on either side of the wall. Once the assembly of the wall was complete, he used a light-sensitive emulsion paint to print the photographs directly onto each of the respective block's surfaces (figures 6.8–6.9). As a result, each of the 105 blocks carried a photograph "of its own construction or deconstruction."[43] Hoffman's wall of blocks and photos describes an open secret about the built environment that is both obvious and yet not consciously noticed: the city is in a continuous state of becoming built and being torn down.

In each of these examples, familiar objects or actions have been displaced from their original contexts by juxtaposing, multiplying, or combining them with others in order to develop a figurative description about the making, practice, or experience of architecture. In this way they become assemblies, which by their very nature are not limited to a single comparative description of architecture as is seen, for example, in the construction of a door that is like a mouth at Parco dei Mostri in the Garden of Bomarzo (1552). Rather, as Fredric Jameson has argued, they extend the metaphor into a continuous series of associations that reinforce the primary representation and take on the role of a narrative.[44] Because the materials or methods for constructing models can be endowed with figurative meanings, the allegorical model maker's task is to weave those meanings with architecture in order to express an idea about it. The efficacy of the allegorical model therefore depends on the familiarity of its user with the figurative meanings shared by a particular group of people, at a particular time or place.

| 6.8 |

Dan Hoffman, *Recording Wall* before reconstruction, 1992.

| 6.9 |

Dan Hoffman, *Recording Wall* after reconstruction with emulsified photographs on block surfaces, 1992.

ANALOGICAL MODELS

The 2018 online *Oxford English Dictionary* defines "analogy" as a correspondence, correlation, similarity, or resemblance between the features of two things and their respective attributes. An analogy differs from a metaphor in that in the latter, an object or idea is used in place of another to suggest a likeness (e.g., "the curtain of night fell upon us," a phrase that contains an implicit comparison between darkness and a curtain that obscures what can be seen). In the design of architecture, an analogical comparison involves a similar transfer of comparable qualities, here of the physical features of a particular subject—a model—to the target or building. One of the earliest analogical models for the design of architecture was nature. For example, Vitruvius asserts in his treatise on architecture that when the "men of old" gathered around a fire for warmth, they developed language and invented architecture by imitating what they found in nature.[45] Whereas analogy is a relation or association between two things, imitation is the act by which a similarity or correlation is created in architecture.

During the eighteenth century, Marc-Antoine Laugier provided his own account for how architecture began as an imitation of nature in his *Essai sur l'architecture* (*Essay on Architecture*, 1753). For Laugier, the first architecture was not a consequence of community and comfort, as Vitruvius had imagined, but a response to natural conditions. As Laugier explained, it was because forests were not sufficiently dry and caves lacked ventilation that humans imitated the superior qualities of both as models for the design of the first primitive hut.[46] To illustrate his concept, Laugier used an image from Charles Eisen as a frontispiece for his 1755 edition of *Essai sur l'architecture.* In Eisen's drawing a woman, presumably Lady Architecture, is reclining on fragments of Greek columns and cornices, directing the attention of an amazed putto toward a grouping of four trees in which the trunks, branches, and leaves are organized into the appearance of a Greek temple's columns, entablature, and pediment (figure 6.10). During Laugier's own lifetime, one can find examples of columns made to look like trees or women from Caryae, men from Persia, or even giants, while a dome added in 1777 to a hothouse at the Dunmore Estate in Falkirk, Scotland, had been given the appearance of a pineapple and Claude-Nicolas Ledoux made the entryway to the Saline Royale (Royal Saltworks) in Arc-et-Senans, France, recall the encrusting of salt crystals in the factory (1775–1779).[47] Unlike Laugier's "rustic hut," these examples have less to do with the analogical imitation of a model's principles of construction or composition than with the ascription of a visual or figurative meaning onto architecture.

One example for the use of nature as a model for the construction of architecture is given by the English gardener and designer Joseph Paxton, who introduced significant advances in glass greenhouse design during the late 1840s by imitating the structure of the *Victoria amazonica* waterlily leaf (figure 6.11). This was a period of

| 6.10 |

Charles Eisen, Vitruvian primitive hut, frontispiece of Marc-Antoine Laugier's *Essai sur l'architecture*, 2nd ed., 1755.

| 6.11 |

Sir Joseph Paxton showing a leaf of the *Victoria regia* waterlily (later named the *Victoria amazonica*), ca. 1849.

architectural history that witnessed the revival of Greek, Gothic, and Renaissance designs alongside an increased production of cast iron for new industrial structures—bridges, factories, warehouses, railway terminals, and also glass greenhouses. The most prominent contemporary discussion of the imitation of nature was by the French armchair archaeologist and architectural theorist Quatremère de Quincy, in the context of the design of classical ornament.[48] Paxton's approach to nature—using it as a model to design a new structural rather than a new aesthetic solution—was innovative compared to Quatremère de Quincy's. The moment of inspiration for Paxton's tectonic insight occurred while he was employed as head gardener at Chatsworth House in Derbyshire, England. There Paxton developed an interest in greenhouses and designed a series of structures made with cast iron and used for the cultivation of exotic plants, especially the *Victoria amazonica* water lily. When Paxton examined the underside of the water lily's huge leaves, he found they were supported by fibrous extensions stiffened by slender cross ribs. Struck by the rigidity of this configuration, which he called a "natural feat of engineering,"[49] Paxton imitated the water lily's ribs in weight-bearing iron struts, and the leaves themselves became the glass panes in his design of a second conservatory at Chatsworth—the Lily House (1849).

It was only after the end of the First World War that questions about the imitation of nature began to focus not on the propriety of one architectural style over another but on its use as an exemplar for those working with new materials and methods of construction. One of the most vocal proponents of the latter approach was László Moholy-Nagy, the director of the German Weimar and later Dessau Bauhaus's *Vorkurs* (preliminary course). During his tenure at these institutions and later as director of the Chicago Bauhaus, Moholy-Nagy published two books: *Von Material zu Architektur* (From material to architecture, 1929) and *Vision in Motion* (1947).[50] In both monographs, Moholy-Nagy argued at length that the intellectual foundation for Bauhaus pedagogy was the Hungarian botanist Raoul Francé's concept of "bio-technique," which, like Paxton's concept, idealized "the possibilities of using nature as a constructional model in creative technique."[51] Echoing Francé, Moholy-Nagy claimed that man has used functional suggestions of nature innumerable times, and many of our utensils, appliances, containers and tools are based upon

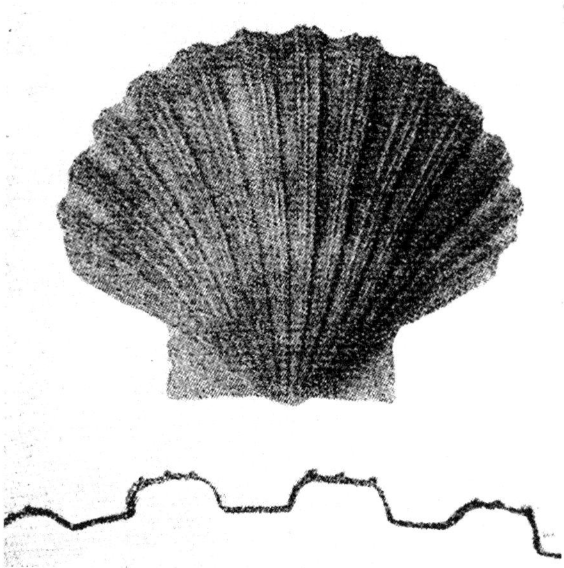

| 6.12 |

László Moholy-Nagy, biotechnical adaptation of a scallop shell to corrugated sheets of metal, 1929.

observations of nature.[52] Pointing to a series of examples—comparing the grip of a hand with a pair of pliers, the strength of an eggshell with a "Horton Spheroid" oil tank, and a scallop shell with metal corrugation (figure 6.12)—Moholy-Nagy reasoned that in all fields of creation, designers are using suggestions of nature to find functional solutions of a technical biological kind.[53] But unlike Paxton and his water lily, Moholy-Nagy draws analogical associations not from the actual models employed in designing these structures and devices but from didactic examples meant to demonstrate the practical application of his proposed use of models. As he explained, "The problem will be, of course, as everywhere else, to find the right ways of application."[54] In practice, however, analogical architectural models are less often found or reasoned after the fact but are frequently imagined from memory, and employed as an ideal in design.

Throughout his career, Moholy-Nagy's contemporary Le Corbusier developed a practice of employing analogies as models for his designs and as means for promoting his architectural ideas among his peers. In these instances, Le Corbusier's models are not objects that he holds in his hands but items familiar in everyday experience and recalled from memory. With the exception of the "stomach," which Le Corbusier used to describe the space of his 1958 Philips

from visible to invisible is a vestige of the term's beginnings in early Greek thought.

"Anagogy" or "anagoge" derives from ἀναγωγή (*anagōgē*), which in late Greek took on the meaning of a mystical or ecstatic elevation, and ultimately from the verb ἀνάγειν (*anagein*), "to lead up," "to elevate."[81] This early sense of physical elevation was expanded to include the elevation of something intellectually and later, by extension, mystically. Plato uses a word with the same prefix, *ana-*, to describe the epistemological ascent (*anabasis*) from a contemplation of physical particulars to their higher, invisible, eternal archetypes or *eidea*.[82] When Aristotle discusses the notion of *eidos*, he includes it as one of the causes of natural and man-made things. Following Aristotle's distinction, to interpret the "how and why" of a thing, its movement or change, was to *agagein* or to elevate an understanding of it intellectually according to four levels of causation: the material of which it is made; the form (*eidos*) or characteristics of its shape, arrangement, or appearance; the agent that produces the effect and starts the material on its way to the product; and the end or purpose (*telos*) for which a thing is what it is.[83] The final cause is that for the sake of which everything else was done—for example, to support a body, in the case of a carpenter making a chair; in the case of a living being, the fully developed form and the end are the same. For the medieval scholastic and theologian St. Bonaventure, the four interpretive levels of the "book of Scripture"—the literal, tropological, allegorical, and anagogical—could likewise be applied to nature as a "book of creation" to elucidate its material, formal, efficient, and final causes, respectively.[84] To return to architectural models, Le Corbusier's crab shell was not made as a model for the structure of his chapel roof, but the end or purpose of its unique combination of material and formal causes was interpreted anagogically as such.

The process by which architects temporarily suspend their identification of a found object in order to interpret it as a model of architecture can be described in philosophical terms as a phenomenological reduction or bracketing. Established by the German philosopher Edmund Husserl, phenomenology is a branch of philosophy that systematically reflects on and studies the structures of experience by investigating phenomena as consciously experienced. To determine the essential properties and structures of experience, Husserl promoted the act of suspending judgment about the natural world to examine phenomena as they are originally given to consciousness: he called this process *Einklammerung* or *epoché*, phenomenological reduction.[85] For example, the act of seeing a house qualifies as an experience, whether one sees that house in physical form, in the imagination, or in a hallucination. By "bracketing" an ice block, one suspends any judgment concerning the objective existence or nonexistence of the ice (the *noumenon*) and instead analyzes only one's experience of it. The French philosopher Maurice Merleau-Ponty, a student of Husserl, described this process as a "*return to things* themselves": "To *return to things* themselves is to *return* to that world which precedes knowledge, of which knowledge always speaks, and in relation to which every scientific schematization is an abstract and derivative sign language, as is geography in relation to the countryside in which we have learnt beforehand what a forest, a prairie or a river is."[86] This "unpacking" of phenomena—the systematic peeling away of their individual or cultural meanings like the layers of an onion, until only the thing itself as experienced remains—is the first act of a modeler with their modeling materials. It is an experience that is particularly familiar to a child playing with a found object.

A critical point of similarity between the child's use of found objects in play and the architect's in making an anagogical model of architecture is that in both cases, an individual's imagination is encouraged to interpret things as something other than what they are. A writer of children's books, Jean Fondin, along with a scholar on the history of toys, Jac Remise, observe: "Children are no respecters of property[;] ... costliness usually means nothing to them. ... Favorite toys are often mere *objets trouvés* [found objects], fugitives from the trash-can."[87] Kendall Walton, a philosopher who explores the points of coincidence between toys and art, has argued that a found object that children play with as a "prop" will "prompt" them to imagine what they might not otherwise be imaginative enough to invent on their own. By interpreting a pile of snow as a prop, they do not merely imagine it as, say, a fort with turrets, a tower, and a moat. Rather, they imagine that the heap of snow is *itself* a fort.[88] Hence, when it is true in a game of make-believe that the pile of snow is a fort, it is *fictional*, and because it is fictional, it is a *fictional truth.*[89] Artists employ this same form of interpretation when they use, for example, a bicycle seat

| 6.20 |

Kurt Schwitters, assemblage (now missing), *Schloss und Kathedrale mit Hofbrunnen* (Castle and Cathedral with Courtyard Well), 1922.

to make the face of a bull or, for our purposes, also a crab shell as a model of architecture.[90] While the crab shell is an ad hoc prop pressed into service for a single game of make-believe, the German artist Kurt Schwitters, discussed earlier in this chapter, encouraged architects to use found materials as a modeling method to find inspiration for new architectural designs.

In the spring 1922 issue of Bruno Taut's architectural journal, *Frühlicht*, Schwitters published an article titled "Schloss und Kathedrale mit Hofbrunnen" (Castle and Cathedral with Courtyard Well) promoting the use of found objects in the design practices of architects (figure 6.20).[91] Its primary aim was to extend his Merz method for making art to architects as an approach for "enriching" their imagination. As Schwitters explained, *Schloss und Kathedrale mit Hofbrunnen* is a "Merzentwurf für die Architektur" (Merz design for architecture): it

> uses any material with architectural feeling, in order to obtain an effect, which architecture can copy/re-create. The use of arbitrarily selected materials means an enriching of the imagination. The imagination works in this case rhythmically with rhythms already given. The transfer of the design onto representative material as well as onto constructive possibilities is a question of working through it. The design gives the stimulation.[92]

Schloss und Kathedrale mit Hofbrunnen is missing today, but from the photograph of the assemblage one can judge that it consisted of three objects: a cylindrical piece of cork, surrounded by a rough decaying organic mass, set vertically next to a smooth horizontal object. Schwitters claims in the opening paragraph of "Schloss und Kathedrale mit Hofbrunnen" that these items were "a medicine cork, a beech log, and pine stump on a diagonal board so that the whole gives the impression of a castle-like arrangement by a mountain slope."[93] The lack of visual correspondence between Schwitters's *Schloss und Kathedrale mit Hofbrunnen* and the miniature version of a conventional castle, cathedral, and courtyard well suggests that for Schwitters, the use of a found object in the design of architecture was not necessarily based on any resemblance to architecture in its appearance. Rather, because his modeling materials were found medicine corks, beech logs, or pine stumps, they encourage what Schwitters described as the "enriching of the [architect's] imagination" to discover new designs. As noted above, Schwitters explained that in order for a found object to become material for one of his Merz models, it had to undergo a process similar to a phenomenological reduction: its identification or purpose (its *Eigengift*) as a medicine cork, beech log, or pine stump had to be lost. Unlike Finsterlin's building blocks mentioned in chapter 2, Schwitters's found objects were not made to represent parts of known architectural structures. As if acknowledging this limitation, Finsterlin introduced a second set of building blocks, called *Formdomino*, with which he abandoned reliance on existing architectural forms.[94]

Like Schwitters's *Schloss und Kathedrale mit Hofbrunnen*, the examples Finsterlin chose for his *Formdomino* set possessed only a vague resemblance to conventional architectural structures (figure 6.21). Finsterlin planned to promote his building set in "Formdomino und Zukunftsarchitektur" (Formdomino and future architecture), an article in the never-published fifth issue of *Frühlicht*.[95] As Finsterlin explained, his *Formdomino* building blocks were derived from basic geometric and irregularly shaped masses that, like the *Stilspiel* before them, were intended to enhance the imagination of the architect. The model itself was "above all above all the bridge from the imagination to the materially grown-up final form, corrected according to the visibilities of the scale: the counter examination of the spirit in material, a unique asylum of preformation."[96] In "Schloss und Kathedrale mit Hofbrunnen," Schwitters also claimed that the use of found objects as architectural modeling material was intended to

| 6.21 |

Hermann Finsterlin, an architectural composition using the *Formdomino* set (now missing), 1922–1923.

enrich the imagination of the architect in such a way that what is transposed "onto representative material as well as onto constructive possibilities" depends on how the Merz design is interpreted as architecture.

At the end of the twentieth century, the Swiss architect Peter Zumthor developed a method of construing his Vals Thermal Bathhouse design with models that embodied many of the characteristics promoted by Schwitters and Finsterlin. Completed in 1996, the Bathhouse is known for its use of long, thin horizontal slabs of local Valser quartzite stone to create a series of fifteen monolithic structures that house baths at different temperatures, showers, steam rooms, and resting spaces in a rich sensorial environment of sight, sound, and scent. Initially referred to as "quarry sketches" or "block drawings," Zumthor's preliminary drawings of the Bathhouse consist predominantly of rectangular black and blue blocks created by dragging

the shaft of a pastel crayon from top to bottom of each piece of tracing paper.[97] The lack of any eraser marks indicates that the architect did not reconsider or rework the drawing on the page. Rather, each drawing embodies the same compositional limitations as a 1:50 scale model that Zumthor made of stone blocks assembled at right angles to one another, with each block supporting a cantilevered slab (figure 6.22).[98] As a composition, this model demonstrates his initial desire to quarry monolithic stone blocks that would be used to construct the bathhouse by a process of building up and hollowing out.[99] This method of construction proved to be too expensive, and he later replaced it with an additive method of forming the masses by horizontally stacking slabs of Valser quartzite stone. Nevertheless, the stone model so closely resembles both the preliminary drawings and the image of the completed construction that it is hard to imagine it did not come first in the design process.

| 6.22 |
Peter Zumthor, stone model of Thermal Bath House, Vals, Switzerland, ca. 1990.

By not using an eraser in his drawings and by using stone to assemble his model, Zumthor aims to reverse the standard practice of design development from idea to plan to concrete object. As Zumthor argues, "The concrete, sensuous quality of our inner image helps us here. It helps us not to lose track of the concrete qualities of architecture. It helps us not to fall in love with the graphic quality of our drawings and to confuse it with real architectural quality."[100] In these instances, the facture of a plan drawing without recourse to an eraser has the same effect as the use of large unwieldy stone to create an architectural model, since stone cannot be cut or manipulated into desired configurations of form. Rather, the concreteness of the stones used in the model determine particular configurations of architectural forms and spaces that are not predetermined by the architect.

As anagogical models of architecture, the models of Finsterlin, Schwitters, and Zumthor are not fashioned according to a prior idea but are found in the critical assemblage of the modeling materials. For Aristotle, the *eidos* (form or idea) of a house is in the builder's mind, whose final cause as "a receptacle for containing goods and bodies"[101] is intimately connected to it, and "the stones, bricks and wood" are selected and transformed to achieve this end. But the formal cause of Le Corbusier's crab shell was created to demonstrate not a preexisting architectural idea but one that is found and interpreted as a strategy for constructing the chapel roof's structure. Conversely, the final cause for a castle and cathedral with courtyard well or bathhouse is interpreted anagogically in the material and formal causes of the assemblage of building blocks or found materials. To interpret a model as its construction is to consider it as a record of how it was "factured."

The word "facture," as noted in chapter 3, derives from a Latin verb that means both "to make" and "to do." On a construction site, the craftsman utilizes different materials that require different methods to be transformed and assembled into architecture. Like buildings, models are also constructed of different materials that create different kinds of factures. Every cut of the knife or saw, tear, layer, fold, cast, fastening, and method of assembly or decomposition in the model has a signaling function and a meaning for the final cause of a proposed building. In this way, an anagogical model tells you not what the building looks like or how to get there, although it surely can, but instead models where your material and its organization into

structure(s) are aiming. Zumthor's and Allied Works Architecture's preliminary models for the Bruder Klaus Field Chapel in Mechernich, Germany, and the National Music Centre of Canada, respectively, demonstrate this use of a facture as an anagogical model in practice.

| 6.23 |

Peter Zumthor, clay model, of Bruder Klaus Field Chapel, 2007.

In the example of the Zumthor chapel model, the space of the chapel was described as an absence left by wood branches that had been cast and later removed from a mass of earth (clay?) (figure 6.23). This method of constructing the space of the chapel was emulated in the final chapel by burning away a conical arrangement of wooden poles inside a rammed earthen mass. For the National Music Centre

of Canada, the architects found a trombone at a thrift store, cut it up, and cast the brass into a square of nine concrete blocks (figure 6.24). The resulting design is also composed of interlocking towers, now adjusted to a site that spans a street connected by a large sky bridge. The spaces of the towers that were defined by the trombone became acoustically distinct volumes or "stages" in the completed structure; the spaces between are wrapped inside and outside with glazed terracotta, both to evoke the earth and light of the prairie and also to enable the sounds of the towers to resonate throughout the structure.

| 6.24 |

Allied Works Architecture, concept model of National Music Centre, 2009.

ALTHOUGH THEY ARE OFTEN assumed to transform materials into illustrations of already existing ideas, models can engage the architect's imagination in a variety of ways; their primary aim is to encourage the user to speculate on new and unexpected solutions. Keeping in mind the four different levels of biblical exegesis helps us understand that a model, like a text, may be subject to different levels of interpretation, both intended and accidental, that can aid architects in their conception and delineation of architecture. Of these, the literal meaning of a text is similar to the ordinary ("historical") function of manufactured and found modeling materials. By embracing the singular use value and significance of everyday things, architects can also speculate on the allegorical implications of their modeling materials for developing a broader description or critique of architecture. But once a modeling material is "cleansed" of these everyday associations, the imagination can freely speculate about analogical comparisons between its formal, material, or constructive properties and those of the proposed design. This fundamental shift in perception opens a modeling material to different levels of meaning beyond its everyday significance, permitting the imagination to anagogically discover how different properties of and associations between modeling materials can represent new architectural ideas about material and constructive experience. Although this process of interpreting models has its intellectual origins in the exegesis of religious texts and is thereby tied to an assumption of transcendence beyond the physical realm, these examples demonstrate a search for the invisible within the visible, whose source need not be divine revelation but can instead be found in the active imagination of the architect.

NOTES

FOREWORD

1. Maniaque Benton writes that Le Corbusier conceived the construction site of the Maisons Jaoul as a full-scale model for experimentation. Caroline Maniaque Benton, *Le Corbusier and the Maisons Jaoul* (New York: Princeton Architectural Press, 2009), 84, 106.
2. Since this mailbox appeared at a time when deadly anthrax was being sent by mail, the model house may have been considered apotropaic.
3. François Rabelais, *Gargantua and Pantagruel* [1542], trans. Burton Raffel (New York: Norton, 1990), 51–56.
4. Ludwig Wittgenstein, quoted in N. O'C. Drury, "Conversations with Wittgenstein," in *Ludwig Wittgenstein, Personal Recollections*, ed. Rush Rhees (Oxford: Blackwell, 1981), 121.
5. Marjorie Perloff, *Wittgenstein's Ladder: Poetic Language and the Strangeness of the Ordinary* (Chicago: University of Chicago Press, 1996), 60.
6. Ludwig Wittgenstein, *Philosophical Investigations*, trans. G. E. M. Anscombe, 2nd ed. (1958; reprint, Oxford: Blackwell, 1997), 43.
7. Françoise Frontisi-Ducroux, *Daedale: Mythologie de l'artisan en Graece ancienne* (Paris: F. Maspero, 1975); Alberto Pérez-Gómez, "The Myth of Daedalus," *AA Files* 10 (Autumn 1985): 49–52.
8. Adolf Behne, *The Modern Functional Building*, trans. Michael Robinson (Santa Monica, CA: Getty Research Center for the History of Art and the Humanities, 1996).
9. Wittgenstein, *Philosophical Investigations*, 206.

INTRODUCTION

1. Ulrike Fauerbach, "Concevoir les détails: Les maquettes de l'Égypte ancienne," in *La maquette, un outil au service du projet architectural* (Paris: Cité de l'architecture & du patrimoine, 2015), 30–31.
2. Corinna Rossi, *Architecture and Mathematics in Ancient Egypt* (Cambridge: Cambridge University Press, 2004), 96–127; Mark Wilson Jones, *Principles of Roman Architecture* (New Haven: Yale University Press, 2000), 26–32.
3. Leo Battista Alberti, *On the Art of Building in Ten Books* 2.1, trans. Joseph Rykwert, Neil Leach, and Robert Tavenor (Cambridge, MA: MIT Press, 1996), 33–35.

4. Sir John Soane, *Sir John Soane: The Royal Academy Lectures*, ed. David Watkin (Cambridge: Cambridge University Press, 2000), 273–274; *A New Description of Sir John Soane's Museum*, 10th ed. (Marlborough: Libanus Press, 2001), 17–19, 83–88; Helene Furján, *Glorious Visions: John Soane's Spectacular Theater* (Abingdon, Oxon.: Routledge, 2011), 28–32; Helen Dorey, "Soane's Pasticcio," *The Georgian*, November 2003, 14–17.

5. Kurt Schwitters, "Schloss und Kathedrale mit Hofbrunnen," *Frühlicht* 1, no. 3 (Spring 1922): 87; reprinted in *Frühlicht, 1920–1922: Eine Folge für die Verwirklichung des neuen Baugedankens*, ed. Bruno Taut (Berlin: Ullstein, 1963), 166–167.

6. Frei Otto, ed., *Tensile Structures*, [trans. D. Ben-Yaakov and T. Pelz] (Cambridge, MA: MIT Press, 1973), 10–11.

7. Edmund Husserl, *Ideen zu einer reinen Phänomenologie und Phänomenologischen Philosophie*, book 1, *Allgemeine Einführung in die reine Phänomenologie* (Halle: Verlag von Max Niemeyer, 1913), 31–32.

8. Cesare Guasti, *La Cupola di Santa Maria del Fiore illustrata con i documenti dell'archivio dell'opera secolare: Saggio di una compiuta illustrazione dell'opera secolare e del tempio di Santa Maria del Fiore* (Florence: Barbera, Bianchi e comp., 1857), 22–25.

9. For the terms *exemplum*, *forma*, *muster*, *Visierung*, and *patron*, see Franz Bischoff, "'... das verkleinert opus recht vor Augen gestellt': Zur Geschichte und Bedeutung des Architekturmodells von der Frühzeit bis zur Gegenwart," in *Rom über die Alpen tragen: Fürsten sammeln antike Architektur: Die Aschaffenburger Korkmodelle*, ed. Werner Helmberger and Valentin Kockel (Landshut: Arcos, 1993), 36, no. 30; Joseph Neuwirth, *Geschichte der Bildenden Künste in Böhmen*, vol. 1 (Prague: Calve, 1893), 321, cited by F. Bischoff, "Les Maquettes d'architecture," in *Les Bâtisseurs des cathédrales gothiques*, ed. Roland Recht (Strasbourg: Editions Les Musées de la ville de Strasbourg, 1989), 287 n. 5. For the use of the term "model" to refer to a drawing as "designum seu modellum," see Cesare Guasti, *Santa Maria del Fiore: La costruzione della Chiesa e del Campanile secondo i documenti tratti dall'Archivio nell'Opera Secolare e da quello di Stato* (Florence: M. Ricci, 1887), 167, doc. 142; Francesco Talenti's 1353 wood model for the Florence Duomo is described as "disegniamento asempro di legniame" on 29 May 1355 (see ibid., 81); Francesco Talenti and Lapo Ghini were asked to make a model in brick called "disegno di mattoni" for their design on 24 July 1367 (see ibid., 191–192., doc. 174).

10. On 24 May 1488, a model built by Pietro da Gorgonzola was destroyed in his absence to make another model with its materials. See *Annali della Fabbrica del Duomo di Milano: Dall'origine fino al presente*, vol. 3 (Milan: G. Brigola, 1880), 42, cited by Luisa Giordano, "Wooden Architectural Models in Lombardy," in *The Renaissance from Brunelleschi to Michelangelo: The Representation of Architecture*, ed. Henry A. Millon and Vittorio Magnago Lampugnani (Milan: Bompiani, 1994), 462.

11. See Millon and Lampugnani, *The Renaissance from Brunelleschi to Michelangelo*; Henry A. Millon, ed., *The Triumph of the Baroque: Architecture in Europe, 1600–1750* (New York: Rizzoli, 1999).

12. Andres Lepik, *Das Architekturmodell in Italien, 1335–1550* (Worms: Wernersche Verlagsgesellschaft, 1994); Peter Cachola Schmal, Teresa Fankhänel, Michael Stöneberg, and Philipp Sturm, *Das Architektur Modell: Werkzeug, Fetisch, kleine Utopie = The Architectural Model: Tool, Fetish, Small Utopia* (Frankfurt am Main: DAM, Deutsches Architekturmuseum, 2012); Sabine Frommel with Raphaël Tassin, eds., *Les maquettes d'architecture: Fonction et évolution d'un instrument de conception et de réalisation* (Paris: Picard; Rome: Campisano Editore, 2015).

13. See, e.g., Tom Porter and John Neale, *Architectural Supermodels: Physical Design Simulation* (Oxford: Architectural Press, 2000); Mark Morris, *Models: Architecture and the Miniature* (Chichester, West Sussex: Wiley-Academy, 2006); Karen Moon, *Modelling Messages: The Architect and the Model* (New York: Monacelli Press, 2005).
14. Ludwig H. Heydenreich, "Architekturmodell," in *Reallexikon zur Deutschen Kunstgeschichte*, vol. 1, ed. Otto Schmitt (Stuttgart: J. B. Metzlersche Verlagsbuchhandlung, 1937), 918–940.
15. Heydenreich suggests that during the fifteenth century, the architectural model became a representation of the "mathematsich-rationalen Gesamtplanung" (mathematical-rational entire planning) of planned constructions. Ibid., 924.
16. Hans Reuther follows Heydenreich's typology, questioning only his distinction between *Idealmodelle* and *Phantasiemodelle*. Hans Reuther, "Wesen und Wandel des Architekturmodells in Deutschland—The Origin and Development of the Architectural Model in Germany," *Daidalos* 2 (1981): 109; see also Bischoff, "Les Maquettes d'architecture," 287.
17. Wassili Luckhardt, "Vom Entwerfen," *Stadtbaukunst alter und neuer Zeit* 11 (1921), reprinted in *Brüder Luckhardt und Alfons Anker: Berliner Architekten der Moderne* (Berlin: Akademie der Künste, 1990), 122; Schwitters, "Schloss und Kathedrale mit Hofbrunnen"; Hermann Finsterlin, "Die Genesis der Weltarchitektur oder die Deszendenz der Dome als Stilspiel: Ein Lehr-, Spiel- und Versuchsbaukasten," *Frühlicht* 1, no. 3 (Spring 1922): 86–87, reprinted in Taut, *Frühlicht, 1920–1922*, 149–158.
18. John Elsner, "A Collector's Model of Desire: The House and Museum of Sir John Soane," in *The Cultures of Collecting*, ed. John Elsner and Roger Cardinal (London: Reaktion Books, 1994), 155–176.
19. Francois Bucher, "Micro-Architecture as the 'Idea' of Gothic Theory and Style," *Gesta* 15, no. 1/2 (1976): 71–89.
20. Architects other than those cited here also adopted such building blocks. See Finsterlin, "Die Genesis der Weltarchitektur oder die Deszendenz der Dome als Stilspiel"; Blanche Mahlberg and Bruno Taut, "*Dandanah der Märchenpalast: Baustein aus massiven Glas*," in *Wege zu einer neuen Baukunst: Bruno Taut: Frühlicht: Konzeptionskritik H. 1–4 und Rekonstruktion H. 5*, by Manfred Speidel, Karl Kegler, and Peter Ritterbach (Berlin: Mann, 2000), 86–87. Working together with the Hungarian architect Fréd Forbát, Walter Gropius sought to base his plan for the estate on "the standardization of individual components from which different types of buildings could be composed." Fréd Forbát, *Erinnerungen eines Architekten aus vier Ländern*, copy of the typographic text and the manuscript, ca. 1967–1969, at the BauhausArchiv, Berlin, 66; translated by Winfried Nerdinger in Winfried Nerdinger, *Walter Gropius* (1969; reprint, Berlin: Gebr. Mann, 1985), 58 n. 3, cited by Magdalena Droste, *Bauhaus, 1919–1933* (Cologne: Taschen, 2002), 111–112.
21. Claude Lévi-Strauss, *The Savage Mind* (Chicago: University of Chicago Press; London: Weidenfeld & Nicolson, 1966), 17–33.
22. Umberto Eco, "The Poetics of the Open Work," in *The Open Work*, trans. Anna Cancogni (Cambridge, MA: Harvard University Press, 1989), 1–24.
23. Ibid., 4, 19.
24. Ibid., 5.
25. Dean MacCannell, *The Tourist* (Berkeley: University of California Press, 1999), 147–151; David Weingarten and Margaret Majua, *Monumental Miniatures: Souvenir Buildings from the Collection of Ace Architects* (Norfolk, VA: Antique Trader Books, 1999).

26. On models in personal collections during the Renaissance, see Samuel Quiccheberg, *The First Treatise on Museums: Samuel Quiccheberg's Inscriptiones, 1565*, trans. Mark A. Meadow and Bruce Robertson (Los Angeles: Getty Research Institute, 2014); Joseph Furttenbach, *Architectura Privata* (Augsburg: Johann Schultes, 1641), 37, 40; Monique Mosser, "Französische Architekturmodelle im Zeitalter der Aufklärung," *Daidalos* 2 (1981): 86; see also Hubertus Günther, "La presentazione dei modelli: Il primo museo del Rinasciamento dedicato all'architettura," in Frommel with Tassin, *Les maquettes d'architecture*, 173–188. On models in municipal collections, see Ekhart Berckenhagen, "Das deutsche Architekturmodell," in *Deutsche Architekturmodelle: Projekthilfe zwischen 1500 und 1900*, by Hans Reuther and Ekhart Berckenhagen (Berlin: Deutscher Verlag für Kunstwissenschaft, 1994), 7–9; see also Stephan Hoppe, "German Architectural Models in the Renaissance (1500–1620)," in Frommel with Tassin, *Les maquettes d'architecture*, 131–142. On models as a didactic tool, see Heinrich Rockstroh, *Anweisung zum Modelliren aus Papier oder aus demselben allerley Gegenstände im Kelinen nachzuahmen, Ein nütlicher Zeitreib für Kinder* (Weimar: Verlag des Landes, 1802); Friedrich Fröbel, *Pedagogics of the Kindergarten*, trans. Josephine Jarvis (New York: D. Appleton, 1896). See also Werner Oechslin, "Le modèle architectural: 'Idea Materialis,'" in Frommel with Tassin, *Les maquettes d'architecture*, 103–120.
27. Alberti, *On the Art of Building in Ten Books* 1.1, 7; 9.10, 317.
28. Ibid.
29. For example, Criss B. Mills, *Designing with Models: A Studio Guide to Making and Using Architectural Models*, 2nd ed. (Hoboken, NJ: John Wiley & Sons, 2005), 14, or Nick Dunn, *The Ecology of the Architectural Model* (Oxford: Peter Lang, 2007), 59.

CHAPTER 1

1. Sir John Soane, "Lecture XII," in *Sir John Soane: The Royal Academy Lectures*, ed. David Watkin (Cambridge: Cambridge University Press, 2000), 274.
2. *A New Description of Sir John Soane's Museum*, 10th ed. (Marlborough: Libanus Press, 2001), 17–19, 83–88; Helene Furján, *Glorious Visions: John Soane's Spectacular Theater* (Abingdon, Oxon.: Routledge, 2011), 28–32.
3. Dean MacCannell, *The Tourist* (Berkeley: University of California Press, 1999), 147–151.
4. Brian Spencer, *Pilgrim Souvenirs and Secular Badges* (London: Stationery Office, 1998), 1–24.
5. MacCannell, *The Tourist*, 147–148.
6. Susan Stewart, *On Longing: Narratives of the Miniature, the Gigantic, the Souvenir, the Collection* (Durham: Duke University Press, 1993), 136.
7. Robin Osborne, "Hoards, Votives, Offerings: The Archaeology of the Dedicated Object," *World Archaeology* 36 (2004): 2–3; Marcel Mauss, *The Gift: The Form and Reason for Exchange in Archaic Societies*, trans. W. D. Halls (London: Routledge, 1990), 41–44.
8. Charles Sanders Peirce, "Excerpts from Letters to Lady Welby (1906–08)," in *The Essential Peirce: Selected Philosophical Writings*, vol. 2, *1893–1914*, ed. the Pierce Edition Project (Bloomington: Indiana University Press, 1998), 478.
9. See, e.g., Artur Simões Rozestraten, "Learning with Arkhanes' Model," *Acta Scientiarum: Education* [online] 32 (July–December 2010): 265–266, http://dx.doi.org/10.4025/actascieduc.v32i2.9774; Thomas Schattner, *Griechische Hausmodelle*

(Berlin: Gebr. Mann, 1990), 205; Carmelo G. Malacrino, *Constructing the Ancient World: Architectural Techniques of the Greeks and Romans* (Los Angeles: J. Paul Getty Museum, 2010), 81–83.

10. Martin Heidegger, "The Origin of the Work of Art," in *Poetry Language Thought*, trans. Albert Hofstadter (New York: Harper & Row, 2001), 41.

11. Umberto Eco, "The Poetics of the Open Work," in *The Open Work*, trans. Anna Cancogni (Cambridge, MA: Harvard University Press, 1989), 3–4, 19.

12. Marija Gimbutas, *The Goddesses and Gods of Old Europe: Myths and Cult Images*, updated ed. (1982; reprint, Berkeley: University of California Press, 2007), 67–69.

13. Ibid.

14. W. M. Flinders Petrie, "The Soul-House in Egypt," *Man* 7 (1907): 113–114; Ilse Schoep, "'Home Sweet Home': Some Comments on the So-Called House Models from the Prehellenic Aegean," *Opuscula Atheniensia* 20 (1994): 198.

15. Rozestraten, "Learning with Arkhanes' Model," 265–267.

16. Jens David Baumbach, *The Significance of Votive Offerings in Selected Hera Sanctuaries in the Peloponnese, Ionia and Western Greece*, BAR International Series 1249 (Oxford: Archaeopress, 2004), 1.

17. Schattner, *Griechische Hausmodelle*, 205.

18. Small models of temples were also votive offerings; see W. M. Ramsay, *The Church in the Roman Empire before A.D. 170* (New York: G. P. Putman's Sons, 1893), 123–126, 134. For the lighthouse model: A. M. McCann, *The Roman Port and Fishery of Cosa* (Rome: Academy in Rome, 2002), 25. For the Nemi model: Axel Boëthius, Roger Ling, and Tom Rasmussen, *Etruscan and Early Roman Architecture*, 2nd ed. (New Haven: Yale University Press, 1992), 54–60.

19. See Appian, *History of Rome, The Punic Wars* 9.66.

20. Thomas Whittemore, *The Mosaics of St. Sophia at Istanbul: Second Preliminary Report, Work Done in 1933 and 1934: The Mosaics of the Southern Vestibule* (Boston: J. Johnson, 1936), 21.

21. Provost Heinrich is credited with the reconstruction and foundation of a new church in Ardagger, Austria. See *Vitrea Dedicata* (Berlin: Deutscher Verlag für Kunstwissenschaft, 1975), 67–68.

22. Ludwig H. Heydenreich, "Architekturmodell," in *Reallexikon zur Deutschen Kunstgeschichte*, ed. Otto Schmitt, vol. 1 (Stuttgart: J. B. Metzlersche Verlagsbuchhandlung, 1937), 934.

23. The cathedral of St. Blaise was finished in 1195, while the Elisabethkirche in Marburg was built 1235–1285. Sauerländer observes that the model of Henry the Lion has reproduced the cathedral of St. Blaise in all of its details. Lipsmeyer argues that it could have been executed to copy the cathedral itself. See W. Sauerländer, "Grabmal Heinrichs des Löwen und seiner Gemahlin Mathilde," in *Die Zeit der Staufer*, 5 vols. (Stuttgart: Württembergisches Landesmuseum, 1977), 1:325–327, and vol. 2, pl. 248; Elisabeth Lipsmeyer, "The Donor and His Church Model in Medieval Art from Early Christian Times to the Late Romanesque Period" (Ph.D. diss., Rutgers, the State University of New Jersey, 1981), 184–187 n. 113, 203. There are a number of sculptures and reliefs of St. Elisabeth von Thüringen at the Marburg cathedral. Of particular interest are two very precise cathedral models, the so-called French Elisabeth from 1470 and another from 1520, now found in the cathedral. See Hermann Bauer, *St. Elisabeth und die Elisabethkirche zu Marburg* (Marburg: Dr. Wolfram Hitzeroth Verlag, 1990), 99–102, and *700 Jahre*

Elisabethkirche in Marburg: 1283–1983 [Ausstellungen 30. April–31. July 1983 in Marburg] (Marburg: Komm. N. G. Elwert, 1983), 8:20–22.

24. For this observation regarding donor models in general, see Heydenreich, "Architekturmodell," 934.

25. Reinhard Wortman, "Hallenplan und Basilikabau der Parler in Ulm," in *600 Jahre Ulmer Münster* (Stuttgart: Kohlhammer, 1977), 106, 111. For a discussion of the Ulmer relief in reference to similar symbolic forms in the visual culture of medieval Europe, see Gaus Joachim, "Dedicatio Ecclesiae: Zum Grundsteinlegungsrelief im Münster zu Ulm," in ibid., 59–85.

26. The model held by Jean Tissandier represents the Rieux chapel, which was destroyed around 1871. In 1804 an engineer by the name of Laferrie had made a detailed record of the chapel, which indicates, as Barbara Mundt observes, that the model is a very precise portrait of the architecture. For Laferrie's report, see Jean-Jacques Esquié, *L'église et le monastère des Cordeliers: Mémoires de l'Academie des Sciences, Inscriptions et Belles Lettres* (Toulouse: Douladoure, 1876), 395, cited in a description of the history of the bishop and the making of the Rieux Chapel by Barbara Mundt, "Der Zyklus der Chapelle de Rieux und seine künstlerische Nachfolge," *Jahrbuch der Berliner Museen* 9 (1967): 26–80.

27. A. Jiménez Martín, *La catedral gótica de Sevilla: Fundación y fábrica de la obra nueva* (Seville: Editorial Universidad de Sevilla-Secretariado de Publicaciones, 2006), 388–394.

28. Kurt Gerstenberg, "Baumeisterbildnis," in *Reallexikon zur Deutschen Kunstgeschichte*, vol. 2, ed. Otto Schmitt (Stuttgart: J. B. Metzler, 1937), 96. For a similar interpretation, see also Spiro Kostof, "The Architect in the Middle Ages, East and West," in *The Architect: Chapters in the History of the Profession*, ed. Spiro Kostof (New York: Oxford University Press, 1977), 78.

29. For the condition of the architect and representations of them with these tools, see Pierre du Colombier, *Les chantiers des cathédrales*, 2nd ed. (Paris: Picard, 1973), 96–105. Lon Shelby has written two articles on the compass, square, measuring stick, and plumb line as the tools of the architect: see "Medieval Mason's Tools: The Level and the Plumb Rule," *Technology and Culture*, no. 2 (1961): 127–130, and "Medieval Mason's Tools II: Compass and Square," *Technology and Culture*, no. 6 (1965): 236–248. See also Günther Binding, *Der mittelalterliche Baubetrieb nördlich der Alpen in zeitig enössischen Darstellungen* (Darmstadt: Wissenschaftliche Buchgesellschaft, 1978), 43–45.

30. Gerstenberg ("Baumeisterbildnis," 96) claims that this is the only tombstone of an architect with a model in Germany.

31. Maryse Bideault and Claudine Lautier, "Saint-Nicaise de Reims, Chronologie et nouvelles remarques sur l'architecture," *Bulletin Monumental*, no. 135 (1977): 295–330; Charles Givelet, *L'eglise et l'abbaye de St. Nicaise de Reims* (Reims: F. Michaud, 1897); *Cartulaire de Saint-Nicaise de Reims*, ed. Jeannine Cossé-Durlin (Paris: Editions du Centre national de la recherche scientifique, 1991).

32. The Reims Palimpsest was created in the early thirteenth century. See Robert Branner, "Drawings from a Thirteenth-Century Architect's Shop: The Reims Palimpsest," *Journal of the Society of Architectural Historians*, no. 18 (1958): 9–21. Günther Binding observes the inclusion of drawing boards in the depictions of architects after the thirteenth century; see *Der mittelalterliche Baubetrieb nördlich der Alpen in zeitig enössischen Darstellungen*, 45.

33. Dennis Geronimus, *Piero di Cosimo: Visions Beautiful and Strange* (New Haven: Yale University Press, 2006), 45.

34. Monique Mosser, *"Französische* Architekturmodelle im Zeitalter der Aufklärung," *Daidalos* 2 (1981): 83–97, esp. 92.

35. *Time* magazine cover of 8 January 1979. Accompanying article: Robert Hughes, "Doing Their Own Thing: U.S. Architects: Goodbye to Glass Boxes and All That," *Time*, 8 January 1979, 52.

36. Gottfried Semper, *Der Stil in den technischen und tektonischen Künsten oder praktische Ästhetik: Ein Handbuch für Techniker, Künstler und Kunstfreunde*, vol. 2 (Frankfurt: Verlag für Kunst und Wissenschaft, 1863), 276.

37. Patrick Geary, *Furta Sacra: Thefts of Relics in the Central Middle Ages* (Princeton, NJ: Princeton University Press, 2001), 7.

38. Ibid., 33.

39. Richard Krautheimer, "Introduction to an 'Iconography of Mediaeval Architecture,'" *Journal of the Warburg and Courtauld Institutes* 5 (1942): 3–5.

40. Ibid., 17.

41. Ibid., 9–11.

42. Aristotle's concept of a nontranscendental "inner form" or idea belonging to the artist was most explicitly incorporated as "quasi-ideas" in the *Summa Theologica* of St. Thomas Aquinas. See Thomas Aquinas, *Summa Theologica* II.1.93.1 and *Quodlibeta* IV.1.1, cited by Erwin Panofsky, *Idea: A Concept of Art Theory*, trans. Joseph J. S. Peake (Columbia: University of South Carolina Press, 1968), 39–43. However, the relationship between a work *in mente* and its transference into reality was similarly formulated by earlier writers, including William of Conches. See Joseph-Marie Parent, *La doctrine de la création dans l'école de Chartres* (Paris: Vrin; Ottawa: Inst. d'études médiévales, 1938), 143, 149. Grosseteste and Aquinas use Aristotle's analogy of the "architect" who has, respectively, a "Form" or "Idea" of a house in his mind preceding the work. See Thomas Aquinas, *Summa Theologica* I.15.1, and Robert Grosseteste, *De unica forma omnium*, as excerpted by Rosario Assunto in *Die Theorie des Schönen im Mittelalter* (Cologne: DuMont, 1982), 223–224.

43. Robert Grosseteste, *De unica forma omnium*, in *Die philosophischen werke des Robert Grosseteste, Bischofs von Lincoln*, ed. Ludwig Baur (Münster i.W.: Aschendorff, 1912), 109, cited by Władysław Tatarkiewicz, *History of Aesthetics*, ed. C. Barrett, vol. 2, *Medieval Aesthetics* (Warsaw: Polish Scientific Publishers, 1970), 231; I have changed "pattern" to "exemplar" (as it is used in the original Latin text) in italics.

44. Ibid.

45. For the idea that the *forma* of a sensible object was the principle for knowing both the sensible singular thing and its constituent parts, see ibid. For a discussion of this concept, see Steven P. Marrone, *William of Auvergne and Robert Grosseteste: New Ideas of Truth in the Early Thirteenth Century* (Princeton, NJ: Princeton University Press, 1983), 169–170. That we have sensible knowledge of sensible singular things, see Robert Grosseteste, *Commentary on Posterior Analytics* 2.6. That this knowledge of sensible singular things is an idea (thus *forma*) that could serve as a basis for a universal, and that when we have found the same patterns in many singular things, we have knowledge of that universal, see Grosseteste, *Commentary on Posterior Analytics* 1.14.

46. The quotation is part of the inscription from 1491 above the entrance to the chapel that houses the replica of the Holy Sepulcher on the Sacro Monte di Varallo. In

full, it reads: "The Milanese Friar Bernardino Caimi envisioned the sacred places of this mountain so that those who could not make the pilgrimage could see Jerusalem right here." See Stefania Stefani Perrone, "La 'Gerusalemme' delle origini nella secolare vicenda edificatoria del Sacro Monte di Varallo," in *Sacri Monti*, ed. Luciano Vaccaro and Francesca Ricardi (Milan: Jaca Book, 1992), 27–57, esp. 31. This English translation is from Roberta Panzanelli, "Pilgrimage in Hyperreality: Images and Imagination in the Early Phase of the 'New Jerusalem' at Varallo (1486–1530)" (Ph.D. diss., University of California, Los Angeles, 1999), 11.

47. Samuel Butler, *Ex Voto* (1888; reprint, London: J. Cape, 1928), 49.
48. David Leatherbarrow, "The Image and Its Setting: A Study of the Sacro Monte at Varallo," *RES: Anthropology and Aesthetics*, no. 14 (Autumn 1987): 117.
49. Ibid., 115.
50. Jean Baudrillard, "Simulacra and Science Fiction," in *Simulacra and Simulation*, trans. Sheila Faria Glaser (Ann Arbor: University of Michigan Press, 1994), 121–127.
51. Karen Tam, "Dolce & Banana, A Shanzhai Creator's Manual: Production and Consumption of Fake in Contemporary Chinese Art Practices," in *The Changing Landscape of China's Consumerism*, ed. Allison Hulme (Oxford: Chandos Publishing, 2014), 84–85, 95–98.
52. Jean Baudrillard, "The Precession of Simulacra," in *Simulacra and Simulation*, 1. The third order, in which simulacra pretend to be copies but mask the absence of a basic reality, is sorcery (6).
53. Ibid., 7.
54. A. L. Frothingham, "Discovery of an Original Church Model by a Gothic Architect," *Architectural Record* 22 (August 1907): 110–116, originally published in French as Arthur L. Frothingham, "Le modèle de l'église Saint-Maclou à Rouen," *Monuments et mémoires de la Fondation Eugène Piot Année* 12, no. 2 (1905): 211–224.
55. Frothingham, "Le modèle de l'église Saint-Maclou à Rouen," 221.
56. Franz Bischoff, "Les Maquettes d'architecture," in *Les Bâtisseurs des cathédrales gothiques*, ed. Roland Recht (Strasbourg: Les Musées de la Ville, 1989), 287 n. 7.
57. Hans Reuther and Ekhart Berckenhagen, *Deutsche Architekturmodelle: Projekthilfe zwischen 1500 und 1900* (Berlin: Deutscher Verlag für Kunstwissenschaft, 1994), cat. 100, 57.
58. Salesius Hess, "Balthasar Neumanns Kirchenbau in Münsterschwarzach," in *Abtei Münsterschwarzach: Arbeiten aus ihrer Geschichte: Festgabe zur Weihe der Kirche 1938* (Münsterschwarzach: [Missions-verlag], 1938), cited by Hans Reuther, "Wesen und Wandel des Architekturmodells in Deutschland—Origin and Development of the Architectural Model in Germany," *Daidalos* 2 (1981): 109.
59. Samuel Quiccheberg, *The First Treatise on Museums: Samuel Quiccheberg's Inscriptiones, 1565*, trans. Mark A. Meadow and Bruce Robertson (Los Angeles: Getty Research Institute, 2014).
60. Ibid., 63.
61. Katharina Pilaski Kaliardos, *The Munich Kunstkammer: Art, Nature, and the Representation of Knowledge in Courtly Contexts* (Tübingen: Mohr Siebeck, 2013), 41–43.
62. Helmut Puff, *Miniature Monuments: Modeling German History* (Berlin: De Gruyter, 2017), 95–96.
63. Ibid., 96–97.
64. Ibid., 109.

65. This requirement is reflected in the "Regensburger Steinmotzen mauern und deckern Ordnung" from 1514. Over almost 300 years, till the beginning of the nineteenth century, the Nürnberger Handicraft ordinances prescribed the production of part/detail models by stone masons and carpenters seeking to acquire the title "Master." "Ain gewundtenner schnegkhen, mit beeden handhaben abgeriessen in ain model" (a wound snail with both rails separated in a model) would be asked in 1629 of the stone masons in Vienna. Otto E. Plettenbacher, *Geschichte der Steinmetzen von Wien im 17. Jahrhundert* (diss., Universität Wien, 1960), 37, cited by Franz Bischoff, "'... das verkleinert opus recht vor Augen gestellt': Zur Geschichte und Bedeutung des Architekturmodells von der Frühzeit bis zur Gegenwart," in *Rom über die Alpen tragen: Fürsten sammeln antike Architektur: Die Aschaffenburger Korkmodelle*, ed. Werner Helmberger and Valentin Kockel (Landshut: Arcos, 1993), 41 n. 75.

66. François Blondel, *Cours d'architecture enseigné dans l'Académie royale d'architecture*, vol. 1 (Paris, 1675), preface (n.p.).

67. Mosser, "Französische Architekturmodelle," 86.

68. Ibid.; Rune Frederiksen and Eckart Marchand, eds., *Plaster Casts: Making, Collecting and Displaying from Classical Antiquity to the Present* (Berlin: De Gruyter, 2010), 4426–4429.

69. Joseph Furttenbach, *Architectura privata* (Augsburg: Johann Schultes, 1641), 37, 40.

70. Mosser, "Französische Architekturmodelle," 93.

71. Ibid., 86.

72. Helen Dorey, "Sir John Soane's Model Room," *Perspecta* 41, *Grand Tour* (2008): 46.

73. Frederiksen and Marchand, *Plaster Casts*, 427.

74. *A New Description of Sir John Soane's Museum*, 17–19.

75. Margaret Richardson, "John Soane and the Temple of Vesta at Tivoli," *Architectural History* 46 (2003): 127–146.

76. *A New Description of Sir John Soane's Museum*, 83–88.

77. Heinrich Rockstroh, *Anweisung zum Modelliren aus Papier oder aus demselben allerley Gegenstände im Kelinen nachzuahmen, Ein nütlicher Zeitreib für Kinder* (Weimar: S.V. Vorrede, 1802).

78. Friedrich Fröbel, *Pedagogics of the Kindergarten*, trans. Josephine Jarvis (New York: D. Appleton, 1896), 118, cited by Norman Brosterman, *Inventing Kindergarten* (New York: Harry N. Abrams, 1997), 50 n. 5.

79. Hermann Finsterlin, "Die Genesis der Weltarchitektur oder die Deszendenz der Dome als Stilspiel: Ein Lehr-, Spiel- und Versuchsbaukasten," *Frühlicht* 1, no. 3 (Spring 1922): 86–87, reprinted in *Frühlicht, 1920–1922: Eine Folge für die Verwirklichung des neuen Baugedankens*, ed. Bruno Taut (Berlin: Ullstein, 1963), 149–158; see specifically 158.

80. From a speech Winston Churchill gave to the House of Commons on October 28, 1944.

CHAPTER 2

1. Edward Albee, *Tiny Alice* (1965; reprint, [New York]: Dramatists Play Service, 2001), 18–19.

2. Lucinda Lambton, *The Queen's Dolls' House* (London: Royal Collection Enterprises, 2010), 14, 95–97.

3. Johan Huizinga, *Homo Ludens: A Study of the Play-Element in Culture* (1949; reprint, London: Routledge & Kegan Paul, 1980), 7.
4. Ibid., 3–4, 12.
5. Roger Caillois, *Man, Play and Games*, trans. Meyer Barash (New York: Free Press of Glencoe, 1961), 19.
6. Elaine Scarry, *Dreaming by the Book* (New York: Farrar, Straus, Giroux, 1999).
7. Jun Yanagisawa, "A Utopia Called Model," in *Toyo Ito: Blurring Architecture, 1971–2005*, ed. Ulrich Schneider and Manfred Fenstel (Milan: Edizioni Charta, 1999), 155.
8. Italo Calvino, *Invisible Cities*, trans. William Weaver (Orlando: Harcourt, 1972), 32–33.
9. Justina Gregory, "Commentary," in Euripides, *Euripides: "Hecuba": Introduction, Text, and Commentary*, by Justina Gregory (Atlanta: Scholars Press, 1999), 53.
10. Ovid, *Metamorphoses* 11.633–649.
11. William H. Peck, *The Material World of Ancient Egypt* (New York: Cambridge University Press, 2013), 176–177; Richard Tames, *Ancient Egyptian Children* (Chicago: Heinemann, 2003).
12. Vitruvius, *Ten Books on Architecture* 10.16, ed. Ingrid D. Rowland and Thomas Noble Howe (Cambridge: Cambridge University Press, 1999), 133.
13. Matthew Mindrup, "*Bauspiel* as Immaterial Investigation: Avant-garde Experimentations with Generative Architectural Models," in *Materiality in Architecture and Art*, ed. Sandra Katrina Löschke (London: Routledge, 2016), 195–212.
14. Hermann Finsterlin, "Die Genesis der Weltarchitektur oder die Deszendenz der Dome als Stilspiel: Ein Lehr-, Spiel- und Versuchsbaukasten," *Frühlicht* 1, no. 3 (Spring 1922): 86–87; reprinted in *Frühlicht, 1920–1922: Eine Folge für die Verwirklichung des neuen Baugedankens*, ed. Bruno Taut (Berlin: Ullstein, 1963), 149–158.
15. Kurt Schwitters, "Schloss und Kathedrale mit Hofbrunnen," *Frühlicht* 1, no. 3 (Spring 1922): 87; reprinted in Taut, *Frühlicht, 1920–1922*, 166–167.
16. "Der Merzentwurf für die Architektur verwendet jedes beliebige Material nach architektonischem Gefühl, um eine Wirkung zu erzielen, welche die Architektur nachbilden kann. Die Verwendung beliebiger Materialien bedeutet eine Bereicherung der Phantasie. Die Phantasie arbeitet in diesem Falle rhythmisch mit schon gegebenen Rhythmen. Das Transportieren des Entwurfs auf darstellendes Material sowie auf konstruktive Möglichkeiten ist Sache der Durcharbeitung. Der Entwurf gibt die Anregung." Ibid., 86. Unless otherwise indicated, all translations are the author's.
17. Aldo Rossi, *Aldo Rossi,* ed. Nakamura Toshio (Tokyo: A & U, 1982), 104–109.
18. Ibid., 104.
19. Christian Hubert, "The Ruins of Representation," in *Idea as Model*, [ed. Kenneth Frampton and Silvia Kolbowski] (New York: Rizzoli, 1981), 22.
20. Galileo Galilei, *Dialogues Concerning Two New Sciences*, trans. Henry Crew and Alfonso de Salvio (1914; reprint, Evanston, IL: Northwestern University, 1939), 1–108, specifically 90–91.
21. Lebbeus Woods, "Experimental Architecture: A Commentary," *Avant Garde* 2 (Summer 1989): 11.
22. Ibid.

23. Tracy Myers, "'The Possibility of the Exceptional': Lebbeus Woods' Passionate Provocations," in *Lebbeus Woods: Experimental Architecture*, ed. Tracy Myers (Pittsburgh: Carnegie Museum of Art, the Heinz Architectural Center, 2004), 6.

24. Lebbeus Woods and Christoph a. Kumpusch, "A Space of Light," in *The Light Pavilion by Lebbeus Woods and Christoph a. Kumpusch for the Sliced Porosity Block in Chengdu, China, 2007–2012*, ed. Christoph a. Kumpusch (Zurich: Lars Müller, 2013), 10.

25. Karsten Harries, "Taking on Risk: Nine Experimental Scenarios," in Myers, *Lebbeus Woods: Experimental Architecture*, 43.

26. Fenna Wagenaar, quoted in Rem Koolhaas, *Content: Triumph of Realisation* (Cologne: Taschen, 2004), 205.

27. Abbot Suger, *Abbot Suger on the Abbey Church of St.-Denis and Its Art Treasures*, ed. and trans. Erwin Panofsky, 2nd ed. (Princeton, NJ: Princeton University Press, 1979), 46–49, 64–65.

28. Origen, *On First Principles*, trans. G. W. Butterworth (Gloucester, MA: Peter Smith, 1973), 278–279.

29. The high-quality sculptural work in the shrine of the Three Kings is accompanied by a confusion of architectural elements, making it impossible to determine if the arcades in the roof planes symbolize colonnades or clerestories. See W. D. Wixom, "The Greatest of the So Called Minor Arts," in *The Year 1200*, ed. Florens Deuchler, 2 vols. (New York: Metropolitan Museum of Art, 1970), 2:93–132, cited by François Bucher, "Micro-Architecture as the 'Idea' of Gothic Theory and Style," *Gesta* 15, nos. 1–2 (1976): 73 n. 14.

30. This shrine, measuring 1.05 by 0.45 meters, is made out of silver and gilded copper and takes the form of a cathedral transept. Unlike the casket- or coffin-type reliquaries, the shrine clearly is increasingly characterized by many identifiable architectural forms, including pilasters, pinnacles, pignons, columns, arches, pilasters, etc. See *Les Trésors des églises de France*, 2nd ed. (Paris: Caisse nationale des monuments historiques, 1965), 111–112, pl. 113.

31. The stonework in the rood screen recalls metalwork, especially at the central arch. This screen contrasts strongly with the heavy opacity of the rood screen of the Naumburg cathedral (1245–1250). See *700 Jahre Elisabethkirche in Marburg: 1283–1983* [Ausstellungen 30. April–31. Juli 1983 in Marburg] (Marburg: Komm. N. G. Elwert, 1983), 1:153, figs. 94–95.

32. For the Three Towers reliquary of Aachen and its idealization of Gothic design, see Ernst Günther Grimme, *Goldschmiedekunst im Mittelalter: Form und Bedeutung des Reliquiars von 800 bis 1500* (Cologne: M. DuMont Schauberg, 1972), 148–151, pl. 50. For a description of the sacrament tabernacle at St. Peter's Church in Louvain and its use as a model for another in the Netherlands, see R. Maere, "De sacramentstorens van Leuven," in *Studia Eucharistica* (Antwerp: Nederlandsche Boekhandel, 1946), 343–348.

33. Bucher, "Micro-Architecture," 72.

34. Überwasser demonstrated that some of the architectural elements in the 260 sheets of drawings contained in the "Basler Golschmiedrisse" relied on the technique of extracting the elevation from the ground plan. But the drawings also show that the procedures for rotating and manipulating the basic geometrical figures varied from one design to the next, and even within the design of the same objects. See Walter Überwasser, "Spägotische Baugeometrie," *Öffentliche Kunstsammlung Basel* 25–27 (1931): 79–122. In the exhibition catalog for *Die deutschen Zeichnen*

des 15. Jahrhunderts, a working drawing for a monstrance tower and another for a baldachin are placed side by side, and the resemblance is uncanny. See Tilman Falk, *Die deutschen Zeichnen des 15. Jahrhunderts* (Munich: Staatliche Graphische Sammlung, 1994), 120, figs. 385–386, Tafel 91. For similar collections of drawings by architects and goldsmiths, see two works by Hans Koepf, *Die gotischen Planrisse der Wiener Sammlungen* (Vienna, 1969) and *Die gotischen Planrisse der Ulmer Sammlungen* (Ulm: W. Kohlhammer, 1977).

35. Filarete, *Treatise on Architecture: Being the Treatise by Antonio di Piero Averlino, Known as Filarete*, trans. John R. Spencer, vol. 1 (New Haven: Yale University Press, 1965), 176.

36. Alina Payne, "Materiality, Crafting, and Scale in Renaissance Architecture," *Oxford Art Journal* 32, no. 3 (2009): 365–396.

37. Ibid., 376.

38. Frédéric Fayot, "Notice biographique sur Carême," in *Classiques de la table*, ed. Justin Améro, new ed., 2 vols. (Paris: Firmin Didot, 1855), 2:178–179.

39. "La Bibliothèque fut l'objet de toutes mes pensées, et je ne manquais jamais le mardi et le vendredi, jours publics, d'y aller passer quelques heures. Le grand cabinet des estampes et gravures m'inspira le beau sentiment d'émulation; et peu à peu je sortis du néant où le sort m'avait fait naître. … [J]'eus bientôt voyagé d'un pôle a l'autre, sans cependant trop comprendre la narration; mais tout ce qui avait rapport au dessin influa beaucoup sur mon imagination: l'Egypte, la Grèce et l'Italie m'inspirèrent le gout de l'architecture." Marie-Antoine Carême, *Le pâtissier royal parisien ou Traité élémentaire et pratique de la pâtisserie ancienne et moderne* (Paris: J.-G. Dentu, 1815), 277–278.

40. Ibid.

41. Ibid.

42. William Pietz, "The Problem of the Fetish, I," *RES: Anthropology and Aesthetics*, no. 9 (Spring 1985): 6.

43. William Pietz, "The Problem of the Fetish, II: The Origin of the Fetish," *RES: Anthropology and Aesthetics*, no. 13 (Spring 1987): 38–40.

44. Ibid., 38–40, 45.

45. Georg Wilhelm Friedrich Hegel, *Vorlesungen über die Philosophie der Geschichte*, vol. 1, *Die Vernunft in der Geschichte*, ed. J. Hoffmeister, 5th ed. (Hamburg: Felix Meiner, 1955); Georg Wilhelm Friedrich Hegel, *Lectures on the Philosophy of World History*, trans. H. B. Nisbet (Cambridge: Cambridge University Press, 1975), 181–182.

46. At age of seventy, Carl May was honored as "Baurat" (building adviser) while working for Ludwig I of Bavaria. Françoise Lecocq, "Les premières maquettes de Rome: L'exemple des modèles réduits en liège de Carl et Georg May dans les collections européennes aux XVIIIe–XIXe siècles," in *Roma illustrata: Représentations de la ville*, comp. Philippe Fleury and Olivier Desbordes (Caen: Presses Universitaires de Caen, 2008), 237.

47. Werner Helmberger, "Carl Joseph May (1742–1822): Hofkonditor und Korkbildner," in *Rom über die Alpen tragen: Fürsten sammeln antike Architektur: Die Aschaffenburger Korkmodelle*, ed. Werner Helmberger and Valentin Kockel (Landshut: Arcos, 1993), 77.

48. The supposed inventor of modeling antique ruins in cork is the Roman architect Augusto Rosa (1738–1816), but in fact only one model has been preserved with his signature: a model of the Poseidon Temple in Paestum, Italy, created in 1777.

49. Claude Lévi-Strauss, *The Savage Mind* (Chicago: University of Chicago Press; London: Weidenfeld & Nicolson, 1966), 17.

50. Review of John Britton, *The Union of Architecture, Sculpture, and Painting* (1827), in *Gentleman's Magazine* 97, no. 2 (1827): 129.

51. "Under the pedestal are Models in wood of the south-east angle of the Bank of England and the Three per Cent Reduced Office; the Bank Stock Office; the original Design for the New Board of Trade and Privy Council Offices, at Whitehall; a Model of the national Debt Redemption Office, in which is a bronze statue of William Pitt, by Westmacott; of a Machine for driving piles; of a design in Gothic style for the Exterior of the buildings connected with the Court of King's Bench, next New Palace Yard; and a Model in Plaster of part of the New State Paper office, as originally designed." Sir John Soane, *Description of the House and Museum on the North Side of Lincoln's Inn* (London: James Moyes, 1830), 88.

52. Walter Benjamin, "Unpacking My Library: A Talk about Book Collecting," in *Illuminations*, ed. Hannah Arendt, trans. Harry Zohn (New York: Schocken Books, 1969), 59–67.

53. Isaiah Berlin, Arthur O. Lovejoy, and Jean-Marie Schaeffer discuss this tendency of the Enlightenment and its effects on the making and experience of art in Isaiah Berlin, *The Roots of Romanticism*, ed. Henry Hardy (London: Chatto & Windus, 1999), 21–26; Arthur O. Lovejoy, *The Great Chain of Being: A Study of the History of an Idea* (1936; reprint, Cambridge, MA: Harvard University Press, 2001), 288–289; and Jean-Marie Schaeffer, *Art of Modern Age: Philosophy of Art from Kant to Heidegger*, trans. Steven Rendall (Princeton, NJ: Princeton University Press, 2000), 67.

54. August K. Wiedmann, *Romantic Roots in Modern Art: Romanticism and Expressionism: A Study in Comparative Aesthetics* (Old Woking [Eng.]: Gresham, 1979), 4–7.

55. Berlin, *Roots of Romanticism*, 114.

56. Le Corbusier, "Les objets à réaction poétique," in *L'Atelier de la recherche patiente* (Paris: Vincent et Fréal, 1960), 209.

57. Le Corbusier, *The Chapel at Ronchamp* (New York: Frederick A. Praeger, 1957), 89–90.

58. Le Corbusier, *Le Corbusier Talks with Students from the Schools of Architecture*, trans. Pierre Chase (New York: Princeton Architectural Press, 1999), 70–71.

59. Louis Pasteur, "Dans les champs de l'observation le hazard ne favorise que les esprits reéparés." Inaugural lecture presented at the University of Lille, Douai, France, on 7 December 1854; reprinted in *A Treasury of the World's Great Speeches*, ed. Houston Peterson (New York: Simon & Schuster, 1954), 473.

60. Charles Sanders Peirce, "Pragmatism as the Logic of Abduction (Lecture VII)," in *The Essential Peirce: Selected Philosophical Writings*, vol. 2, *1893–1914*, ed. the Pierce Edition Project (Bloomington: Indiana University Press, 1998), 227.

61. Charles Sanders Peirce, "A Neglected Argument for the Reality of God," in ibid., 436.

62. In the *Apology*, Plato argues that the work of poets was not the result of their genius, a tutelary spirit, since "what they composed they composed not by wisdom [*sophia*], but by nature [*physis*] and because they were inspired [*enthousiazontes*], like the prophets and givers of oracles" (22c). For Plato, "[T]he poet is a light and winged and holy thing, and there is no invention in him until he has been inspired and is out of his senses, and the mind is no longer in him" (*Ion* 534b). As Plato makes clear in the *Phaedrus*, the poet is not insane in the modern sense but is overcome by divine madness sent by the Muses (see 245a). For the

translation of *Apology*, see *Plato in Twelve Volumes*, vol. 1, *Euthyphro; Apology; Crito; Phaedo; Phaedrus*, trans. Harold North Fowler, Loeb Classical Library (1914; reprint, Cambridge, MA: Harvard University Press, 1966), 81; *Ion* is translated by Benjamin Jowett in *The Dialogues of Plato*, 3rd ed., 5 vols. (New York: Macmillan, 1892), 1:502.

63. Peirce, "A Neglected Argument for the Reality of God," 436.

CHAPTER 3

1. Cesare Guasti, *La Cupola di Santa Maria del Fiore illustrata con i documenti dell'Archivio dell'Opera secolare: Saggio di una compiuta illustrazione dell'opera secolare e del tempio di Santa Maria del Fiore* (Florence, Barbera: Bianchi E. Comp, 1857), 15–25.
2. Giorgio Vasari, *Lives of the Painters, Sculptors and Architects*, trans. Gaston du C. de Vere, 2 vols. (1912–15; reprint, New York: Alfred A. Knopf: Distributed by Random House, 1996), 1:334–337.
3. Ibid., 122.
4. Ibid., 123.
5. Ibid., 124.
6. Diogenes Laertius, "Thales," in *Lives of Eminent Philosophers* 1.28, trans. R. D. Hicks, vol. 1, Loeb Classical Library (London: W. Heinemann; New York: Putnam's Sons, 1925), 29.
7. Plutarch, "The Dinner of the Seven Wise Men," in *Moralia* 147A, trans. Frank Cole Babbitt, vol. 2, Loeb Classical Library (London: W. Heinemann; New York: Putnam's Sons, 1928), 353.
8. Corinna Rossi, *Architecture and Mathematics in Ancient Egypt* (Cambridge: Cambridge University Press, 2004). For the use of cubits to determine geometric shapes, see 96–147; for the use of cords in planning the building, see 148–173.
9. Ibid., 148–173.
10. H. S. Smith and H. M. Stewart, "The Gurob Shrine Papyrus," *Journal of Egyptian Archaeology* 70 (1984): 54–64.
11. Ulrike Fauerbach, "Concevoir les détails: Les maquettes de l'Égypte ancienne," in *La maquette, un outil au service du projet architectural* (Paris: Cité de l'architecture & du patrimoine, 2015), 35.
12. Ibid., 36–37.
13. Ibid., 38–39.
14. Dieter Arnold and Rainer Stadelmann, "Dahschur: Zweiter Grabungsbericht," *Mitteilungen des Deutschen Archäologischen Instituts, Abteilung Kairo* 33 (1977): 15–20, fig. 3b; Dieter Arnold, *Der Pyramidenbezirk des Königs Amenemhet III. in Dahschur* (Mainz am Rhein: P. von Zabern, 1987), 86–88, pl. 35, figs. 66–68.
15. Fauerbach, "Concevoir les détails," 30–31.
16. James Weinstein, "Foundation Deposits in Ancient Egypt" (Ph.D. diss., University of Pennsylvania, 1973), xxiv; Faiza Mahmoud Sakr, "New Foundation Deposits of Kom el-Hisn," *Studien zur Altägyptischen Kultur* 33 (2005): 353; Rossi, *Architecture and Mathematics in Ancient Egypt*, 155; John Steele Gordon, *Washington's Monument and the Fascinating History of the Obelisk* (New York: Bloomsbury, 2016), 179.

17. J. J. Coulton understands *paradeigma* as meaning "scale model," but argues that Herodotus must have meant to say *synagraphē* (specification), since the Alcmaeonidae changed the material rather than the structure, a substitution easier to make from a description than from a model. Coulton, *Ancient Greek Architects at Work: Problems of Structure and Design* (Ithaca, NY: Cornell University Press, 1977), 57. Herodotus is also cited by Robert Hahn, *Anaximander and the Architects* (Albany: State University of New York Press, 2001), 132 n. 88.
18. Coulton, *Ancient Greek Architects at Work*, 55–58, 71–72.
19. Ibid., 56 n. 20. Gorham P. Stevens, "A Tile Standard in the Agora of Ancient Athens," *Hesperia* 19, no. 3 (1950): 174–188.
20. Burckhardt Wesenberg, "Das Paradeigma des Eupalinos," *Jahrbuch des Deutschen Archäologischen Instituts* 122 (January 2007): 33–49.
21. John Onians, *Bearers of Meaning: The Classical Orders in Antiquity, the Middle Ages, and the Renaissance* (Princeton, NJ: Princeton University Press, 1988), 19.
22. Vitruvius, *Ten Books on Architecture* 4.1, ed. Ingrid D. Rowland and Thomas Noble Howe, trans. Ingrid D. Rowland (New York: Cambridge University Press, 1999), 55. I have replaced the word "model" with "exemplar."
23. Vitruvius, *The Ten Books on Architecture* 1.2, trans. Morris Hickey Morgan (1914; reprint, New York: Dover, 1960), 14.
24. Ibid., 1.2, 14; 106.
25. Mark Wilson Jones, *Principles of Roman Architecture* (New Haven: Yale University Press, 2000), 43.
26. Lothar Haselberger, "Architectural Likenesses: Models and Plans of Architecture," *Journal of Roman Archaeology* 10 (1997): 89–90.
27. Patrizio Pensabene, "Maqueta de templo en mármol de Luna," in *Las casas del alma* (Barcelona: Fundación Caja de Arquitecto, 1997), 132.
28. Pensabene ponders whether the ratio is a 1:24 or 1:32 ratio. See ibid., 130–132.
29. For the comparison of the typology of the plan in this model with that of the Temple of Portunus and the Maison Carrée, see Wilson Jones, *Principles of Roman Architecture*, 55, figs. 3.26, 2.10.
30. In an article dedicated to the classification of assembly markings from schools of Roman architects and masons, Haroutune Kalayan first mentions the discovery of a second-century CE stone model in limestone that was made to study and visualize the Great Temple of Niha (Beqaa) near Syria. Haroutune Kalayan, "Notes on Assembly Marks, Drawings and Models Concerning the Roman Period Monuments in Lebanon," *Les Annales archéologiques de Syrie* 21 (1971): 269–273, figs. 9–11.
31. Ibid., 272.
32. The variations are in the number of stairs, their general configuration, and a number of architectural elements at the top of the podium, including a bench and the design of column bases. For these observations, see Ernest Will, "La maquette de l'adyton au temple A de Niha (Beqaa)," in *Le dessin d'architecture dans les sociétés antiques: Actes du Colloque de Strasbourg, 26–28 janvier 1984* ([Leiden]: E. J. Brill, 1985), 277–281, and Wilson Jones, *Principles of Roman Architecture*, 55.
33. Kalayan first suggested that the Greek letters indicated horizontal distances measured in feet. See Kalayan, "Notes on Assembly Marks," 272. Ernest Will observes that these measurements are instead corrections to the stair depths. See Ernest Will, "La maquette de l'adyton au temple A de Niha (Beqaa)."

34. Kalayan, “Notes on Assembly Marks,” 272.

35. Marica S. Tacconi, *Cathedral and Civic Ritual in Late Medieval and Renaissance Florence* (Cambridge: Cambridge University Press, 2005), 3.

36. Ibid.

37. Ibid., 25.

38. Vasari, *Lives of the Painters, Sculptors and Architects*, 1:69. Contradicting this account, Rolf Bernzen makes three arguments against the existence of Arnolfo’s model. See Rolf Bernzen, *Die praktische und theoretische Konstitution des Modellverfahrens* (Bern: Peter Lang, 1986), 72–78, 316–319.

39. The 1353 model for the campanile was previously attributed to Giotto, but Marvin Trachtenberg has argued that it should be assigned to Talenti. See Marvin Trachtenberg, *The Campanile of Florence Cathedral: “Giotto’s Tower”* (New York: New York University Press, 1971), 114. Further confirmation is provided by a note from Filippo Marsili dated 29 May 1355. See Cesare Guasti, *Santa Maria del Fiore: La costruzione della Chiesa e del Campanile secondo i documenti tratti dall’Archivio nell’Opera Secolare e da quello di Stato* (Florence: M. Ricci, 1887), 81.

40. For the invitation from the Opera to a cooperative effort by the painters’, masons’, and goldsmiths’ guilds to issue a proposal for completing Santa Maria del Fiore and their submission of a “designum seu modellum,” see Guasti, *Santa Maria del Fiore*, docs. 140–142, cited by Bernzen, *Die praktische und theoretische Konstitution des Modellverfahrens*, 91. On 13 August 1366 there was a discussion regarding the draft from the guilds, a drawing by Simone di Francesco Talenti, and a model from Ghini (Guasti, *Santa Maria del Fiore*, 174, doc. 150). By 24 July 1367, it was clear that Talenti and Ghini were asked to make a model in brick for their design (see ibid., 191ff., doc. 174).

41. The final decision to construct the church after the drawings and model of Neri occurred on 19 November 1367 (see Guasti, *Santa Maria del Fiore*, 207, doc. 192). “On August 3, 1366, it was decided that no further work be done on the small church made as a model by Giovanni di Lapo”; Frank D. Praeger, “Brunelleschi’s Inventions and the ‘Renewal of Roman Masonry Work,’” *Osiris* 9 (1950): 531.

42. Guasti, *Santa Maria del Fiore*, 192–220, docs. 174–214.

43. “E che ongni altro disengnamento, si di mattoni chome di lengname e di charta, si deba disfare, e quello rimangha fermo.” Ibid., 207, doc. 192.

44. Andreas Grote, *Florenz: Gestalt und Geschichte eines Gemeinwesens*, 4th ed. (Munich: Prestel, 1976), 229.

45. Jules Quicherat, *Mélanges d’archéologie et d’histoire*, 2 vols. (Paris: Alphonse Picard, 1885–1886), 2:205–206. The original French is “dans les combles de l’église” and probably refers to the covered workshops on the building site.

46. Pierre du Colombier, *Les chantiers des cathédrales*, 2nd ed. (Paris: Picard, 1973), 96 n. 127.

47. Bucher mentions this model in reference to the use of a low graffito technique in a tracing he attributes to Villard de Honnecourt. See François Bucher, “A Rediscovered Tracing by Villard de Honnecourt,” *Art Bulletin*, no. 59 (September 1977): 315–319.

48. The original contract between the Fabbrica and Antonio is in Archivio della fabbrica di San Petronio (AFSP), Bologna, *Liber compoxicionum*, vol. 372, fols. 2–3. He is named chief architect in AFSP, *Liber compoxicionum*, vol. 372, fol. 11. Anna Laura Trombetti Budriesi, “I primi anni del cantiere di San Petronio (1390–1397),” in *Una*

basilica per una città: sei secoli in San Petronio: Atti del convegno di studi per il sesto centenario di Fondazione della basilica di San Petronio, 1390–1990, ed. Mario Fanti and Deanna Lenzi (Bologna: Istituto per la storia della Chiesa di Bologna, 1994), 52–57, cited by David Drogin, "Art Patronage and Civic Identities in Renaissance Bologna," in *The Court Cities of Northern Italy*, ed. C. M. Rosenberg (Cambridge: Cambridge University Press, 2010), 254 n. 54.

49. Paul Booz, *Der Baumeister der Gotik* (Munich: Deutscher Kunst-verlag, 1956), 14–15.

50. Among these architects from north of the Alps are Nicolas de Bonaventure in 1389 from France and Annas de Firimburg (Freiburg) in 1391 from Germany, who was followed by Heinrich Parler at the end of 1391 and Ulrich of Ensingen in 1395. In 1399 a French engineer named Jean Mignot is mentioned. For a discussion of these architects and their involvement with the work at the Milan cathedral during this time, see James Ackerman, "'Ars sine scientia nihil est': Gothic Theory of Architecture at the Cathedral of Milan," *Art Bulletin*, no. 31 (1949): 84–116. As recorded in the *Annali*, on 2 February 1392, Heinrich Parler from Gmünd was asked to show the wood model he made to the building masters and other experts of the Opera. See *Annali della Fabbrica del Duomo di Milano: Dall'origine fino al presente*, vol. 1 (Milan: G. Brigola, 1877), 64, cited in Andreas Lepik, "Der Mailänder Dom," chap. 3 of *Das Architekturmodell in Italien, 1335–1550* (Worms: Wernersche Verlagsgesellschaft, 1994), 46 n. 16.

51. Sir James George Frazer, *The Golden Bough: A Study in Magic and Religion*, abridged by Robert K. G. Temple (New York: Simon & Schuster, 1996), 14.

52. Giambattista Vico, *On the Most Ancient Wisdom of the Italians*, trans. L. M. Palmer (Ithaca, NY: Cornell University Press, 1988), 45–47.

53. For the term "facture," I owe a debt to Marco Frascari for introducing me to Summers's discussion of painting as dependent on the combination of material and technique. See David Summers, *Real Spaces: World Art History and the Rise of Western Modernism* (London: Phaidon, 2003), 74.

54. Vasari, *Lives of the Painters, Sculptors and Architects*, 2:56.

55. Ibid., 55.

56. Ibid., 57.

57. Nicholas Penny, Peter Schade, and Harriet O'Neill, *The Sansovino Frame* (Washington, DC: National Gallery, 2015).

58. A public call for designs to solve the construction of the dome project was issued in August 1418. See Guasti, *La cupola di Santa Maria del Fiore*, 15–16, docs. 11–14. For the argument that this competition was not for a new form of the cupola but only for a solution to the problems of how to construct the existing plan, see Cornel von Fabriczy, *Filippo Brunelleschi: Sein Leben und seine Werke* (Stuttgart: J. G. Cotta, 1892), 67.

59. Guasti, *La cupola di Santa Maria del Fiore*, 17–25, docs. 16–42.

60. This document is found in ibid., 17, doc. 16; for this translation of doc. 16, see Praeger, "Brunelleschi's Inventions," 470 n. 16. For Brunelleschi's four models, see Guasti, *La cupola di Santa Maria del Fiore*, 19–21, docs. 21, 22, 24–28, cited by Praeger, "Brunelleschi's Inventions," 541 n. 240.

61. Guasti, *La cupola di Santa Maria del Fiore*, 17, doc. 16.

62. Praeger, "Brunelleschi's Inventions," 541.

63. Vasari, *The Lives of the Painters, Sculptors and Architects*, 1:335.

64. Quoted in Ross King, *Brunelleschi's Dome: How a Renaissance Genius Reinvented Architecture* (New York: Walker, 2000), 1.
65. Guasti, *La cupola di Santa Maria del Fiore*, 21.
66. Wooden models are indicated by, for example, "modello di lengiame" (doc. 22), "modellum de lignamine" (doc. 24), and "modello di lingo" (doc. 26), while Brunelleschi's brick model is "modello di mattoni" (doc. 43). Guasti, *La Cupola di Santa Maria del Fiore*, 17–26.
67. In December 1418, eleven other models were being considered by the Opera del Duomo in the competition for the construction of the dome. Cesare Guasti and Howard Saalman have documented the separate payment receipts for these, in which a number are referred to as a *modello*. Guasti, *La Cupola di Santa Maria del Fiore*, 22–25; Howard Saalman, *Filippo Brunelleschi: The Cupola of Santa Maria del Fiore* (London: Zwemmer, 1980), 250.
68. Vasari, *The Lives of the Painters, Sculptors and Architects*, 1:348.
69. Eugenio Battisti, *Filippo Brunelleschi*, trans. Robert Erich Wolf (London: Thames & Hudson, 1981), 132.
70. Antonio Manetti, *The Fat Woodworker*, trans. Robert L. Martone and Valerie Martone (New York: Italica Press, 1991), 1–2.
71. Ibid., 3.
72. Katalin Prajda, "Manetto di Jacopo Ammanatini, the Florentine Woodcarver-architect and Pippo Scolari's Castle in Ozora," in *Art and Architecture around 1400: Global and Regional Perspectives*, ed. Marjeta Ciglenečki and Polona Vidmar (Maribor: Faculty of Arts of the University of Maribor, 2012), 75–78.
73. Guasti, *La Cupola di Santa Maria del Fiore*, 24, doc. 39.
74. Antonio Manetti, *The Life of Brunelleschi*, trans. Catherine Enggass (University Park: Pennsylvania State University Press, 1970), 116.
75. Leo Battista Alberti, *On the Art of Building in Ten Books* 2.1, trans. Joseph Rykwert, Neil Leach, and Robert Tavernor (Cambridge, MA: MIT Press, 1996), 34.
76. Sir John Soane Museum Library, anonymous manuscript English translation (ca. 1680) of Vicenzo Scamozzi's *L'idea della architettura universale* (1615), 52.
77. Gülru Necipoğlu-Kafadar, "Plans and Models in 15th- and 16th-Century Ottoman Architectural Practice," *Journal of the Society of Architectural Historians* 45, no. 3 (September 1986): 239.
78. Monique Mosser, "Französische Architekturmodelle im Zeitalter der Aufklärung," *Daidalos* 2 (1981): 83–97, 95.
79. Ibid., 92.
80. Architecture Départment de l'Hérault (Arch. Dép. Hérault), D 123, cited by Jean-Luc Pissaloux, "'Le Grand Giral,' Jean-Antoine Giral (1713–1787): L'Architecte de l'embellissement du Peyrou de Montpellier," 2 vols. (thèse de doctorat de l'Ecole Practique des Hautes Etudes, 2013), 1:308–313, itself cited by Raphaël Tassin, "Le rôle de la maquette dans le processus de conception architecturale en France au XVIIIe siècle," in *Les maquettes d'architecture: fonction et évolution d'un instrument de conception et de réalisation*, ed. Sabine Frommel with Raphaël Tassin (Paris: Picard; Rome: Campisano Editore, 2015), 239 n. 55.
81. Arch. Dép. Hérault, D 124 fol. 41v, cited by Tassin, "Le rôle de la maquette," 239 n. 56.

82. Elisabeth Kieven, "'Mostrar l'inventione'—The Role of Roman Architects in the Baroque Period: Plans and Models," in *Triumph of the Baroque: Architecture in Europe, 1600–1750*, ed. Henry A. Millon (New York: Rizzoli, 1999), 204.

83. Manetti, *The Life of Brunelleschi*, 116.

84. Costantino Baroni, ed., *Documenti per la storia dell'architettura a Milano nel Rinascimento e nel Barocco*, 2 vols. (Florence: Sansoni, 1940), 1:253, cited by Luisa Giordano, "Wooden Models in Lombardy," *The Renaissance from Brunelleschi to Michelangelo: The Representation of Architecture*, ed. Henry A. Millon and Vittorio Magnano Lampugnani (New York: Rizzoli, 1994), 461.

85. Abbot Matteo Valerios, quoted in "Mémoire inédite sulla Certosa di Pavia," in *Archivo Storici Lombardo VI* (Milan: Società Storica Lombarda, 1879), 138, cited by Giordano, "Wooden Models in Lombardy," 462.

86. Baroni, *Documenti per la storia dell'architettura a Milano*, 1:58, cited by Giordano, "Wooden Models in Lombardy," 462.

87. Margaret Richardson, "Model Architecture," *Country Life*, 21 September 1989, 224–227, cited by Karen Moon, *Modelling Messages: The Architect and the Model* (New York: Monacelli Press, 2005), 34.

88. Hans Reuther and Ekhart Berckenhagen, *Deutsche Architekturmodelle: Projekthilfe zwischen 1500 und 1900* (Berlin: Deutscher Verlag für Kunstwissenschaft, 1994), 81, fig. 168.

89. Eugene Clute, "Models, Their Making and Their Use," chap. 8 of *Drafting Room Practice* (New York: Pencil Points Press, 1928), 43.

90. Henry A. Millon, "Models in Renaissance Architecture," in Millon and Lampugnani, *The Renaissance from Brunelleschi to Michelangelo*, 19.

91. *Annali della Fabbrica del Duomo di Milano: Dall'origine fino al presente*, vol. 3 (Milan: G. Brigola, 1880), 42, cited by Giordano, "Wooden Models in Lombardy," 462.

92. Millon and Lampugnani, *The Renaissance from Brunelleschi to Michelangelo*, cat. 246, 248, 250, 254.

93. Ibid., cat. 56.

94. Baroni, *Documenti per la storia dell'architettura a Milano*, 1:238, cited by Giordano, "Wooden Architectural Models in Lombardy," 462.

95. Millon and Lampugnani, *The Renaissance from Brunelleschi to Michelangelo*, cat. 142.

96. Scamozzi, anonymous translation of *L'idea della architettura universale*, 51.

97. Howard Saalman, "S. Maria del Fiore and St. Peter's," *Art Bulletin* 57, no. 3 (September 1975): 381.

98. Vasari, *Lives of the Painters, Sculptors, and Architects*, 2:720.

99. Mosser, "Französische Architekturmodelle," 85.

100. Réne Maere, "Maquette des tours de l'église St. Pierre de Louvain et l'emploi des Maquettes en architecture," *Annales de la Société Royale d'Archéologie de Bruxelles* 40 (1939): 55–64.

101. Franz Bischoff, "'... das verkleinert opus recht vor Augen gestellt': Zur Geschichte und Bedeutung des Architekturmodells von der Frühzeit bis zur Gegenwart," in *Rom über die Alpen tragen: Fürsten sammeln antike Architektur: Die Aschaffenburger Korkmodelle*, ed. Werner Helmberger and Valentin Kockel (Landshut: Arcos, 1993), 33–48.

102. Peter Murray, *The Saga of Sydney Opera House: The Dramatic Story of the Design and Construction of the Icon of Modern Australia* (New York: Spon Press, 2004), 87.

103. Ludwig Mies van der Rohe, "Hochhäuser," *Frühlicht* 1, no. 4 (Summer 1922): 122–124.

104. Detlef Mertins, *Mies* (London: Phaidon, 2014), 58–81.

105. See Thomas L. Schumacher, *The Danteum: A Study in the Architecture of Literature* (Princeton, NJ: Princeton Architectural Press, 1985).

106. Tom Porter and John Neale, *Architectural Supermodels: Physical Design Simulation* (Oxford: Architectural Press, 2000), v.

107. The photograph was taken for the 11 September 1950 issue of *Life* magazine but was not included in the article, "A Designer's Home of His Own: Charles Eames Builds House of Steel and Glass," *Life*, 11 September 1950, 148–152. See Eames House: Ray Eames at home in California, photo by Peter Stackpole, 1950. —The LIFE Picture Collection/Getty Images.

108. Millon and Lampugnani, *Renaissance from Brunelleschi to Michelangelo*, cat. 144, 145.

109. Ibid.

110. Alberti, *On the Art of Building in Ten Books* 2.1, 34.

111. Richard J. Tuttle, "The Basilica of S. Petronio in Bologna," in Millon and Lampugnani, *The Renaissance from Brunelleschi to Michelangelo*, 522–523, cat. 151.

112. Peter W. Parshall and Rainer Schoch, *Origins of European Printmaking: Fifteenth-Century Woodcuts and Their Public* (Washington, DC: National Gallery of Art, in association with Yale University Press, 2005), 61–62; Martha Easton, "The Wound of Christ, the Mouth of Hell: Appropriation and Inversions of Female Anatomy in the Later Middle Ages," in *Tributes to Jonathan J. G. Alexander: The Making and Meaning of Illuminated Medieval and Renaissance Manuscripts Art and Architecture*, ed. Susan L'Engle and Gerald Guest (London: Miller, 2006), 406, cited by Paul Emmons, "A Window to the Soul: Depth in Early Modern Section Drawing," in *Architecture Post Mortem*, ed. Donald Kunze, Charles Bertolini, and Simone Brott (Burlington, VT: Ashgate, 2013), 160 n. 52.

113. Ellen Spolsky, "Doubting Thomas and the Senses of Knowing," *Common Knowledge* 3, no. 2 (1994): 114.

114. Millon and Lampugnani, *The Renaissance from Brunelleschi to Michelangelo*, cat. 152, 253.

115. Sir Roger Pratt, *The Architecture of Sir Roger Pratt, Charles II's Commissioner for the Rebuilding of London after the Great Fire: Now Printed for the First Time from His Note-books*, ed. R. T. Gunther (London: Oxford University Press, 1928), 23, cited by Moon, *Modelling Messages*, 62.

116. Millon, *Triumph of the Baroque*, 567.

117. Jacques Guillerme and Hélène Vérin, "The Archaeology of the Section," *Perspecta* 25 (1989): 226–257.

118. Guillerme and Vérin make a similar observation in ibid., 228.

119. Johann Friedrich Penther, *Zweyter Theil der ausführlichen Anleitung zur Bürgerlichen Baukunst* (Augspurg: Verlegts Johann Andreas Pfeffel, weil. Kayserl. Hof-Kupferstecher, 1762).

120. AFSP, *Liber compoxicionum*, vol. 372, fols. 2–3.

121. Giuseppe Zander, "Il colore della Basilica di S. Pietro secondo il probabile pensiero di Antonio da Sangallo," in *Antonio da Sangallo il Giovane—La vita e l'opera*, ed. Gianfranco Spagnesi (Rome: Centro di studi per la storia dell'architettura, 1986), 175–186, cited by Millon, "Models in Renaissance Architecture," 41 n. 21.

122. Ibid.

123. Sir Christopher Wren, quoted in *Wren Society* [Oxford] 13 (1936): 17, cited by Kerry Downes, *The Architecture of Wren*, rev. ed. (Reading, Eng.: Redhedge, 1988), 48.

124. Mosser, "Französische Architekturmodelle," 94.

125. John Wilton-Ely, "The Architectural Model: I. English Baroque," *Apollo* 88, no. 80 (October 1968): 254.

126. Millon, *Triumph of the Baroque*, 411, 587.

127. "On the Proper Display of Models," *The Builder* 1 (1843): 317–318.

128. Ibid., 317.

129. William Boring, "Use of Models in the Study of Architecture," *Architect and Engineer* 60 (1920): 100.

130. Edward W. Hobbs, *Pictorial House Modelling* (London: C. Lockwood and Son, 1926), 11.

131. Reuther and Berckenhagen, *Deutsche Architekturmodelle*, 82, cat. 173, and Ulrich Bauche, Gisela Jaacks, and Ute Scheurlen, *Gärten, Landhäuser und Villen des hamburgischen Bürgertums* (Hamburg: Museum für Hamburgische Geschichte, 1975), 146–176, cat. 435.

132. J. S. Ackerman, *The Architecture of Michelangelo*, 2 vols. (London: Zwemmer, 1961), 2:72, cited by George Bauer, "From Architecture to Scenography: The Full-Scale Model in the Baroque Tradition," in *La scenografia barocca*, ed. Antoine Schnapper (Bologna: CLUEB, 1982), 143.

133. Bruce Boucher, ed., *Earth and Fire: Italian Terracotta Sculpture from Donatello to Canova*, (New Haven: Yale University Press, 2001), 35–36.

134. Ackerman, *Architecture of Michelangelo*, 144.

135. Ibid., 143–144.

136. Jacques-François Blondel, *Cours d'architecture, ou, Traité de la décoration, distribution & construction des bâtiments: contenant les leçons données en 1750, & les années suivantes*, 6 vols. (Paris: Chez Desaint, Libraire, rue du Foin-S.-Jacques, 1771–1777), vol. 4, chap. 2, 158–162, cited by Mosser, "Französische Architekturmodelle," 88.

137. Mosser, "Französische Architekturmodelle," 95.

138. Franz Schulze, *Mies van der Rohe: A Critical Biography*, rev. ed. (Chicago: University of Chicago Press, 2012), 38–43.

139. Steven Holl, interview with Stanley Collyer, *Competitions* 8, no. 2 (Summer 1998): 57, 59.

140. Egerton Swartwout, "The Use of Large Scale Models in Architecture," *Architecture* 24 (1911): 132.

141. Ibid.

142. Frederic C. Hirons, "The Use of Scale Models," *Pencil Points* 1 (November–December 1920): 5.

143. Jonathan Lipman, *Frank Lloyd Wright and the Johnson Wax Buildings* (New York: Rizzoli, 1986), 51–62.

25. Peter Springer, *Modelle und Muster, Vorlage und Kopie, Serien*, exh. cat., vol. 1 (Cologne, 1985), 301–314. See also F. M. Fritz, *Goldschmiedekunst der Gotik in Mitteleuropa* (Munich: C. H. Beck, 1982), 119ff., cited by Franz Bischoff, "Les Maquettes d'architecture," in *Les Bâtisseurs des cathédrales gothiques*, ed. Roland Recht (Strasbourg: Les Musées de la Ville, 1989), 293 n. 52.
26. Reuther and Berckenhagen, *Deutsche Architekturmodelle*, 35–36, cat. 33. Stephan Hoppe argues that the simplicity of the model, which depicts only the external visible shape of the tower, was intended to assist in finding a solution to satisfy the tower's symbolic significance. Hoppe, "German Architectural Models in the Renaissance (1500–1620)," in Frommel with Tassin, *Les maquettes d'architecture*, 131–142.
27. One can find a number of plain and simple working models (*Entwurfsmodell*) in Hans Reuther and Ekhart Berckenhagen's exhibition catalog: *Deutsche Architekturmodelle: Projekthilfe zwischen 1500 und 1900*. Of particular interest are those by Adolf Daucher for the Lugisland-Turms (1514) and Elias Holl for the Augsburg Rathaus (1614/15). See *Deutsche Architekturmodelle*, 35–36, cat. 31–33; 43–44, cat. 46–48.
28. Ibid., 43–44, cat. 46–48. See also Hans Reuther, "Wesen und Wandel des Architekturmodells in Deutschland—Origin and Development of the Architectural Model in Germany," *Daidalos* 2 (1981): 98–110.
29. *Deutsche Architekturmodelle*, 43, cat. 46.
30. "Oultre plus, tous les modelles que je faisoys faire, tant pour le service du Roy que de ceulx qui estoyent aupres de luy, l'on ne m'en payoit pas ung denier, et si j'en ay faict tels qui a couste deux ou troys cens escuz." Philibert de l'Orme, "Instruction de M. d'Yvry," in *Les grands architectes français de la Renaissance*, by Adolphe Berty (Paris: C. A. Aubry, 1860), 50.
31. Philibert de l'Orme, *Le premier tome de l'architecture* (Paris: F. Morel, 1567), 23v–25v, cited by Philippe Potié, *Philibert de L'Orme: Figures de la pensée constructive* (Marseille: Editions Parenthèses, 1996), 68.
32. "I'ay beaucoup conduict de grandes edifices & petis en mon temps, & de diueries fortes, voire autát ou plus qu'homme que ie cognoisse, comme aussi plusieurs forteresse de guerre, quoy saisant i'ay veritablement aperceu, que par tout il n'y a chose tant necessaire que un bon modelle." De l'Orme, *Le premier tome de l'architecture*, 23v.
33. "Le veux encores dire d'auantage, zu'un bon Architecte desirant representer au naturel un bastiment, ne doit jamais faire, comme nous auons dict, un modelle sarde, ou si voulez, enrichy de peinture, ou dore d'or moulu, ou illustre de couleurs, ainsi que font ordinairement ceux qui veulent tromper les homes." Ibid.
34. Jacques Androuet du Cerceau, *Livre d'architecture* (Paris: B. Prevost, 1559).
35. See, e.g., lessons 40–45, 50–51, 53–54, and 56–57 in Jacques Androuet du Cerceau, *Leçons de perspective positive* (Paris: Mamert Patisson imprimeur, 1576).
36. "J'en ai facit en carton des villes entieres fortifiees et de chasteaux, temples, pavillions et autres bastiments particulieres de ce livre qui ne sont plus grands que leurs perspectives." Jacques Perret, *Des fortifications et artifices, architecture et perspective* (Paris, 1601), 26r, cited by Jean Guillaume, "Les maquettes d'architecture en France au XVIe siècle," in Frommel with Tassin, *Les maquettes d'architecture*, 127 n. 42.
37. Richard Cleary, "Paris, VI. Institutions, 2. Académie Royale d'Architecture," in *The Dictionary of Art*, ed. Jane Turner, 34 vols. (New York: Grove, 1996), 24:169–171.
38. Anthony Gerbino, *François Blondel: Architecture, Erudition, and the Scientific Revolution* (Abingdon, Oxon.: Routledge, 2010), 41–70, specifically 57.

39. Bibliothèque nationale, MS ital. 2083, 27, letter of Matthia de Rossi to Bernin, 3 December 1666 ; cited by Léon Mirot, "Le Bernin en France," *Mémoires de la Société de l'histoire de Paris et de l'Ile-de-France* 31 (1904): 272 n. 2, which is cited by Alexandre Cojannot, "En petit ou en grand: 'Modèles' et maquettes dans la practique architecturale française du XVIIe siècle," in Frommel with Tassin, *Les maquettes d'architecture*, 205 n. 37.

40. From the minutes of a 27 January 1710 meeting at the Académie Royale d'Architecture; cited by Monique Mosser, "Französische Architekturmodelle im Zeitalter der Aufklärung," *Daidalos* 2 (1981): 85.

41. See two portraits: one of Lequeux de Lille in front of a reduced portal of the Hotel Asselin and the other of Perronet, whom Roslin shows laying a final hand on the orangery model. Ibid., 92.

42. Henry Wotton, *The Elements of Architecture* (1624; facsimile reprint, Farnborough, Hants.: Gregg International Publishers, 1969), 65.

43. Ibid.

44. Howard Colvin, *Unbuilt Oxford* (New Haven: Yale University Press, 1983), 9–10.

45. Howard Colvin, *The Canterbury Quadrangle: St. John's College, Oxford* (Oxford: Oxford University Press, 1988), 44 n. 23.

46. Anna Boato and Anna Decri, "Disegni e contratti edili nel Fondo Notai dell'Archivio di Stato di Genova (XVI–XVII sec.)," *Il Disegno di architettura*, no. 5 (1992): 11–17.

47. Margaret Whinney, *Wren* (1971; reprint, London: Thames & Hudson, 1998), 83–84.

48. Sir John Soane, *Sir John Soane: The Royal Academy Lectures*, ed. David Watkin (Cambridge: Cambridge University Press, 2000), 273.

49. Henry Liddell, "To the Editor of the Builder," *The Builder* 1 (27 May 1843): 198.

50. Edwin S. Parker, "The Model for Architectural Representation," *Architectural Forum* 30 (April 1919): 120.

51. Maurice Gauthier, "Studying in Three Dimensions," *Pencil Points* 7 (July 1926): 416.

52. Henry Rutgers Marshall, "The Architect's Tools," *Architectural Review* 4 (November 1897): 55; William Boring, "Use of Models in the Study of Architecture," *Architecture* 45 (1922): 200.

53. This critique of orthogonal drawings and perspective is often found in introductions to the value and use of models to visualize the design from many angles. See Berthold Audsley, "Miniatures and Their Value in Architectural Practice," *Brickbuilder*, no. 23 (September 1914): 213; Parker, "The Model for Architectural Representation," 119; Boring, "Use of Models in the Study of Architecture," 200, and a shorter article with the same title in *Architect and Engineer* 60 (1920): 100; William Harvey, *Models of Buildings: How to Make and Use Them* (London: Architectural Press, 1927), 1. Philip McDonnell admits the advantages of perspective but also its limitations in depicting buildings that have salient projections, unusual heights, curved lines, or oblique angles; see Philip McDonnell, "Models and Their Making," *American Architect* 107, no. 2054 (May 1915): 277.

54. Boring, "Use of Models in the Study of Architecture" (*Architecture*), 200–202.

55. For the value of using models to study and develop ideas, see Parker, "The Model for Architectural Representation," 119–120; Boring, "Use of Models in the Study of Architecture" (*Architect and Engineer* and *Architecture*); Audsley, "Miniatures and Their Value in Architectural Practice," 213; McDonnell, "Models and Their

Making," 277; William, *Models of Buildings*, 2–4; Eugene Clute, "Models, Their Making and Their Use," chap. 8 of *Drafting Room Practice* (New York: Pencil Points Press, 1928), 57. For arguments that preliminary study models should be plain and simple, see William, *Models of Buildings*, 26, 31; Parker, "The Model for Architectural Representation," 121; Audsley, "Miniatures and Their Value in Architectural Practice," 213–214.

56. Royal Rook, "Model Making in the Drafting Room," *American Architect* 117, no. 2227 (August 1918): 247; Gauthier, "Studying in Three Dimensions," 416; J. Price Nunn, "Models and Their Making," *Builder* 162 (26 June 1942): 553.

57. The architect is advised to draw the model on a sheet of paper, cut it, fold it, and then add on additional layers, including columns, cornices, and moldings. Clute, "Models, Their Making and Their Use," 50–59, 63; McDonnell, "Models and Their Making," 278–279; William, *Models of Buildings*, 26–40; Parker, "The Model for Architectural Representation," 121; Percival Marshall, *Wonderful Models* (New York: Spon & Chamberlain, 1928), 177.

58. William, *Models of Buildings*, 26–34; Clute, "Models, Their Making and Their Use," 48.

59. Ethel Bartholomew, "Architectural Model Making as Part of the Technique of the Drafting-Room," *Architecture* 54 (December 1926): 283–285.

60. Gauthier, "Studying in Three Dimensions," 410–411; Rook, "Model Making in the Drafting Room," 250; Margaret J. Postgate, "Architectural Models from Bar Soap," *Pencil Points* 10 (June 1929): 392–396.

61. Christa Schreiber, "Das Berlinische Rathaus: Versuch einer Entsehungs- und Ideengeschichte," in *Das Rathaus im Kaiserreich: Kunstpolitische Aspeke einer Bauaufgabe des 19. Jahrhunderts*, ed. Ekkehard Mai, Kunst, Kultur und Politik im Deutschen Kaiserreich 4 (Berlin: Mann, 1982), 95–100, specifically 99; Ingrid Bartmann-Kompa, *Das Berliner Rathaus* (Berlin: Henschel Verlag, 1991), 49.

62. Kathy Martin, *Famous Brand Names and Their Origins* (Barnsley, South Yorkshire: Pen & Sword History, 2016), 143.

63. Eva Afuhs and Andres Strohl, "Erste grundlagen zu einem fragmente Werk (First Principles for a Fragmented Oeuvre)," in *Hermann Obrist: Skulptur, Raum, Abstraktion um 1900* (Zurich: Scheidegger & Spiess, 2009), 24–28.

64. Robert Schmutzler, *Art Nouveau* (London: Thames & Hudson, 1978), 135–140.

65. "Wie der lebendige Organismus Erhöhungen und Vertiedungen gegliesdert aus sich herauswachsen lässt, so wachsen aus der Wand die Formen heraus und die Wand wird damit zu einem Lebendigen." Rudolf Steiner, *Wege zu einem neuen Baustil: Fünf Vorträge gehalten während der Arbeit am ersten Goetheanum in Dornach zwischen dem 7. Juni und 26. Juli 1914* (1926; reprint, Stuttgart: Verlag Freies Geistesleben, 1957), 35.

66. "Das, was hier umschlossen ist in den Raumformen, was darin gesprochen und getrieben wird, soll sich so anpassen, wie sich der Napfkuchenteig anpaßt der Negativform des Napfkuchentopfes." Ibid., 23.

67. Bruno Taut, "Ein Architektur-Programm," *Mitteilungen des deutschen Werkbundes*, no. 4 (1918): 16–19, and Bruno Taut, "Eine Notwendigkeit," *Der Sturm* 4, nos. 196–197 (February 1914): 174–175.

68. "[G]anz anderen gerüstlosen, untektonischen Bauart, die wie mit Riesenhänden einem Mauerblock aushöhlt und aus der Höhlung den Raum schafft." Paul

Klopfer, "Über Apollinisches und Dionysisches in der Baukunst," *Stadtbaukunst alter und neuer Zeit* 1 (1920): 161.

69. The work for the exhibition was screened and accepted by an "Architektenausschuss" led by Gropius. See Adolf Behne, "Kurze Chronik," *Sozialistische Monatshefte* 25, no. 2–3 (10 February 1919): 136, and Adolf Behne, "Unbekannte Architekten," *Sozialistische Monatshefte* 25, no. 10 (28 April 1919): 422–423, both cited by Marcel Franciscono, *Walter Gropius and the Creation of the Bauhaus in Weimar: The Ideals and Artistic Theories of Its Founding Year* (Urbana: University of Illinois Press, 1971), 145 n. 41.

70. "Im Innenraum des neuen Hauses wird man sich nicht nur als Insasse einer märchenhaften Kristalldruse fühlen, sondern als interner Bewohner eines Organismus, wandernd von Organ zu Organ, ein gebender und empfangender Symbiote eines fossilen Riesenmutterleibes." Hermann Finsterlin, "Innenarchitektur" (1921/1922), reprinted in *Frühlicht, 1920–1922: Eine Folge für die Verwirklichung des neuen Baugedankens*, ed. Bruno Taut (Berlin: Ullstein, 1963), 107.

71. "Man lege Bleistift und Lineal beiseite, nehme Ton oder Plastelin und fange an, ganz von vorn, ganz unvermittelt und unbeeinflusst zu kneten und man wird erstaunt sein über die ungefügen Klumpen, die da zunächst auf dem Modelliertisch zu sehen sind, und die nichts von den schönen Proportionen auf dem Reißbrett an sich haben. Aber man wird zu seinem Erstaunen bemerken, daß das Licht in diesen Formen spielt, daß ein Luftraum diese Form umgibt. Man wird beim Weiterschreiten der Arbeit sehen, wie diese Formen in den Luftraum hineinwachsen und ihn anderseits wieder umfangen und ihn einschließen." Wassili Luckhardt, "Vom Entwurfen," *Stadtbaukunst alter und neuer Zeit* 11 (1921), reprinted in *Brüder Luckhardt und Alfons Anker: Berliner Architekten der Moderne* (Berlin: Akademie der Künste, 1990), 122.

72. Fritz Schumacher, "Das Entstehen des baulichen Kunstwerks," in *Handbuch für Architektur*, part 4, *Entwerfen, Anlage und Einrichtung der Gebaude* (Leipzig: J. M. Gebhardt's Verlag, 1926), 41–63.

73. Ibid., 41–43.

74. Ibid., 47.

75. Gustaf Stotz, leader of the Württemberg chapter of the Werkbund and editor of the Werkbund's national newsletter, hatched the plan for the Weissenhof Siedlung and chose Mies as its artistic director. See Richard Pommer and Christian F. Otto, *Weissenhof 1927 and the Modern Movement in Architecture* (Chicago: University of Chicago Press, 1991), 20 n. 2.

76. Ibid., 24 n. 28.

77. Mies first completed a drawing of the site plan (now lost) without knowing the terrain, and at the request of Gustaf Stotz he visited Stuttgart shortly thereafter to modify the drawing in accordance with a model of the terrain being produced by the city. Paul Otto's plan of the Siedlung closely corresponds with the photographs of the clay model. Ibid., 24 nn. 29–32.

78. Milka Bliznakov, "The Rationalist Movement in Soviet Architecture of the 1920's," in *Russian Formalism*, ed. Stephen Bann and John W. Bowlt (Edinburgh: Scottish Academic Press, 1973), 152–160.

79. While Walter Gropius's initial Bauhaus program from 1919 proposed to erase "the essential difference between the artist and the craftsman" and called on architects, sculptors, and painters to "return to the crafts," Vkhutemas's mission,

according to Lenin, was to "prepare master artists of the highest qualifications for industry." By 1926 Gropius would recast the school's workshops as "laboratories in which prototypes of products suitable for mass production and typical of our time are carefully developed and constantly improved," and the demand for the new aesthetic paradigm was reflected in its curricular structures in different ways. See Walter Gropius, "Programme of the Staatliches Bauhaus Weimar" (1919) and "Principles of Bauhaus Production" (1926), reprinted and translated in *Programs and Manifestoes on 20th Century Architecture*, trans. Michael Bullock, ed. Ulrich Conrads (1970; reprint, Cambridge, MA: MIT Press, 2002), 49–53, 95–97. The design school was established in Soviet Russia by a decree from Lenin—"подготовить художников-мастеров высшей квалификации для промышленности, а также конструкторов и руководителей для профессионально-технического образования (to prepare master artists of the highest qualifications for industry, and builders and managers for professional-technical education)"; Собрание узаконений и распоряжений Рабочего и Крестьянского Правительства (Collection of laws and regulations of the Workers' and Peasants' Government of the Union of Soviet Socialist Republics), 19 December 1920, no. 98, art. 522, p. 540.

80. Kestutis Paul Zygas, *Form Follows Form: Source Imagery of Constructivist Architecture, 1916–1925* (Ann Arbor, MI: UMI Research Press, 1981), 55–58.

81. Ibid., 60–62.

82. Audsley, "Miniatures and Their Value in Architectural Practice," 213–214.

83. "Model Making by Architects: An Interesting Communication from a Reader Who Strongly Approves the Work Begun at Columbia University," *American Architect* 118 (8 December 1920): 749–750; Boring, "Use of Models in the Study of Architecture" (*Architecture*), 202.

84. Nunn, "Models and Their Making," 553.

85. Frank H. Bosworth and Roy C. Jones, *A Study of Architecture Schools* (New York: Charles Scribner's Sons, 1932), 45, cited by Hyungmin Pai, *The Portfolio and the Diagram: Architecture, Discourse, and Modernity in America* (Cambridge, MA: MIT Press, 2002), 105 n. 29.

86. Ernest Pickering, *Architectural Design* (New York: J. Wiley; London: Chapman & Hall, 1933), 294–295.

87. Ernest Pickering, *Architectural Design*, 2nd ed. (New York: J. Wiley; London: Chapman & Hall, 1941), 311–312.

88. Ibid., 312.

89. LeRoy Grumbine, "The Use of Scale Models as an Aid to the Architect," *Western Architect* 34 (June 1925): 61.

90. Kenneth McCutchon, "Architectural Models," *Architects' Journal* 84 (1 October 1936): 459.

91. Nunn, "Models and Their Making," 553.

92. Franz Schulze, *Mies van der Rohe: A Critical Biography*, rev. ed. (Chicago: University of Chicago Press, 2012), 246, 273.

93. Jane Jacobs, "The Miniature Boom," *Architectural Forum* 108, no. 5 (May 1958): 106–111

94. The earliest reference to Theodore Conrad as the "dean of the model makers" is probably Carter E. Horsley, "Modelmakers' Work Gaining New Recognition,"

New York Times, 28 July 1974, 283. For more on Theodore Conrad's repertoire, see Teresa Fankhänel, "Introducing Theodore Conrad or Why Should We Look at the Architectural Model Maker?" in Frommel with Tassin, *Les maquettes d'architecture*, 259–268.

95. P. R. Wickham, *Commercial Model Making* (London: Vawser & Wiles, 1945); T. W. Hendrick, *The Modern Architectural Model* (London: Architectural Press, 1957); H. J. Cowan and R. W. Muncey, *Models in Architecture* (Amsterdam: Elsevier, 1968).

96. Jasper Cepl, *Oswald Mathias Ungers: Eine Intellectuelle Biographie* (Cologne: Verlag der Buchhandlung Walther König, 2007), 89.

97. Ibid.

98. "Dow Plastic Gets Boost from Telaflora Shop," *Telegraph Delivery Spirit* 24, no. 8 (August 1957): 22.

99. Axel Schultes and Charlotte Frank, "Leuchtmodelle (Light Models)," in *The Architectural Model: Tool, Fetish, Small Utopia*, ed. Peter Cachola Schmal and Oliver Elser (Zurich: Scheidegger, 2012), 262–264.

100. Charlotte Frank, ed., *Axel Schultes in Bangert, Jansen, Scholz, Schultes: Projekte, 1985–1991* (Berlin: Ernst & Sohn, 1992).

101. See *OMA/Rem Koolhaas, 1987–1998* (Madrid: El Croquis Editorial, 1998); Michele Costanzo, *MVRDV: Works and Projects, 1991–2006*, trans. Marco Migotto and Robert Burns (Milan: Skira; New York: Rizzoli, 2006); *Ben van Berkel, 1990/1995* (Madrid: El Croquis Editorial, 1995).

102. Mark Morris, *Models: Architecture and the Miniature* (Chichester, West Sussex: Wiley-Academy, 2006), 46–49.

103. Steven Holl, *Steven Holl: Written in Water* (Baden: Lars Müller, 2002).

104. Steven Holl, *Intertwining* (New York: Princeton Architectural Press, 1996), 88–90.

105. Ben van Berkel and UN Studio, *Buy Me a Mercedes-Benz: The Book of the Museum* (Barcelona: Actar, 2006).

106. Ibid., 62–65.

107. Ibid.

108. The new reliance on digital tools is made particularly clear by a comparison of the sections on computer modeling in the first and second editions of the popular architectural modeling handbook *Designing with Models*. See in the chapter titled "Expand" in Criss B. Mills, *Designing with Models: A Studio Guide to Making and Using Architectural Design Models* (New York: John Wiley, 2000), 180–181, and the second edition (2005), 230–232.

109. Mills, *Designing with Models* (2005), 231.

110. In *Phenomenology of Perception*, "être-au-monde" is frequently translated as "being in the world," as if to suggest that "being" is placed in a container. Yet our bodily tasks and engagements always occur in the mode of being-to or being-toward. Maurice Merleau-Ponty, *Phenomenology of Perception*, trans. Colin Smith (London: Routledge & Kegan Paul, 1962), 95–97. See also Edward S. Casey, "Habitual Body and Memory in Merleau-Ponty," *Man and World* 17 (1984): 279–297.

111. Merleau-Ponty, *Phenomenology of Perception*, 129.

112. Vicenzo Scamozzi, *L'idea della architettura universale* (1615), anonymous manuscript translation (ca. 1680), Sir John Soane Museum Library, 52.

CHAPTER 5

1. See Philip Urspring, ed., *Herzog & de Meuron: Natural History*, exh. cat. (Baden: Lars Müller, 2002), published to accompany the exhibition *Herzog & de Meuron: Archaeology of the Mind*, organized by the Canadian Centre for Architecture (CCA), Montreal, 2002.
2. Herzog & de Meuron, "Just Waste (2002)," in ibid., 74.
3. For the models of the de Young Museum, see Urspring, *Herzog & de Meuron*, 94–97, specifically 94; for models of the Prada Aoyama, see ibid., 370–375, specifically 371. Figure 5.1 above is the second of four pages that trace the evolution of the latter project.
4. Vitruvius, *Ten Books on Architecture* 10.16, ed. Ingrid D. Rowland and Thomas Noble Howe, trans. Ingrid D. Rowland (New York: Cambridge University Press, 1999), 133.
5. Leon Battista Alberti, *On the Art of Building in Ten Books* 2.1, trans. Joseph Rykwert, Neil Leach, and Robert Tavenor (Cambridge, MA: MIT Press, 1996), 34.
6. Michelangelo Buonarroti, *The Letters of Michelangelo*, trans. and ed. E. H. Ramsden, 2 vols. (Stanford, CA: Stanford University Press, 1963), 2:186.
7. Scholars discussing the Laurentian staircase have often pointed to the strong resemblance of the central portion of the staircase to flowing water. See, for example, John Templar, *The Staircase: History and Theories* (Cambridge, MA: MIT Press, 1992), 32; Angelo Tartuferi, *Michelangelo: Painter, Sculptor, and Architect* (Rome: A.T.S., 1993), 36; Kirsten Bradbury, *Michelangelo* (Bath: Parragon Books, 2000), 158.
8. Tartuferi briefly summarizes Michelangelo's preoccupations during this time. Tartuferi, *Michelangelo*, 36.
9. Like his approach to sculpture, Michelangelo's working method permitted time for decision making and alterations in midcourse. Robin O'Bryan, "The Source of the Laurentian Staircase," *Rutgers Art Review* 17 (1977): 23, cited by William Wallace, *Michelangelo at San Lorenzo: The Genius as Entrepreneur* (Cambridge: Cambridge University Press, 1994), 137.
10. Benvenuto Cellini, *La Vita di Benvenuto Cellini: I Trattati della Oreficeria e della Scultura e gli scritti sall'Arte*, ed. Arturo Jahn Rusconi and A. Valeri (Rome: Società Editrice Nazionale, 1901), 778–779, cited by Frederick Hartt, *David by the Hand of Michelangelo* (New York: Abbeville Press, 1987), 131, 59–64. See also Ludwig Goldscheider, *A Survey of Michelangelo's Models in Wax and Clay* (London: Phaidon Press, 1962), 1–3.
11. Vicenzo Scamozzi, *L'idea della architettura universale* (1615), anonymous manuscript translation (ca. 1680), Sir John Soane Museum Library, 203.
12. Vicenzo Scamozzi, *L'idea della architettura universale* (Venice, 1615), 1.15, 49ff.; translated by Marco Frascari in *Eleven Exercises in the Art of Architectural Drawing: Slow Food for the Architect's Imagination* (New York: Routledge, 2011), 188.
13. "[A]ssalito da una febbre che diede segni di qualche violenza e malignità"; Giovanni Battista Passeri, *Vite de pittori, scultori ed architetti: Che anno lavorato in Roma, morti dal 1641 fino al 1673* (Rome: Presso Natale Barbiellini mercante di libria Pasquino, 1772), 388.
14. Orietta Verdi and Simonetta Ceglie, *La fabbrica della Sapienza: L'università al tempo di Borromini* (Rome: Croma-Università degli Studi Roma Tre, 2015), 95–97.

15. Giorgio Vasari, *Vasari on Technique: Being the Introduction to the Three Arts of Design, Architecture, Sculpture and Painting, Prefixed to the Lives of the Most Excellent Painters, Sculptors and Architects*, trans. Louisa S. Maclehose, ed. with intro. G. Baldwin Brown (1907; reprint, New York: Dover Publications, 1960), chap. 2, §42, 148–149.
16. Federico Bellini, *Le cupole di Borromini: La "scientia" costruttiva in età barocca* (Milan: Electa, 2004), 102–104.
17. Anita Büttner, "Korkmodelle," in *Antike Bauten in Modell und Zeichnung um 1800*, ed. Peter Gercke (Kassel: Staatliche Kunstsammlungen Kassel, 1986), 10–19; Valentin Kockel, "Rom über die Alpen tragen: Korkmodelle antiker Architektur im 18. und 19. Jahrhundert," in *Rom über die Alpen tragen: Fürsten sammeln antike Architektur: Die Aschaffen-burger Korkmodelle*, ed. Werner Helmberger and Franz Bischoff (Landshut: Arcos, 1993), 11–13; Richard Gillespie, "The Rise and Fall of Cork Model Collections in Britain," *Architectural History* 60 (November 2017): 117–146.
18. Ian Jenkins, "Drawings by Vincenzo Brenna," in *Grand Tour: The Lure of Italy in the Eighteenth Century*, ed. Andrew Wilton and Ilaria Bignamini, exh. cat. (London: Tate Gallery Publishing, 1996), 236, nos. 185–189, cited by Valentin Kockel, "Plaster Models and Plaster Casts of Classical Architecture and Its Decoration," in *Plaster Casts: Making, Collecting, and Displaying from Classical Antiquity to the Present,* ed. Rune Frederiksen and Eckart Marchand (Berlin: De Gruyter, 2010), 421.
19. The minute ornamental capitals, friezes, and figural reliefs continued to be modeled in plaster. Kockel, "Plaster Models and Plaster Casts," 423.
20. Geneviève Cuisset, "Jean-Pierre et François Fouquet, artistes modeleurs," *Gazette des beaux-arts*, 6th ser., 115 (1990): 227–240, cited by Kockel, "Plaster Models and Plaster Casts," 423 n. 15.
21. Kockel, "Plaster Models and Plaster Casts," 423 n. 16; he there cites J. G. Legrand, *Collection des chefs d'oeuvre de l'architecture des différents peuples, exécutés en modèles, sous la direction de L. F. Cassas* (Paris: Treuttel & Würtz, 1806), xix–xxii.
22. Bertus Mulder and Ida van Zijl, *The Rietveld Schröder House*, trans. Lynn George (New York: Princeton Architectural Press, 1999).
23. Rietveld later built a second model of cardboard, glass, and matchsticks, which unfortunately was destroyed. Paul Overy et al., *The Rietveld Schröder House* (Wiesbaden: Vieweg, 1988), 33 n. 42.
24. Marijke Küper and Ida van Zijl, *Gerrit Th. Rietveld, 1888–1964: The Complete Works* (Utrecht: Centraal Museum, 1992), 91; Eld Hoek, ed., *Theo van Doesburg: Oeuvre catalogue* (Utrecht: Centraal Museum, 2000), 343–344.
25. Thomas Kuhn, *The Structure of Scientific Revolutions*, 2nd ed. (Chicago: University of Chicago Press, 1970); Gaston Bachelard, *The Philosophy of No: A Philosophy of the New Scientific Mind*, trans. G. C. Waterston (New York: Orion Press, 1968). See also Matthew Mindrup and Paul Emmons, "Material Models and Immaterial Paradigms," *Journal of Architectural Education* 62, no. 2 (November 2008): 42–52.
26. Juhani Pallasmaa and Andrei Gozak, *The Melnikov House: Moscow, 1927–1929* (London: Academy Editions, 1996), 15–16.
27. Terence Riley, *The International Style: Exhibition 15 and The Museum of Modern Art* (New York: Rizzoli, 1992), 81.
28. Johnson's statement was part of a seven-page press release from the Museum of Modern Art announcing the exhibition that would be touring the United States for three years. See, for example, *Arts Magazine* 6 (1931): 12.

29. Henry-Russell Hitchcock and Philip Johnson, *The International Style* (1932; reprint, New York: Norton, 1995), 59, 56.
30. Riley, *The International Style*, 81.
31. Frank Lloyd Wright, "The Cardboard House," in *Frank Lloyd Wright: Collected Writings*, vol. 2, *1930–1932*, ed. Bruce Brooks Pfeiffer (New York: Rizzoli, 1992), 51.
32. Le Corbusier, *Towards a New Architecture*, trans. Frederick Etchells (1931; reprint, New York: Dover, 1986), 21; Jean-Louis Cohen, introduction to *Toward an Architecture*, by Le Corbusier, trans. John Goodman (Los Angeles: Getty Research Institute, 2007), 49.
33. The phrase is "Meine Versuche an einem Glasmodell" (My experiments with a glass model). See Ludwig Mies van der Rohe, "Hochhäuser," *Frühlicht* 1, no. 4 (Summer 1922): 122–124, specifically 124.
34. Architects used a variety of materials in place of glass, including mica, celluloid, and acetate sheets. For mica, see Harvey Wiley Corbett, "Architectural Models of Cardboard, pt. 2," *Pencil Points* 3 (May 1922): 29; for celluloid, see Berthold Audsley, "Miniatures and Their Value in Architectural Practice," *The Brickbuilder*, no. 23 (September 1914): 215; for acetate sheets, see Steven H. Waring, "Improved Techniques in Architectural Modelling," *Royal Architectural Institute of Canada* 25, no. 2 (February 1948): 60.
35. Küper and van Zijl, *Gerrit Th. Rietveld*, 124; Gilbert Lupfer and Paul Sigel, *Walter Gropius, 1883–1969: The Promoter of a New Form* (Cologne: Taschen, 2004), 59–62.
36. Federico Neder, *Fuller Houses: R. Buckminster Fuller's Dymaxion Dwellings and Other Domestic Adventures*, trans. Elsa Lam (Baden: Lars Müller, 2008), 36–40.
37. Joseph Rosa, *Albert Frey, Architect* (New York: Rizzoli International, 1990), 23–24.
38. Jane Jacobs, "The Miniature Boom," *Architectural Forum* 108 (May 1958): 109. See also Theresa Fankhänel, "Introducing Theodore Conrad or Why Should We Look at the Architectural Model Maker?," in *Les maquettes d'architecture: Fonction et évolution d'un instrument de conception et de réalisation*, ed. Sabine Frommel with Raphaël Tassin (Paris: Picard; Rome: Campisano Editore, 2015), 259–260.
39. Jacobs, "The Miniature Boom," 109–110; see also Arthur E. Herman, "Models of Plastics and Aluminum" *Progressive Architecture* 40 (December 1959): 9–11.
40. Jacobs, "The Miniature Boom," 109–111.
41. Ibid., 107.
42. Friedrich Kiesler, "On Correalism and Biotechnique: A Definition and Test of a New Approach to Building Design," *Architectural Record* 86 (September 1939): 67.
43. Friedrich Kiesler, *Inside the Endless House* (New York: Simon & Schuster, 1966), 566.
44. Stephen J. Phillips, *Elastic Architecture: Frederick Kiesler and Design Research in the First Age of Robotic Culture* (Cambridge, MA: MIT Press, 2017), 249–250.
45. "Soleri's Cities on Display," *Progressive Architecture* 51 (April 1970): 29; "Soleri's Urban Utopia Comes to New York," *Interiors* 130 (August 1970): 6.
46. Frank Gehry, quoted in Bjørn Normann Sandaker, *On Span and Space: Exploring Structures in Architecture* (London: Routledge, 2008), 32.
47. Bruce Lindsey, *Digital Gehry: Material Resistance, Digital Construction* (Basel: Birkhäuser, 2001), 32–47.
48. Ibid., 65–69.
49. Ibid., 69–74.

50. Gaston Bachelard, *Water and Dreams*, trans. Edith R. Farrell (1983; reprint, Dallas: Pegasus Foundation, 1999), 1.

51. Alberti, *On the Art of Building in Ten Books* 1.1, 7.

52. Aristotle, *De Anima* 2.1, 412a15–16.

53. Aristotle identifies it as "that in virtue of which we say an image presents itself to us occurs in us": *De anima* 3.2, 428a1–2, in Aristotle, *De anima*, trans. R. D. Hicks (Cambridge: Cambridge University Press, 1907), 125.

54. David Pye, *The Nature and Art of Workmanship* (Cambridge: Cambridge University Press, 1968), 20–24.

55. Ibid., 20.

56. Gilbert Simondon, *L'individuation à la lumière des notions de forme et d'information* (Grenoble: Editions Jérôme Millon, 2005), 41–42.

57. Ibid., 46.

58. Lars Spuybroek, *The Sympathy of Things: Ruskin and the Ecology of Design* (Rotterdam: V2_Publishing, 2011), 160.

59. In the case of the Luxor obelisk, this curvature seems to have been an unwanted rather than a desired outcome. Denys A. Stocks, "Scientific Evaluation of Experiments in Egyptian Archaeology," in *Mummies, Magic, and Medicine in Ancient Egypt: Multidisciplinary Essays for Rosalie David*, ed. Campbell Price, Roger Forshaw, Andrew Chamberlain, and Paul T. Nicholson (Manchester: Manchester University Press, 2016), 453; Denys A. Stocks, *Experiments in Egyptian Archaeology: Stoneworking Technology in Ancient Egypt* (London: Routledge, 2003), 189–191.

60. Vitruvius, *The Ten Books on Architecture* 3.4.

61. Oscar Broneer, "Measurements and Refinements at the South Stoa at Corinth," *AJA* 53 (1949): 146–147.

62. Roland Martin, *L'Agora*, Études thasiennes 6 (Paris: E. de Boccard, 1959); Dieter Mertens, "Die Herstellung der Kurvatur am Tempel von Segesta," *Mitteilungen des Deutschen Archäologischen Instituts, Römische Abteilung* 81 (1974): 107–114.

63. Lothar Haselberger, "Curvature: The Evidence at Didyma," in *Appearance and Essence: Refinements of Classical Architecture—Curvature: Proceedings of the Second Williams Symposium on Classical Architecture Held at the University of Pennsylvania, Philadelphia, April 2–4, 1993*, ed. Lothar Haselberger (Philadelphia: University Museum, University of Pennsylvania, 1999), 173–184.

64. Leonardo da Vinci, manuscript notebooks, MS Inst. France A, fol. 48r, Bibliothèque de l'Institut de France, Paris. See also fol. 61v.

65. Galileo Galilei, *Dialogues Concerning Two New Sciences*, trans. Henry Crew and Alfonso de Salvio (1914; reprint, Evanston, IL: Northwestern University, 1939), 149.

66. The term "catenary" is the English version of the Latin *catenaria*, originally coined by Huygens in an 18 November 1690 letter to Gottfried Leibniz. Christiaan Huygens, letter no. 2633, in *Œuvres complètes*, vol. 9, *Correspondance, 1685–1690*, published by Société hollandaise des sciences (La Haye: M. Nijhoff, 1901), 537.

67. Robert Hooke, *A Description of Helioscopes, and Some Other Instruments* (London: T.R. for John Martyn, 1676), 31. This English translation is by Clifford Truesdale in *The Rational Mechanics of Flexible or Elastic Bodies, 1638–1788* (Basel: Birkhäuser, 1960), 57.

68. Stanley B. Hamilton, "The Place of Sir Christopher Wren in the History of Structural Engineering," *Newcomen Society Transactions* 14 (1933–1934): 27–42;

W. Godfrey Allen and Captain C. Stanley Peach, "The Preservation of St. Paul's Cathedral," *Journal of the RIBA* 37 (August 1930): 655–676.

69. Giovanni Poleni, *Memorie istoriche della gran cupola del tempio vaticano* (Padua: Stamperia del Seminario, 1748).

70. This way of working with arches would be disseminated by John Robison in the 1801 supplement to the *Encyclopaedia Britannica*. See John Robison, "Arch," in *Encyclopaedia Britannica: Supplement*, 3rd ed., 2 vols. (Edinburgh: Thomson Bonar, 1801), 1:21–38, 4 plates; Thomas Young, *Lectures on Natural Philosophy and the Mechanical Arts* (London: Johnson, 1807), 160–161.

71. Bernard Forest de Belidor, *La science des ingénieurs dans la conduite des travaux de fortification et architecture civile* (Paris: C. Jombert, 1729), book 2, chap. 3, 5th proposition; Amédée-François Frézier, *La théorie de la pratique de la coupe des pierres et des bois, pour la construction des voûtes et autres parties de bâtiments civils et militaires ou traité de stéréotomie à l'usage de l'architecture*, 3 vols. (Strasbourg: Doulsseker; Paris, Guérin, 1737–1739).

72. Wilhelm Tappe, *Darstellung einer neuen äußerst wenig Holz erfodernden höchst feuersicheren Bauart*, 6 vols. (Essen: Baedeker, 1818–1821), cited by Ludwig Schreiner, "Der Lüdenscheider Baumeister Wilhelm Tappe (1769–1823)," *Der Reidemeister*, nos. 49/50 (April 28, 1970): 381–396.

73. Heinrich Hübsch, *Bauwerke*, 2 vols. (Karlsruhe: Veith, 1838), 2:53–56.

74. Ibid., 40–53.

75. Ibid., 46.

76. J. Tomlow, "Die Kuppel des Gießhauses der Firma Henschel in Kassel (1837): Eine frühe Anwendung des Entwurfsverfahrens mit Hängemodellen," *Architectura* 23 (1993): 151–172.

77. Robert Descharnes and Clovis Prévost, *Gaudí: The Visionary*, trans. Frederick Hill (London: Patrick Stephens, 1971), 41.

78. Jos Tomlow, "L'esperit del càlcul en l'obra arquitectònica de Gaudí," in *Gaudí 2002: Miscelánia*, by Oriol Bohigas et al., 2nd ed. (Barcelona: Planeta; Ajuntament de Barcelona, 2002), 189 n. 45.

79. José Luis González Moreno-Navarro and Albert Casals Balagué, *Gaudí y la razon constructiva: Un legado inagotable* (Madrid: Akal, 2002), cited by Santiago Huerta, "Structural Design in the Work of Gaudí," *Architectural Science Review* 49, no. 4 (December 2006): 332–333.

80. Antoni Gaudí, quoted in Maria Antonietta Crippa, "Sagrat i profà en l'obra de Gaudí," in Bohigas et al., *Gaudí 2002*, 309.

81. Claudia Alsina and Josep Gómez, "Gaudí: Geometria, estructura i construcció," in ibid., 153–154.

82. Terence Riley and Barry Bergdoll, *Mies in Berlin* (New York: Museum of Modern Art, 2001), 44–46.

83. Iain Boyd Whyte and David Frisby, "Planning the World City," in *Metropolis Berlin: 1880–1940*, ed. Iain Boyd Whyte and David Frisby (Berkeley: University of California Press, 2011), 316.

84. Mies van der Rohe, "Hochhäuser," trans. by Philip Johnson as "Two Glass Skyscrapers," in *Mies van der Rohe*, by Philip Johnson, 3rd ed., rev. (New York: Museum of Modern Art, 1978), 187.

85. Ibid.

86. R. H. Francé, *Plants as Inventors* (New York: Albert & Charles Boni, 1923), 11.

87. Raoul Heinrich Francé, "Die sieben technischen Grundformen der Natur," *Das Kunstblatt* 8, no. 1 (January 1923): 5–11.

88. Marc Treib, *Space Calculated in Seconds: The Philips Pavilion, Le Corbusier, Edgard Varèse* (Princeton, NJ: Princeton University Press, 1996), 19.

89. Ibid., 3.

90. Ibid.

91. Felix Candela, "Understanding the Hyperbolic Paraboloid: Part 2," *Architectural Record* 124 (August 1958): 205.

92. Eero Saarinen, quoted in Michael J. Crosbie, "Is It a Catenary? New Questions about the Shape of Saarinen's St. Louis Arch," *AIA Journal*, June 1983, 78–79.

93. Kevin Roche, quoted in Hart Laubkeman, "Form Swallows Function," *Progressive Architecture* (May 1992): 108, cited by Jayne Merkel, *Eero Saarinen* (London: Phaidon, 2005) 209 n. 8.

94. Ibid., n. 9.

95. "TWA's Graceful New Terminal," *Architectural Forum* 108 (January 1958): 82.

96. Ibid.

97. John Chilton, *Heinz Isler* (London: Thomas Telford, 2000), 14–17.

98. Heinz Isler, "New Shapes for Shells," *Bulletin of the International Association for Shell Structures* 8 (1960): 123–130.

99. John Chilton, "Form-finding and Fabric Forming in the Work of Heinz Isler," in *Proceedings of the Second International Conference on Flexible Formwork*, ed. John Orr, Mark Evernden, Antony Darby, and Timothy Ibell (University of Bath, 2012), 84–91.

100. Frei Otto, *Das Hängende Dach: Gestalt und Struktur* (Dresden: Verlag der Kunst, 1954).

101. Conrad Roland, *Frei Otto—Structures*, trans. C. V. Amerongen (London: Longman, 1972), 18–21.

102. S. Adriaenssens, S. Gabriele, P. Magrone, and V. Varano, "Revisiting the Form Finding Techniques of Sergio Musmeci: The Bridge over the Basento River," in *Structures and Architecture—Proceedings of the 3rd International Conference on Structures and Architecture, ICSA 2016* (Leiden: CRC Press/Balkema, 2016), 545–546.

103. Sergio Musmeci, quoted in Luigi Spinelli, "Quando l'infrastruttura diventa paesaggio," *Domus* 907 (2007): 80.

104. Rinaldo Capomolla, "Le forme organiche strutturali: Materie e spazio nelle opere di Sergio Musmeci," *Rassegna di Architettura e Urbanistica*, nos. 121–122 (2007): 135–148.

105. Sergio Musmeci, "Ponte sul Basento a Potenza," *L'Industria Italiana del Cemento* 2 (1977): 77–98.

106. Emilio Pérez Piñero, "Teatro ambulante," *Arquitectura*, no. 30 (July 1961): 26–29.

107. E. P. Piñero, Three dimensional reticular structure, US Patent 3,185,164, filed 15 November 1961, and issued 25 May 1965.

108. F. Escrig, "Emilio Pérez Piñero: Inventor of Deployability," in *Structures and Architecture: Concepts Applications and Challenges*, ed. Paulo J. da Sousa Cruz (London: Taylor & Francis, 2013), 42–57.

109. In reference to the aesthetic effect of his airship hangars at Orly (1921–1923), Freyssinet remarked, "After a lot of trial and error, I managed to combine shapes, previously unadopted, which could be built by mechanical means with little labour and were such that ample solidity of the edifice could be achieved with very little expenditure on materials. I didn't search any further, and not for a second did I give any thought to the possible artistic effects." In *Eugène Freyssinet: A Revolution in the Art of Construction* (Paris: Presses de l'École nationale des ponts et chaussées, 2004), 174.

110. Eugène Freyssinet, "Ma vie: Naissance du béton précontraint" (1954), in *Un amour sans limite* (Paris: Editions du Linteau, 1993), 34–36.

111. Peter Sulzer, *Jean Prouvé, Highlights: 1917–1944* (Basel: Birkhäuser, 2002), 15–17; Alois Diethelm, "Steel: Systems in Architecture: Folding and Bending," in *Constructing Architecture: Materials, Processes, Structures*, ed. Andrea Deplazes (Basel: Birkhäuser, 2005), 133.

112. Ronald D. Resch, Self-supporting structural unit having a series of repetitious geometrical modules, US Patent 3,407,558, filed 24 January 1966, and issued 29 October 1968.

113. Cheng Lv, Deepakshyam Krishnaraju, Goran Konjevod, Hongyu Yu, and Hanqing Jiang, "Origami Based Mechanical Metamaterials," *Scientific Reports* 4, art. no. 5979 (August 2014), http://dx.doi.org/10.1038/srep05979; Tomohiro Tachi, "Freeform Variations of Origami," *Journal of Geometry and Graphics*14, no. 2 (2010): 203–215; Tomohiro Tachi, "Designing Freeform Origami Tessellations by Generalizing Resch's Patterns" *Journal of Mechanical Design* 135, no. 11 (October 2013): 1–10. For Tomohiro Tachi's software, see http://tsg.ne.jp/TT/software/.

114. Lisa Iwamoto, *Digital Fabrications: Architectural and Material Techniques* (New York: Princeton Architectural Press, 2009), 11–12.

115. Christopher Beorkrem, *Material Strategies in Digital Fabrication* (New York: Routledge, 2013), 46–50.

116. Adolf Loos, *Ins Leere Gesprochen, 1897–1900* (1921; reprint, Vienna: Prachner, 1981), 163–164, cited by David Leatherbarrow, *The Roots of Architectural Invention: Site, Enclosure, Materials* (Cambridge: Cambridge University Press, 1993), 210.

CHAPTER 6

1. Françoise Fromonot, *Jørn Utzon: The Sydney Opera House*, trans. Christopher Thompson (Corte Madera, CA: Electa/Gingko, 1998), 19–27.

2. Ibid., 81–83.

3. Yuzo Mikami, *Utzon's Sphere: Sydney Opera House: How It Was Designed and Built* (Tokyo: Shokokuska, 2001), 65.

4. Matthew Mindrup, "The Resistance and Factures in Drawing-out Architectural Constructions," in *The Material Imagination: Reveries on Architecture and Matter*, ed. Matthew Mindrup (London: Routledge, 2017), 57–68, specifically 64–65.

5. Raymond Queneau, quoted by Marcel Bénabou, "Rule and Constraint," in *Oulipo: A Primer of Potential Literature*, ed. and trans Warren F. Motte (Lincoln: University of Nebraska Press, 1986), 41.

6. Italo Calvino, "Cybernetics and Ghosts," in *The Uses of Literature: Essays*, trans. Patrick Creagh (San Diego: Harcourt Brace, 1986), 13.

7. Raymond Queneau, quoted by Warren F. Motte, introduction to Motte, *Oulipo*, 22.

8. Italo Calvino, *The Castle of Crossed Destinies*, trans. William Weaver (New York: Harcourt Brace Jovanovich, 1976).
9. Peter Eisenman, "Misreading," in *House of Cards* (New York: Oxford University Press, 1987), 167.
10. Ibid.
11. Ibid., 181.
12. Peter Eisenman, "Cardboard Architecture," *Casabella*, no. 374 (1973): 24.
13. Eisenman, "Misreading," 174.
14. Angus Fletcher, *Allegory, the Theory of a Symbolic Mode* (Ithaca, NY: Cornell University Press, 1964), 2.
15. Philibert de l'Orme, *Le premier tome de l'architecture* (Paris: F. Morel, 1567), 51v.
16. "[P]our signifier qu'il doit mesurer & compasser tous ses affaires & toutes ses œuures & ouurages, auecques vne preudence & meure deliberation, a fin de se pouuoir asseurer du chemin qu'il doit tenir ... picques, enuies, haines, deceptions, iniures, trauerses & empeschemens." Ibid., 50r–50v.
17. Plato, *Republic* 7, 514a2–517a7.
18. "En premier lieu docques ie figure vn Architecte habillé ainsi qu'vn homme docte & sage (tel qu'il doit estre) & comme sortant d'une cauerne ou lieu obseur, c'est a fire de contemplation, solitude, & lieu d'estude, a fin de pouuoir a la vraye cognoissance & perfection de son art." L'Orme, *Le premier tome de l'architecture*, 50r.
19. Ibid., 23r.
20. Gualtherus Hermenius Rivius, *Der furnembsten notwendigsten der gantzen Architectur angehörigen mathematischen und mechanischen Künst eygentlicher Bericht und verstendliche Unterrichtung* (1547; facsimile reprint, Hildesheim: George Olms, 1981), title page verso; book 1, LIXv; book 3, IVr. The second edition was published as *Der Architectur furnembsten, notwendigsten, angehörigen mathematischen und mechanischen Künst* (Nuremberg: Gabriel Heyn, 1548). See also idem, *Vitruvius Teutsch* (Nuremberg: Johann Petreius, 1548), xi; Harry Francis Mallgrave, Gerald Beasley, Claire Baines, and Henry Raine, *Northern European Books, Sixteenth to Early Nineteenth Centuries*, vol. 3 of *The Mark J. Millard Architectural Collection* (Washington, DC: National Gallery of Art, 1998), 329–330.
21. Paul Emmons, "Architectural Encounters between Material and Idea," in Mindrup, *The Material Imagination*, 92.
22. Andrea Alciati, *A Book of Emblems: The Emblematum Liber in Latin and English*, trans. and ed. John F. Moffitt (Jefferson, NC: McFarland, 2004), 143, emblem 120.
23. Rivius, *Vitruvius Teutsch*, introduction [n.p.], cited by Emmons, "Architectural Encounters," 92 n. 19.
24. Matthew D. Mindrup, "Assembling the Ineffable in Kurt Schwitters' Architectural Models" (Ph.D. diss., Virginia Tech, 2007); idem, "The Merz Mill and the Cathedral of the Future," *Interstices* 14 (November 2013): 49–58; idem, "Kurt Schwitters' Architectural Models," *Journal of the Kurt Schwitters Society* 4 (2014): 23–38.
25. Joan Weinstein, *The End of Expressionism: Art and the November Revolution in Germany, 1918–19* (Chicago: University of Chicago Press, 1990), 1–25; Ida Katherine Rigby, "Critics, Artists and the Revolution," in *German Expressionism: Documents from the End of the Wilhelmine Empire to the Rise of National Socialism*, ed. Rose-Carol Washton Long (New York: G. K. Hall; Toronto: Maxwell Macmillan,

1993), 173–174; Iain Boyd Whyte, *Bruno Taut and the Architecture of Activism* (Cambridge: Cambridge University Press, 1982), 95–102.

26. Walter Gropius, "Speech to Bauhaus Students (July 1919)," trans. Rose-Carol Washton Long, in Long, *German Expressionism*, 251.

27. Kurt Schwitters, "Merz," *Der Ararat* 2, no. 1 (January 1921): 3–9, reprinted in Kurt Schwitters, *Das Literarische Werk*, ed. Friedhelm Lach, vol. 5 (Cologne: DuMont, 1981), 79.

28. Ibid., 76.

29. Kurt Schwitters, "Die Bedeutung des Merzgedankens in der Welt," *Merz: Holland Dada*, no. 1 (1923): 8–11, reprinted in *Literarische Werk*, 5:134.

30. Ibid.; Mindrup, "The Merz Mill and the Cathedral of the Future," 52–55.

31. Daniel Libeskind, *Three Lessons on Architecture*, installation at Venice Biennale, 1985.

32. Jacques Derrida, *Of Grammatology*, trans. Gayatri Chakravorty Spivak (Baltimore: Johns Hopkins University Press, 1976).

33. Francis A. Yates, *The Art of Memory* (1966; reprint, London: Routledge, 1999), 130–131.

34. Daniel Libeskind, "Three Lessons in Architecture: The Machines," in *Daniel Libeskind: The Space of Encounter* (New York: Universe Publishing, 2000), 180–181.

35. Ibid., 181.

36. Ibid., 192.

37. K. Michael Hays, *Modernism and the Posthumanist Subject: The Architecture of Hannes Meyer and Ludwig Hilberseimer* (Cambridge, MA: MIT Press, 1992), 281–282.

38. Libeskind, "Three Lessons in Architecture: The Machines," 180.

39. Ben Nicholson, *The Appliance House* (Cambridge, MA: MIT Press, 1990), 37.

40. Ibid., 50.

41. Ibid., 37.

42. Dan Hoffman, *Architecture Studio: Cranbrook Academy of Art, 1986–1993* (New York: Rizzoli, 1994), 169–171.

43. Ibid., 169.

44. Fredric Jameson, "From Metaphor to Allegory," in *Anything*, ed. Cynthia C. Davidson (Cambridge, MA: MIT Press, 2001), 24–37.

45. Vitruvius, *Ten Books on Architecture* 2.1, trans. Morris Hickey Morgan (1914; New York: Dover Publications, 1960), 38–9.

46. Marc-Antoine Laugier, *An Essay on Architecture*, trans. Wolfgang and Anni Herrmann (Los Angeles: Hennessey & Ignalls, 1977), 11–12.

47. Claude Nicolas Ledoux, Yvan Christ, Ionel Schein, and Jacques Ohayo, *L'Oeuvre et les rêves de Claude-Nicolas Ledoux* (Paris: Chêne, 1971), 56–68.

48. Quatremère de Quincy, *Essai sur la nature, le but et les moyens de l'imitation dans les beaux-arts* (Paris: Treuttel & Würtz, 1823).

49. Josephine Kamm, *Joseph Paxton and the Crystal Palace: A Story Biography* (London: Methuen, 1967), 66.

50. László Moholy-Nagy, *Von Material zu Architektur* (Munich: Albert Langen Verlag, 1929), published in English as *The New Vision: Fundamentals of Bauhaus Design,*

Painting, Sculpture, and Architecture, trans. Daphne M. Hoffmann (1938; reprint, Mineola, NY: Dover, 2012); László Moholy-Nagy, *Vision in Motion* (Chicago: P. Theobald, 1947).

51. Moholy-Nagy, *The New Vision*, 60.
52. Moholy-Nagy, *Vision in Motion*, 44.
53. Ibid., 53.
54. Moholy-Nagy, *The New Vision*, 54.
55. Le Corbusier, *Toward an Architecture*, trans. John Goodman (Los Angeles: Getty Research Institute, 2007), 87, 151.
56. Le Corbusier, *Le Corbusier, My Work* (London: Architectural Press, 1960), 160–161.
57. H. Allen Brooks, *Le Corbusier's Formative Years: Charles-Edouard Jeanneret at La Chaux-de-Fonds* (Chicago: University of Chicago Press, 1997), 162.
58. Paul Emmons, "Le Corbusier's Serious Game of Dominos," in *The Cultural Role of Architecture : Contemporary and Historical Perspectives*, ed. Paul Emmons, Jane Lomholt, and John Hendrix (Hoboken: Taylor & Francis, 2012), 132–140.
59. Le Corbusier, *Precisions on the Present State of Architecture and City Planning: With an American Prologue, a Brazilian Corollary, Followed by The Temperature of Paris and The Atmosphere of Moscow*, trans. Edith Schreiber Aujame (Cambridge, MA: MIT Press, 1991), 92.
60. Barry Bergdoll and Peter Christensen, eds., *Home Delivery: Fabricating the Modern Dwelling* (New York: Museum of Modern Art, 2008), 15–17.
61. Steven Holl, *Anchoring* (New York: Princeton Architectural Press, 1989), 126–127.
62. Ibid., 150–155.
63. Steven Holl, "Phenomenon and Idea" (1983), in Mindrup, *The Material Imagination*, 49–50.
64. Steven Holl, *The Chapel of St. Ignatius* (New York: Princeton Architectural Press, 1999), 14–18.
65. Steven Holl, *Simmons Hall, MIT Undergraduate Residence*, ed. Todd Gannon and Michael Denison (New York: Princeton Architectural Press, 2004), 51–70.
66. Ibid., 56.
67. Santiago Calatrava, *Santiago Calatrava: Secret Sketchbook*, ed. Mirko Zardini, photographs by Paolo Rosselli (New York: Zardelli, 1995), 13.
68. Richard C. Levene and Fernando Marquez Cecilia, *MvRdV 1991–1997: Maas, vanRijs, deVries*, El Croquis 86 (Madrid: El Croquis, 1997), 164–167.
69. Thomas Heatherwick, *Thomas Heatherwick: Making*, rev. ed. (London: Thames & Hudson, 2015), 64–71.
70. Gaston Bachelard, *The Poetics of Space*, trans. Maria Jolas (1964; reprint, Boston: Beacon Press, 1994), 8.
71. George Lakoff and Mark Johnson, *Metaphors We Live By* (Chicago: University of Chicago Press, 1980).
72. V. S. Ramachandran, *A Brief Tour of Human Consciousness: From Imposter Poodles to Purple Numbers* (New York: Pi Press, 2004), 71, cited by Harry Francis Mallgrave, *The Architect's Brain: Neuroscience, Creativity, and Architecture* (Chichester, West Sussex: Wiley-Blackwell, 2010), 174 n. 36.

73. Mark Johnson, *The Body in the Mind: The Bodily Basis of Meaning, Imagination and Reason* (Chicago: University of Chicago Press, 1987), 171, cited by Mallgrave, *The Architect's Brain*, 171 n. 47.

74. Marco Frascari, *Eleven Exercises in the Art of Architectural Drawing: Slow Food for the Architect's Imagination* (New York: Routledge, 2011), 17, 96–102.

75. Ibid., 6.

76. Umberto Eco, *Experiences in Translation*, trans. Alastair McEwen (Toronto: University of Toronto Press, 2001), 74.

77. Robert M. Grant, *A Short History of the Interpretation of the Bible*, rev. ed. (New York: Macmillan, 1963), 76–77.

78. See Henri de Lubac, *Medieval Exegesis*, vol. 1, *The Four Senses of Scripture*, trans. Mark Sebanc (Grand Rapids, MI: Wm. B. Eerdmans; Edinburgh: T&T Clark, 1998), 1–2, 271 n. 1.

79. Abbot Suger, *Abbot Suger on the Abbey Church of St.-Denis and Its Art Treasures*, ed. and trans. Erwin Panofsky, 2nd ed. (Princeton, NJ: Princeton University Press, 1979), 64–65.

80. Frascari, *Eleven Exercises in the Art of Architectural Drawing*, 59–60.

81. *Oxford Dictionary of English Etymology*, ed. C. T. Onions (Oxford: Oxford University Press, 1966), s.v. "anagogy."

82. For Plato, the path taken by a mind that moves from a contemplation of visible things to knowledge of intelligible Ideas is an "ascent" (*anabasis*); see the analogy of the divided line and the allegory of the cave in *The Republic* 6.509d–7.517c, trans. Paul Shorey, 2 vols., Loeb Classical Library (1930–1935; reprint, Cambridge, MA: Harvard University Press; London: William Heinemann, 1969), 2:108–131.

83. Aristotle, *The Physics* 2.3, 194b24–35, trans. Philip H. Wicksteed and Francis M. Cornford, rev. ed., 2 vols., Loeb Classical Library (1957–60; reprint, Cambridge, MA: Harvard University Press, 1980), 1:128–131.

84. St. Bonaventure, prologue in *Breviloquium* 4.1, 5; ed. min. 20–23; *In Hexaemeron* 2.15–18, 13.11–33, t. v, 338–339, 389–392; *De reductione atrium* 5, t. v, 321, et ed. min., 372, cited by Etienne Gilson, *The Philosophy of St. Bonaventure*, trans. Illtyd Trethowan and Frank J. Sheed (1938; reprint, Patterson, NJ: St. Anthony Guild Press, 1965), 208 nn. 38–39.

85. Edmund Husserl, *Ideen zu einer reinen Phänomenologie und Phänomenologischen Philosophie*, book 1, *Allgemeine Einführung in die reine Phänomenologie* (Halle: Verlag von Max Niemeyer, 1913), §§31–32.

86. Maurice Merleau-Ponty, *Phenomenology of Perception*, trans. Colin Smith (London: Routledge & Kegan Paul, 1962), ix (emphasis added).

87. Jean Fondin and Jac Remise, *The Golden Age of Toys*, trans. D. B. Tubbs (Lausanne: Edita, 1967), 12.

88. Kendall L. Walton, *Mimesis as Make-Believe: On the Foundations of the Representational Arts* (1990; reprint, Cambridge, MA: Harvard University Press, 2004), 25.

89. Ibid., 35.

90. Ibid., 276–277.

91. Kurt Schwitters, "Schloss und Kathedrale mit Hofbrunnen," *Frühlicht* 1, no. 3 (Spring 1922): 87, reprinted in *Frühlicht, 1920–1922: Eine Folge für die Verwirklichung des neuen Baugedankens*, ed. Bruno Taut (Berlin: Ullstein, 1963), 166–167.

92. "Der Merzentwurf für die Architektur verwendet jedes beliebige Material nach architektonischem Gefühl, um eine Wirkung zu erzielen, welche die Architektur nachbilden kann. Die Verwendung beliebiger Materialien bedeutet eine Bereicherung der Phantasie. Die Phantasie arbeitet in diesem Falle rhythmisch mit schon gegebenen Rhythmen. Das Transportieren des Entwurfs auf darstellendes Material sowie auf konstruktive Möglichkeiten ist Sache der Durcharbeitung. Der Entwurf gibt die Anregung." Ibid., 166.

93. The entire sentence reads: "Hätte meine Frau gesagt, dass ich als erwachsener Kunstmaler einen Arzneikork, einen Buchen- und einen Kiefernstumpf auf ein schräges Brett genagelt hätte, damit das Ganze den Eindruck einer schlossartigen Anlage am Bergabhang mache, und damit ein Architekt seine Phantasie auffrischen könnte, so würde der Schaffner wahrscheinlich gesagt haben, das hätte er sich auch gedacht, aber das zeuge von einer krankhaft gesteigerten Phantasie." (If my wife had said that I, as an adult painter of art, nailed a medicine cork, a beech log, and a pine stump on a diagonal board so that the whole gives the impression of a castle-like arrangement by a mountain slope to refresh an architect's imagination, the conductor would have probably said, that is what he imagined, but that it looked like an imagination enhanced morbidly.) Ibid.

94. Hermann Finsterlin, "Formdomino und Zukunftsarchitektur," in *Hermann Finsterlin: Eine Annäherung: Monographie, Das literarische Werk, Aquarelle und Modelle*, by Reinhard Döhl (Stuttgart: Staatsgalerie Stuttgart, 1988), 323–329; reprinted in Manfred Speidel, Karl Kegler, and Peter Ritterbach, *Wege zu einer neuen Baukunst: Bruno Taut: Frühlicht: Konzeptionskritik H. 1–4 und Rekonstruktion H. 5* (Berlin: Mann, 2000), 88–94.

95. One of the three examples given with the reproduction of the article shows a horn-shaped block of wood among other cut shapes deriving from cubes, spheres, cones, and cylinders. See ibid., 89, 91, 93.

96. The original German text states: "Das Modell ist uns vor allem die Brücke von der Vorstellung zur stofflich erwachsenen, nach den Sichtverhältnissen der Größe berichtigen Endformen; die Gegenprüfung des Geistes im Stoff, ein einzigartiges Asyl der Präformation." Ibid., 89.

97. Sigrid Hauser describes the material and method used to create the drawings in *Peter Zumthor Therme Vals*, ed. Peter Zumthor (Zurich: Verlag Schneidegger & Speiss, 2007), 38, 58.

98. Peter Zumthor explains that he created the 1:50 scale model for the Thermal Bath House in Vals, Switzerland, and later used it when he met with the community to gain approval for project. Later, during the project's development, its form and construction changed. Peter Zumthor, email to author, 23 June 2004.

99. Hauser, in *Peter Zumthor Therme Vals*, 38, 42.

100. Peter Zumthor, *Thinking Architecture* (Baden: Lars Müller Publishers, 1998), 59.

101. Aristotle gave an example for only the efficient cause of a house in his discussion of the four causes in the *Physics*: "Thus, we may say that 'the builder' caused the house to be built, meaning the man who knew how to build, but it was only when he was in the act of building that he was really causing the house to be built" (2.3, 195b5–7; 1:137). However, one can find examples for the formal, material, and final causes in other locations of the *Physics* and the *Metaphysics*. In the *Physics*, Aristotle gives the formal cause: "As the physician, for instance, must study health and also bile and phlegm, the state of which constitutes health; and the builder must know what the house is to be like [its *eidos*] and also that it is built of bricks and

timber; and so in all other cases" (2.2, 194a23–26; 1:123). In the *Metaphysics*, he elaborates on the location of the formal cause in the mind of the builder: "a house from a house, inasmuch as it is generated by the mind; for the art [of building] is the form [(*eidos*) of the house]." *The Metaphysics* 7.9, 1034a23–24, trans. Hugh Tredennick, Aristotle 17, Loeb Classical Library (1933; reprint, Cambridge, MA: Harvard University Press; London: William Heinemann, 1980), 351. For the material and final causes, see the *Metaphysics:* "Hence in defining the nature of a house, those who describe it as stones, bricks and wood, describe the potential house, since these things are its matter; those who describe it as 'a receptacle for containing goods and bodies,' or something else to the same effect, describe its actuality" (8.2, 1043a15–18; 409).

BIBLIOGRAPHY

700 Jahre Elisabethkirche in Marburg: 1283–1983 [Ausstellungen 30. April–31. July 1983 in Marburg]. 8 vols. Marburg: Komm. N. G. Elwert, 1983.

Ackerman, J. S. *The Architecture of Michelangelo*. 2 vols. London: Zwemmer, 1961.

Ackerman, James. "'Ars sine scientia nihil est': Gothic Theory of Architecture at the Cathedral of Milan." *Art Bulletin*, no. 31 (1949): 84–116.

Adriaenssens, S., S. Gabriele, P. Magrone, and V. Varano. "Revisiting the Form Finding Techniques of Sergio Musmeci: The Bridge over the Basento River." In *Structures and Architecture—Proceedings of the 3rd International Conference on Structures and Architecture, ICSA 2016*, 543–550. Leiden: CRC Press/Balkema, 2016.

Afuhs, Eva, and Andres Strohl. "Erste grundlagen zu einem fragmente Werk (First Principles for a Fragmented Oeuvre)." In *Hermann Obrist: Skulptur, Raum Abstraktion um 1900*, 14–43. Zurich: Scheidegger & Spiess, 2009.

Albee, Edward. *Tiny Alice.* 1965. Reprint, [New York:] Dramatists Play Service, 2001.

Alberti, Leon Battista. *De Pictura*. Ed. and trans. Rocco Sinisgalli. Cambridge: Cambridge University Press, 2011.

Alberti, Leon Battista. *On the Art of Building in Ten Books*. Trans. Joseph Rykwert, Neil Leach, and Robert Tavernor. Cambridge, MA: MIT Press, 1996.

Alciati, Andrea. *A Book of Emblems: The Emblematum Liber in Latin and English*. Trans. and ed. John F. Moffitt. Jefferson, NC: McFarland, 2004.

Allen, W. Godfrey, and Captain C. Stanley Peach. "The Preservation of St. Paul's Cathedral." *Journal of the RIBA* 37 (August 1930): 655–676.

Alsina, Claudia, and Josep Gómez. "Gaudí: Geometria, estructura i construcció." In Bohigas et al., *Gaudí 2002*, 138–157.

Androuet du Cerceau, Jacques. *Leçons de perspective positive*. Paris: Mamert Patisson imprimeur, 1576.

Androuet du Cerceau, Jacques. *Livre d'architecture*. Paris: B. Prevost, 1559.

Aristotle. *De Anima*. Trans. R. D. Hicks. Cambridge: Cambridge University Press, 1907.

Aristotle. *The Metaphysics.* Trans. Hugh Tredennick. Aristotle 17. Loeb Classical Library. 1933. Reprint, Cambridge, MA: Harvard University Press; London: William Heinemann, 1980.

Aristotle. *The Physics*. Trans. Philip H. Wicksteed and Francis M. Cornford. Rev. ed. 2 vols. Loeb Classical Library. 1957–60. Reprint, Cambridge, MA: Harvard University Press, 1980.

Arnold, Dieter. *Der Pyramidenbezirk des Königs Amenemhet III. in Dahschur.* Mainz am Rhein: P. von Zabern, 1987.

Arnold, Dieter, and Rainer Stadelmann. "Dahschur: Zweiter Grabungsbericht." *Mitteilungen des Deutschen Archäologischen Instituts, Abteilung Kairo* 33 (1977): 15–20.

Arnold, T. F. K. "Felloplastik oder die Kunst Modellen von antiken Gebaüden in Kork darzustellen." In *Kork: Geschichte, Architektur, Design*, 130–136. Ostfildern-Ruit: Hatje Cantz, 2002.

Audsley, Berthold. "Miniatures and Their Value in Architectural Practice." *The Brickbuilder*, no. 23 (September 1914): 213–216.

Bachelard, Gaston. *The Philosophy of No: A Philosophy of the New Scientific Mind*. Trans. G. C. Waterston. New York: Orion Press, 1968.

Bachelard, Gaston. *The Poetics of Space*. Trans. Maria Jolas. 1964. Reprint, Boston: Beacon Press, 1994.

Bachelard, Gaston. *Water and Dreams*. Trans. Edith R. Farrell. 1983. Reprint, Dallas: Pegasus Foundation, 1999.

Baroni, Costantino, ed. *Documenti per la storia dell'architettura a Milano nel Rinascimento e nel Barocco*. 2 vols. Florence: Sansoni, 1940.

Bartholomew, Ethel. "Architectural Model Making as Part of the Technique of the Drafting-Room." *Architecture* 54 (December 1926): 283–285.

Bartmann-Kompa, Ingrid. *Das Berliner Rathaus*. Berlin: Henschel Verlag, 1991.

Battisti, Eugenio. *Filippo Brunelleschi*. Trans. Robert Erich Wolf. London: Thames & Hudson, 1981.

Bauche, Ulrich, Gisela Jaacks, and Ute Scheurlen. *Gärten, Landhäuser un Villen des hamburgischen Bürgertums.* Hamburg: Museum für Hamburgische Geschichte, 1975.

Baudrillard, Jean. "The Precession of Simulacra." In *Simulacra and Simulation*, trans. Sheila Faria Glaser, 1–42. Ann Arbor: University of Michigan Press, 1994.

Baudrillard, Jean. "Simulacra and Science Fiction." In *Simulacra and Simulation*, trans. Sheila Faria Glaser, 121–127. Ann Arbor: University of Michigan Press, 1994.

Bauer, George. "From Architecture to Scenography: The Full-Scale Model in the Baroque Tradition." In *La scenografia barocca*, ed. Antoine Schnapper, 142–149. Bologna: CLUEB, 1982.

Bauer, Hermann. *St. Elisabeth und die Elisabethkirche zu Marburg*. Marburg: Dr. Wolfram Hitzeroth Verlag, 1990.

Baumbach, Jens David. *The Significance of Votive Offerings in Selected Hera Sanctuaries in the Peloponnese, Ionia and Western Greece*. BAR International Series 1249. Oxford: Archaeopress, 2004.

Belidor, Bernard Forest de. *La science des ingénieurs dans la conduite des travaux de fortification et architecture civile*. Paris: C. Jombert, 1729.

Bellini, Federico. *Le cupole di Borromini: La "scientia" costruttiva in età barocca*. Milan: Electa, 2004.

Ben van Berkel 1990/1995. Madrid: El Croquis Editorial, 1995.

Bénabou, Marcel. "Rule and Constraint." In Motte, *Oulipo*, 40–47.

Benjamin, Walter. "Unpacking My Library: A Talk about Book Collecting." In *Illuminations*, ed. Hannah Arendt, trans. Harry Zohn, 59–67. New York: Schocken Books, 1969.

Benjamin, Walter. "The Work of Art in the Age of Mechanical Reproduction." In *Illuminations*, ed. Hannah Arendt, trans. Harry Zohn, 217–251. New York: Schocken Books, 1969.

Beorkrem, Christopher. *Material Strategies in Digital Fabrication*. New York: Routledge, 2013.

Berckenhagen, Ekhart. "Das deutsche Architekturmodell." In Reuther and Berckenhagen, *Deutsche Architekturmodelle*, 7–9.

Bergdoll, Barry, and Peter Christensen, eds. *Home Delivery: Fabricating the Modern Dwelling*. New York: Museum of Modern Art, 2008.

Berkel, Ben van, and UN Studio. *Buy Me a Mercedes-Benz: The Book of the Museum*. Barcelona: Actar, 2006.

Berlin, Isaiah. *The Roots of Romanticism*. Ed. Henry Hardy. London: Chatto & Windus, 1999.

Bernzen, Rolf. *Die praktische und theoretische Konstitution des Modellverfahrens*. Bern: Peter Lang, 1986.

Bideault, Maryse, and Claudine Lautier. "Saint-Nicaise de Reims, Chronologie et nouvelles remarques sur l'architecture." *Bulletin Monumental*, no. 135 (1977): 295–330.

Binding, Günther. *Der mittelalterliche Baubetrieb nördlich der Alpen in zeitig enössischen Darstellungen.* Darmstadt: Wissenschaftliche Buchgesellschaft, 1978.

Bischoff, Franz. "Burkhard Engelberg und due Süddeutsche Architektur um 1500: Anmekungen zur sozialen Stellung und zur Arbeitsweise spätgotischer Steinmetzen und Werkmeister." Diss., Philosophy dactylographiée, Bamberg, 1987.

Bischoff, Franz. "Les Maquettes d'architecture." In *Les Bâtisseurs des cathédrales gothiques*, ed. Roland Recht, 287–295. Strasbourg: Editions Les Musées de la ville de Strasbourg, 1989.

Bischoff, Franz. "'... das verkleinert opus recht vor Augen gestellt': Zur Geschichte und Bedeutung des Architekturmodells von der Frühzeit bis zur Gegenwart." In Helmberger and Kockel, *Rom über die Alpen tragen*, 33–48.

Bliznakov, Milka. "The Rationalist Movement in Soviet Architecture of the 1920's." In *Russian Formalism*, ed. Stephen Bann and John W. Bowlt, 147–161. Edinburgh: Scottish Academic Press, 1973.

Blondel, François. *Cours d'architecture enseigné dans l'Académie royale d'architecture*. Vol. 1. Paris, 1675.

Boato, Anna, and Anna Decri. "Disegni e contratti edili nel Fondo Notai dell'Archivio di Stato di Genova (XVI–XVII sec.)." *Il Disegno di architettura*, no. 2 (1992): 11–17.

Boëthius, Axel, Roger Ling, and Tom Rasmussen. *Etruscan and Early Roman Architecture*. 2nd ed. New Haven: Yale University Press, 1992.

Bohigas, Oriol, et al. *Gaudí 2002: Miscelánia*. 2nd ed. Barcelona: Planeta; Ajuntament de Barcelona, 2002.

Booz, Paul. *Der Baumeister der Gotik*. Munich: Deutscher Kunst-verlag, 1956.

Borgo, Ludovico, and Howard Saalman. "1512: Projects for a New Church of San Marco in Florence." In *Essays Presented to Myron P. Gilmore*, ed. Sergio Bertelli and Gloria Ramakus, 2:15–23. 2 vols. Florence: La Nuova Italia Editrice, 1978.

Boring, William. "Use of Models in the Study of Architecture." *Architect and Engineer* 60 (1920): 99–100.

Boring, William. "Use of Models in the Study of Architecture." *Architecture* 45 (1922): 199–202.

Boucher, Bruce, ed. *Earth and Fire: Italian Terracotta Sculpture from Donatello to Canova*. New Haven: Yale University Press, 2001.

Bradbury, Kirsten. *Michelangelo*. Bath: Parragon Books, 2000.

Branner, Robert. "Drawings from a Thirteenth-Century Architect's Shop: The Reims Palimpsest." *Journal of the Society of Architectural Historians*, no. 18 (1958): 9–21.

Broneer, Oscar. "Measurements and Refinements at the South Stoa at Corinth." *AJA* 53 (1949): 146–147.

Brooks, H. Allen. *Le Corbusier's Formative Years: Charles-Edouard Jeanneret at La Chaux-de-Fonds*. Chicago: University of Chicago Press, 1997.

Brosterman, Norman. *Inventing Kindergarten*. New York: Harry N. Abrams, 1997.

Bucher, François. "Micro-Architecture as the 'Idea' of Gothic Theory and Style." *Gesta* 15, nos. 1–2 (1976): 71–89.

Bucher, François. "A Rediscovered Tracing by Villard de Honnecourt." *Art Bulletin*, no. 59 (September 1977): 315–319.

Butler, Samuel. *Ex Voto*. 1888. Reprint, London: J. Cape, 1928.

Büttner, Anita. "Korkmodelle." In *Antike Bauten in Modell und Zeichnung um 1800*, ed. Peter Gercke, 10–19. Kassel: Staatliche Kunstsammlungen Kassel, 1986.

Cachola Schmal, Peter, Teresa Fankhänel, Michael Stöneberg, and Philipp Sturm. *Das Architektur Modell: Werkzeug, Fetisch, kleine Utopie = The Architectural Model: Tool, Fetish, Small Utopia*. Frankfurt am Main: DAM, Deutsches Architekturmuseum, 2012.

Caillois, Roger. *Man, Play and Games*. Trans. Meyer Barash. New York: Free Press of Glencoe, 1961.

Calatrava, Santiago. *Santiago Calatrava: Secret Sketchbook*. Ed. Mirko Zardini. Photographs by Paolo Rosselli. New York: Zardelli, 1995.

Calvino, Italo. *The Castle of Crossed Destinies*. Trans. William Weaver. New York: Harcourt Brace Jovanovich, 1976.

Calvino, Italo. "Cybernetics and Ghosts." In *The Uses of Literature: Essays*, trans. Patrick Creagh, 3–27. San Diego: Harcourt Brace, 1986.

Calvino, Italo. *Invisible Cities*. Trans. William Weaver. Orlando: Harcourt, 1972.

Candela, Felix. "Understanding the Hyperbolic Paraboloid: Part 2." *Architectural Record* 124 (August 1958): 205.

Capomolla, Rinaldo. "Le forme organiche strutturali: Materie e spazio nelle opere di Sergio Musmeci." *Rassegna di Architettura e Urbanistica*, nos. 121–122 (2007): 135–148.

Carême, Marie-Antoine. *Le pâtissier royal parisien ou Traité élémentaire et pratique de la pâtisserie ancienne et moderne*. Paris: J.-G. Dentu, 1815.

Casey, Edward S. "Habitual Body and Memory in Merleau-Ponty." *Man and World* 17 (1984): 279–297.

Cecchi, Alessandro. "Modello della chiesa di San Giuseppe." In *L'Officina della maniera: Varieta e fierezza nell'arte fiorentina del Cinquecento fra le due repubbliche, 1494–1530*, ed. Alessandro Cecchi and Antonio Natali, 220–221. [Florence]: Giunta Regionale Toscana; [Venice]: Marsilio, 1996.

Cecchi, Alessandro. "Percorso di Baccio d'Agnolo legnaiuolo e architetto fiorentino: Dal ballatoio di Santa Maria del Fiore alle ultime opere, 2." *Antichità viva* 29, nos. 2–3 (1990): 40–57.

Cepl, Jasper. *Oswald Mathias Ungers: Eine Intellectuelle Biographie*. Cologne: Verlag der Buchhandlung Walther König, 2007.

Chiappelli, Alessandro. "Il ritrovamento d'un modello inedito di Baccio d'Agnolo." *Bollettino d'Arte* 1 (1921–1922): 563–566.

Chilton, John. "Form-finding and Fabric Forming in the Work of Heinz Isler." In *Proceedings of the Second International Conference on Flexible Formwork*, ed. John Orr, Mark Evernden, Anthony Darby, and Timothy Ibell, 84–91. University of Bath, 2012.

Chilton, John. *Heinz Isler*. London: Thomas Telford, 2000.

Cleary, Richard. "Paris, VI. Institutions, 2. Académie Royale d'Architecture." In *The Dictionary of Art*, ed. Jane Turner, 24:169–171. 34 vols. New York: Grove, 1996.

Clute, Eugene. "Models, Their Making and Their Use." Chapter 8 of *Drafting Room Practice*, 43–67. New York: Pencil Points Press, 1928.

Cohen, Jean-Louis. Introduction to Le Corbusier, *Toward an Architecture*, 1–82.

Cojannot, Alexandre. "En petit ou en grand: 'Modèles' et maquettes dans la practique architecturale française du XVIIe siècle." In Frommel with Tassin, *Les maquettes d'architecture*, 199–218.

Colvin, Howard. *The Canterbury Quadrangle: St. John's College, Oxford*. Oxford: Oxford University Press, 1988.

Colvin, Howard. *Unbuilt Oxford*. New Haven: Yale University Press, 1983.

Conrads, Ulrich, ed. *Programs and Manifestoes on 20th Century Architecture*. Trans. Michael Bullock. 1970. Reprint, Cambridge, MA: MIT Press, 2002.

Corbett, Harvey Wiley. "Architectural Models of Cardboard." Part 1. *Pencil Points* 3 (May 1922): 29–37.

Cossé-Durlin, Jeannine, ed. *Cartulaire de Saint-Nicaise de Reims*. Paris: Editions du Centre national de la recherche scientifique, 1991.

Costanzo, Michele. *MVRDV: Works and Projects, 1991–2006*. Trans. Marco Migotto and Robert Burns. Milan: Skira; New York: Rizzoli, 2006.

Coulton, J. J. *Ancient Greek Architects at Work: Problems of Structure and Design*. Ithaca, NY: Cornell University Press, 1977.

Cowan, H. J., and R. W. Muncey. *Models in Architecture*. Amsterdam: Elsevier, 1968.

Crippa, Maria Antonietta. "Sagrat i profà en l'obra de Gaudí." In Bohigas et al., *Gaudí 2002*.

Crosbie, Michael J. "Is It a Catenary? New Questions about the Shape of Saarinen's St. Louis Arch." *AIA Journal* (June 1983): 78–79.

Diethelm, Alois. "Steel: Systems in Architecture: Folding and Bending." In *Constructing Architecture: Materials, Processes, Structures*, ed. Andrea Deplazes, 133. Basel: Birkhäuser, 2005.

Derrida, Jacques. *Of Grammatology*. Trans. Gayatri Chakravorty Spivak. Baltimore: Johns Hopkins University Press, 1976.

Descharnes, Robert, and Clovis Prévost. *Gaudí: The Visionary*. Trans. Frederick Hill. London: Patrick Stephens, 1971.

"A Designer's Home of His Own: Charles Eames Builds House of Steel and Glass." *Life*, 11 September 1950, 148–152.

Diogenes Laertius. "Thales." In *Lives of Eminent Philosophers* 1.22–44, trans. R. D. Hicks, 1:22–47. Loeb Classical Library. London: W. Heinemann; New York: Putnam's Sons, 1925.

Dorey, Helen. "Sir John Soane's Model Room." *Perspecta* 41, *Grand Tour* (2008): 46 (images on 26, 92–93, 170–171).

Dorey, Helen. "Soane's Pasticcio." *The Georgian*, November 2003, 14–17.

"Dow Plastic Gets Boost from Telaflora Shop." *Telegraph Delivery Spirit* 24, no. 2 (August 1957): 43.

Downes, Kerry. *The Architecture of Wren*. Rev. ed. Reading, Eng.: Redhedge, 1988.

Drogin, David. "Art Patronage and Civic Identities in Renaissance Bologna." In *The Court Cities of Northern Italy*, ed. C. M. Rosenberg, 244–324. Cambridge: Cambridge University Press, 2010.

Droste, Magdalena. *Bauhaus, 1919–1933*. Cologne: Taschen, 2002.

du Colombier, Pierre. *Les chantiers des cathédrales*. 2nd ed. Paris: Picard, 1973.

Dunn, Nick. *The Ecology of the Architectural Model*. Oxford: Peter Lang, 2007.

Eco, Umberto. *Experiences in Translation*. Trans. Alastair McEwen. Toronto: University of Toronto Press, 2001.

Eco, Umberto. "The Poetics of the Open Work." In *The Open Work*, trans. Anna Cancogni, 1–24. Cambridge, MA: Harvard University Press, 1989.

Eisenman, Peter. "Cardboard Architecture." *Casabella*, no. 374 (1973): 17–31.

Eisenman, Peter. "Misreading." In *House of Cards*, 167–186. New York: Oxford University Press, 1987.

Elsner, John. "A Collector's Model of Desire: The House and Museum of Sir John Soane." In *The Cultures of Collecting*, ed. John Elsner and Roger Cardinal, 155–176. London: Reaktion Books, 1994.

Emmons, Paul. "Architectural Encounters between Material and Idea." In Mindrup, *The Material Imagination*, 90–106.

Emmons, Paul. "Le Corbusier's Serious Game of Dominos." In *The Cultural Role of Architecture: Contemporary and Historical Perspectives*, ed. Paul Emmons, Jane Lomholt, and John Hendrix, 132–140. Hoboken: Taylor & Francis, 2012.

Emmons, Paul. "A Window to the Soul: Depth in Early Modern Section Drawing." In *Architecture Post Mortem*, ed. Donald Kunze, Charles Bertolini, and Simone Brott, 153–177. Burlington, VT: Ashgate, 2013.

Escrig, F. "Emilio Pérez Piñero: Inventor of Deployability." In *Structures and Architecture: Concepts Applications and Challenges*, ed. Paulo J. da Sousa Cruz, 42–57. London: Taylor & Francis, 2013.

Eugène Freyssinet: A Revolution in the Art of Construction. Paris: Presses de l'École nationale des ponts et chaussées, 2004.

Euripides. *Euripides: "Hecuba": Introduction, Text, and Commentary*, by Justina Gregory. Atlanta: Scholars Press, 1999.

Fabriczy, Cornel von. *Filippo Brunelleschi: Sein Leben und seine Werke*. Stuttgart: J. G. Cotta, 1892.

Falk, Tilman. *Die deutschen Zeichnen des 15. Jahrhunderts*. Munich: Staatliche Graphische Sammlung, 1994.

Fankhänel, Teresa. "Introducing Theodore Conrad or Why Should We Look at the Architectural Model Maker?" In Frommel with Tassin, *Les maquettes d'architecture*, 259–268.

Fauerbach, Ulrike. "Concevoir les détails: Les maquettes de l'Égypte ancienne." In *La maquette, un outil au service du projet architectural*, 36–51. Paris: Cité de l'architecture & du patrimoine, 2015.

Fayot, Frédéric. "Notice biographique sur Carême." In *Classiques de la table*, ed. Justin Améro, 2:178–179. New ed. Paris: Firmin Didot, 1855.

Ficino, Marsilio. *De Amore (Commentary on the Symposium of Plato)* [1484].Trans. S. E. Jayne. Dallas: Spring Publications, 1985.

Filarete. *Treatise on Architecture: Being the Treatise by Antonio di Piero Averlino, Known as Filarete*. Trans. John R. Spencer. Volume 1. New Haven: Yale University Press, 1965.

Finsterlin, Hermann. "Formdomino und Zukunftsarchitektur." In Speidel, Kegler, and Ritterbach, *Wege zu einer neuen Baukunst*, 88–94.

Finsterlin, Hermann, "Die Genesis der Weltarchitektur oder die Deszendenz der Dome als Stilspiel: Ein Lehr-, Spiel- und Versuchsbaukasten" (1922). Reprinted in Taut, *Frühlicht, 1920–1922*, 149–158.

Finsterlin, Hermann. "Innenarchitektur" (1921/1922). Reprinted in Taut, *Frühlicht, 1920–1922*, 105–108.

Fletcher. Angus *Allegory, the Theory of a Symbolic Mode*. Ithaca, NY: Cornell University Press, 1964.

Flinders Petrie, W. M. "The Soul-House in Egypt." *Man* 7 (1907): 113–114.

Fondin, Jean, and Jac Remise. *The Golden Age of Toys*. Trans. D. B. Tubbs. Lausanne: Edita, 1967.

Francé, R. H.. *Die Pflanze als Erfinder*. Stuttgart: Kosmos, 1920.

Francé, R. H.. *Plants as Inventors*. New York: Albert & Charles Boni, 1923.

Francé, Raoul Heinrich. "Die sieben technischen Grundformen der Natur." *Das Kunstblatt* 8, no. 1 (January 1923): 5–11.

Franciscono, Marcel. *Walter Gropius and the Creation of the Bauhaus in Weimar: The Ideals and Artistic Theories of Its Founding Year.* Urbana: University of Illinois Press, 1971.

Frank, Charlotte, ed. *Axel Schultes in Bangert, Jansen, Scholz, Schultes: Projekte, 1985–1991*. Berlin: Ernst & Sohn, 1992.

Frascari, Marco. *Eleven Exercises in the Art of Architectural Drawing: Slow Food for the Architect's Imagination*. New York: Routledge, 2011.

Frazer, Sir James George. *The Golden Bough: A Study in Magic and Religion.* Abridged by Robert K. G. Temple. New York: Simon & Schuster, 1996.

Frederiksen, Rune, and Eckart Marchand, eds. *Plaster Casts: Making, Collecting and Displaying from Classical Antiquity to the Present.* Berlin: De Gruyter, 2010.

Freyssinet, Eugène. "Ma vie: Naissance du béton précontraint" (1954). In *Un amour sans limite*, 34–36. Paris: Editions du Linteau, 1993.

Frézier, Amédée-François. *La théorie de la pratique de la coupe des pierres et des bois, pour la construction des voûtes et autres parties de bâtiments civils et militaires ou traité de stéréotomie à l'usage de l'architecture*. 3 vols. Strasbourg: Doulsseker; Paris: Guérin, 1737–1739.

Fröbel, Friedrich. *Pedagogics of the Kindergarten*. Trans. Josephine Jarvis. New York: D. Appleton, 1896.

Frommel, Sabine, with Raphaël Tassin, eds. *Les maquettes d'architecture: Fonction et évolution d'un instrument de conception et de réalisation.* Paris: Picard; Rome: Campisano Editore, 2015.

Fromonot, Françoise. *Jørn Utzon: The Sydney Opera House.* Trans. Christopher Thompson. Corte Madera, CA: Electa/Gingko, 1998.

Frothingham, Arthur L. "Discovery of an Original Church Model by a Gothic Architect." *Architectural Record* 22 (August 1907): 110–116.

Frothingham, Arthur L. "Le modèle de l'église Saint-Maclou à Rouen." *Monuments et mémoires de la Fondation Eugène Piot Année* 12, no. 2 (1905): 211–224.

Furján, Helene. *Glorious Visions: John Soane's Spectacular Theater.* Abingdon, UK: Routledge, 2011.

Furttenbach, Joseph. *Architectura private.* Augsburg: Johann Schultes, 1641.

Galilei, Galileo. *Dialogues Concerning Two New Sciences.* Trans. Henry Crew and Alfonso de Salvio. 1914. Reprint, Evanston, IL: Northwestern University, 1946.

Gauthier, Maurice. "Studying in Three Dimensions." *Pencil Points* 7 (July 1926): 407–416.

Geary, Patrick. *Furta Sacra: Thefts of Relics in the Central Middle Ages.* Princeton, NJ: Princeton University Press, 2001.

Gentleman's Magazine. Unsigned review of *The Union of Architecture, Sculpture, and Painting*, by John Britton. 97, no. 2 (1827): 129.

Gerbino, Anthony. *François Blondel: Architecture, Erudition, and the Scientific Revolution.* Abingdon, Oxon.: Routledge, 2010.

Geronimus, Dennis. *Piero di Cosimo: Visions Beautiful and Strange.* New Haven: Yale University Press, 2006.

Gerstenberg, Kurt. "Baumeisterbildnis." In *Reallexikon zur Deutschen Kunstgeschichte*, 96–100. Vol. 2, ed. Otto Schmitt. Stuttgart: J. B. Metzler, 1937.

Gillespie, Richard. "The Rise and Fall of Cork Model Collections in Britain." *Architectural History* 60 (November 2017): 117–146.

Gilson, Etienne. *The Philosophy of St. Bonaventure.* Trans. Illtyd Trethowan and Frank J. Sheed. 1938. Reprint, Patterson, NJ: St. Anthony Guild Press, 1965.

Gimbutas, Marija. *The Goddesses and Gods of Old Europe: Myths and Cult Images.* Updated ed. 1982. Reprint, Berkeley: University of California Press, 2007.

Giordano, Luisa. "Wooden Architectural Models in Lombardy." In Millon and Lampugnani, *The Renaissance from Brunelleschi to Michelangelo*, 461–463.

Givelet, Charles. *L'eglise et l'abbaye de St. Nicase de Reims.* Reims: F. Michaud, 1897.

Goldscheider, Ludwig. *A Survey of Michelangelo's Models in Wax and Clay.* London: Phaidon Press, 1962.

Gordon, John Steele. *Washington's Monument and the Fascinating History of the Obelisk.* New York: Bloomsbury, 2016.

Grant, Robert M. *A Short History of the Interpretation of the Bible.* Rev. ed. New York: Macmillan, 1963.

Grimm, Jacob, and Wilhelm Grimm. *Deutsches Wörterbuch.* 16 vols. Leipzig: Verlag von S. Herzel, 1854–1971.

Grimme, Ernst Günther. *Goldschmiedekunst im Mittelalter: Form und Bedeutung des Reliquiars von 800 bis 1500.* Cologne: M. DuMont Schauberg, 1972.

Gropius, Walter. “Principles of Bauhaus Production” (1926). In Conrads, *Programs and Manifestoes on 20th Century Architecture*, 95–97.

Gropius, Walter. “Programme of the Staatliches Bauhaus Weimar” (1919). In Conrads, *Programs and Manifestoes on 20th Century Architecture*, 49–53.

Gropius, Walter. “Speech to Bauhaus Students (July, 1919).” Trans. Rose-Carol Washton Long. In Long, *German Expressionism*, 246–251.

Grosseteste, Robert. *De generatione sonorum*. In *History of Aesthetics*, by Władysław Tatarkiewicz. Ed. C. Barrett. Vol. 2, *Medieval Aesthetics*, 230–231. Warsaw: Polish Scientific Publishers, 1970.

Grote, Andreas. *Florenz: Gestalt und Geschichte eines Gemeinwesens*. 4th ed. Munich: Prestel, 1976.

Grumbine, LeRoy. “The Use of Scale Models as an Aid to the Architect.” *Western Architect* 34 (June 1925): 59–62.

Guasti, Cesare. *La Cupola di Santa Maria del Fiore illustrata con i documenti dell'archivio dell'opera secolare: Saggio di una compiuta illustrazione dell'opera secolare e del tempio di Santa Maria del Fiore*. Florence: Barbera, Bianchi e comp., 1857.

Guasti, Cesare. *Santa Maria del Fiore: La costruzione della Chiesa e del Campanile secondo i documenti tratti dall'Archivio nell'Opera Secolare e da quello di Stato*. Florence: M. Ricci, 1887.

Guillaume, Jean. “Les maquettes d'architecture en France au XVIe siècle.” In Frommel with Tassin, *Les maquettes d'architecture*, 123–130.

Guillerme, Jacques, and Hélène Vérin. “The Archaeology of the Section.” *Perspecta* 25 (1989): 226–257.

Günther, Hubertus. “La presentazione dei modelli: Il primo museo del Rinasciamento dedicato all'architettura.” In Frommel with Tassin, *Les maquettes d'architecture*, 173–188.

Guillaume, Jean. “Les maquettes d'architecture en France au XVIe siècle.” In Frommel with Tassin, *Les maquettes d'architecture*, 121–130.

Hahn, Robert. *Anaximander and the Architects*. Albany: State University of New York Press, 2001.

Hamilton, Stanley B. “The Place of Sir Christopher Wren in the History of Structural Engineering.” *Newcomen Society Transactions* 14 (1933–1934): 27–42.

Harries, Karsten. “Taking on Risk: Nine Experimental Scenarios.” In *Lebbeus Woods: Experimental Architecture*, ed. Tracy Myers, 24–37. Pittsburgh: Carnegie Museum of Art, the Heinz Architectural Center, 2004.

Hartt, Frederick. *David by the Hand of Michelangelo*. New York: Abbeville Press, 1987.

Harvey, William. *Models of Buildings: How to Make and Use Them*. London: Architectural Press, 1927.

Haselberger, Lothar. “Architectural Likenesses: Models and Plans of Architecture.” *Journal of Roman Archaeology* 10 (1997): 77–94.

Haselberger, Lothar. “Curvature: The Evidence at Didyma.” In *Appearance and Essence: Refinements of Classical Architecture—Curvature: Proceedings of the Second Williams Symposium on Classical Architecture Held at the University of Pennsylvania, Philadelphia, April 2–4, 1993*, ed. Lothar Haselberger, 173–184. Philadelphia: University Museum, University of Pennsylvania, 1999.

Hauser, Sigrid. In *Peter Zumthor Therme Vals*, ed. Peter Zumthor. Zurich: Verlag Schneidegger & Spiess, 2007.

Hays, K. Michael. *Modernism and the Posthumanist Subject: The Architecture of Hannes Meyer and Ludwig Hilberseimer*. Cambridge, MA: MIT Press, 1992.

Heatherwick, Thomas. *Thomas Heatherwick: Making*. Rev. ed. London: Thames & Hudson, 2015.

Hegel, Georg Wilhelm Friedrich. *Lectures on the Philosophy of World History*. Trans. H. B. Nisbet. Cambridge: Cambridge University Press, 1975.

Hegel, Georg Wilhelm Friedrich. *Vorlesungen über die Philosophie der Geschichte*. Vol. 1, *Die Vernunft in der Geschichte*. Ed. J. Hoffmeister. 5th ed. Hamburg: Felix Meiner, 1955.

Heidegger, Martin. "The Origin of the Work of Art." In *Poetry Language Thought*, trans. Albert Hofstadter, 15–86. New York: Harper & Row, 2001.

Helmberger, Werner. "Carl Joseph May (1742–1822): Hofkonditor und Korkbildner." In Helmberger and Kockel, *Rom über die Alpen tragen*, 63–89.

Helmberger, Werner, and Valentin Kockel, eds. *Rom über die Alpen tragen: Fürsten sammeln antike Architektur: Die Aschaffen-burger Korkmodelle.* Landshut: Arcos, 1993.

Hendrick, T. W. *The Modern Architectural Model*. London: Architectural Press, 1957.

Hendrix, John S. "Alberti and Ficino." *School of Architecture, Art, and Historic Preservation Faculty Publications*, no. 25 (2012). https://docs.rwu.edu/saahp_fp/25.

Herder, Johann Gottfried. *Sculpture: Some Observations on Shape and Form from Pygmalion's Creative Dream*. Ed. and trans. Jason Gaiger. Chicago: University of Chicago Press, 2002.

Herman, Arthur E. "Models of Plastics and Aluminium." *Progressive Architecture* 40 (December 1959): 9–11.

Herzog & de Meuron. "Just Waste (2002)." In Ursprung, *Herzog & de Meuron: Natural History*, 74–75.

Heydenreich, Ludwig H. "Architekturmodell." In *Reallexikon zur Deutschen Kunstgeschichte*, vol. 1, ed. Otto Schmitt, 918–940. Stuttgart: J. B. Metzlersche Verlagsbuchhandlung, 1937.

Hirons, Frederic C. "The Use of Scale Models." *Pencil Points* 1 (November–December 1920): 4–10.

Hitchcock, Henry-Russell, and Philip Johnson. *The International Style*. 1932. Reprint, New York: Norton, 1995.

Hobbs, Edward W. *Pictorial House Modelling*. London: C. Lockwood and Son, 1926.

Hoek, Elk, ed. *Theo van Doesburg: Oeuvre catalogue.* Utrecht: Centraal Museum, 2000.

Hoffman, Dan. *Architecture Studio: Cranbrook Academy of Art, 1986–1993*. New York: Rizzoli, 1994.

Holl, Steven. *Anchoring*. New York: Princeton Architectural Press, 1989.

Holl, Steven *The Chapel of St. Ignatius*. New York: Princeton Architectural Press, 1999.

Holl, Steven. *Intertwining*. New York: Princeton Architectural Press, 1996.

Holl, Steven. Interview with Stanley Collyer. *Competitions* 8, no. 2 (Summer 1998): 54–61.

Holl, Steven. "Phenomenon and Idea." In Mindrup, *The Material Imagination*, 49–50.

Holl, Steven. *Simmons Hall, MIT Undergraduate Residence.* Ed. Todd Gannon and Michael Denison. New York: Princeton Architectural Press, 2004.

Holl, Steven. *Steven Holl: Written in Water*. Baden: Lars Müller, 2002.

Hooke, Robert. *A Description of Helioscopes, and Some Other Instruments*. London: T.R. for John Martyn, 1676.

Hoppe, Stephan. "German Architectural Models in the Renaissance (1500–1620)." In Frommel with Tassin, *Les maquettes d'architecture*, 131–142.

Horsley, Carter E. "'Modelmakers' Work Gaining New Recognition." *New York Times*, 28 July 1974, 283.

Hubert, Christian. "The Ruins of Representation." In Richard Pommer, *Idea as Model*, [ed. Kenneth Frampton and Silvia Kolbowski], 17–28. New York: Rizzoli, 1981.

Hübsch, Heinrich. *Bauwerke*. 2 vols. Karlsruhe: Veith, 1838.

Huerta, Santiago. "Structural Design in the Work of Gaudí." *Architectural Science Review* 49, no. 4 (December 2006): 324–339.

Hughes, Robert. "Doing Their Own Thing: U.S. Architects: Goodbye to Glass Boxes and All That." *Time*, 8 January 1979, 52.

Huizinga, Johan. *Homo Ludens: A Study of the Play-Element in Culture.* 1949. Reprint, London: Routledge & Kegan Paul, 1980.

Husserl, Edmund. *Ideen zu einer reinen Phänomenologie und Phänomenologischen Philosophie*. Book 1, *Allgemeine Einführung in die reine Phänomenologie*. Halle: Verlag von Max Niemeyer, 1913.

Huygens, Christiaan. *Œuvres complètes*. Vol. 9, *Correspondance, 1685–1690*, published by Société hollandaise des sciences. La Haye: M. Nijhoff, 1901.

Isler, Heinz. "New Shapes for Shells." *Bulletin of the International Association for Shell Structures* 8 (1960): 123–130.

Iwamoto, Lisa. *Digital Fabrications: Architectural and Material Techniques*. New York: Princeton Architectural Press, 2009.

Jacobs, Jane. "The Miniature Boom." *Architectural Forum* 108, no. 5 (May 1958): 106–111.

Jameson, Fredric. "From Metaphor to Allegory." In *Anything*, ed. Cynthia C. Davidson, 24–37. Cambridge, MA: MIT Press, 2001.

Janner, Ferdinand. *Die Baütten des Deutschen Mittelalters*. Leipzig: E. A. Seemann, 1876.

Joachim, Gaus. "Dedicatio Ecclesiae: Zum Grundsteinlegungsrelief im Münster zu Ulm." In *600 Jahre Ulmer Münster*, 59–85. Stuttgart: Kohlhammer, 1977.

Josephson, Ragnar. "Les maquettes du Bernin pour le Louvre." *Gazette des Beaux-Arts*, ser. 5, 1 (February 1928): 77–92.

Kalayan, Haroutune. "Notes on Assembly Marks, Drawings and Models Concerning the Roman Period Monuments in Lebanon." *Les Annales archéologiques de Syrie* 21 (1971): 269–273.

Kamm, Josephine. *Joseph Paxton and the Crystal Palace: A Story Biography*. London: Methuen, 1967.

Kiesler, Friedrich. *Inside the Endless House*. New York: Simon & Schuster, 1966.

Kiesler, Friedrich. "On Correalism and Biotechnique: A Definition and Test of a New Approach to Building Design." *Architectural Record* 86 (September 1939): 60–75.

Kieven, Elisabeth. "'Mostrar l'inventione'—The Role of Roman Architects in the Baroque Period: Plans and Models." In Millon, *Triumph of the Baroque*, 173–205.

King, Ross. *Brunelleschi's Dome: How a Renaissance Genius Reinvented Architecture*. New York: Walker, 2000.

Klopfer, Paul. "Über Apollinisches und Dionysisches in der Baukunst." *Stadtbaukunst alter und neuer Zeit* 1 (1920): 161–166.

Kockel, Valentin. "Plaster Models and Plaster Casts of Classical Architecture and Its Decoration." In Frederiksen and Marchand, *Plaster Casts*, 417–434.

Kockel, Valentin. "Rom über die Alpen tragen: Korkmodelle antiker Architektur im 18. und 19. Jahrhundert." In Helmberger and Kockel, *Rom über die Alpen tragen*, 11–32.

Koepf, Hans. *Die gotischen Planrisse der Ulmer Sammlungen*. Ulm: W. Kohlhammer, 1977.

Koepf, Hans. *Die gotischen Planrisse der Wiener Sammlungen*. Vienna, 1969.

Koolhaas, Rem. *Content: Triumph of Realisation*. Cologne: Taschen, 2004.

Kostof, Spiro. *The Architect: Chapters in the History of the Profession*. New York: Oxford University Press, 1977.

Kostof, Spiro. "The Architect in the Middle Ages, East and West." In Kostof, *The Architect*, 59–95.

Krautheimer, Richard. "Introduction to an 'Iconography of Mediaeval Architecture.'" *Journal of the Warburg and Courtauld Institutes* 5 (1942): 1–33.

Kuhn, Thomas. *The Structure of Scientific Revolutions*. 2nd ed. Chicago: University of Chicago Press, 1970.

Küper, Marijke, and Ida van Zijl. *Gerrit Th. Rietveld, 1888–1964: The Complete Works*. Utrecht: Centraal Museum, 1992.

l'Orme, Philibert de. "Instruction de M. d'Yvry." In *Les grands architectes français de la Renaissance*, by Adolphe Berty, 49–59. Paris: C. A. Aubry, 1860.

l'Orme, Philibert de. *Le premier tome de l'architecture*. Paris: F. Morel, 1568.

Lakoff, George, and Mark Johnson. *Metaphors We Live By*. Chicago: University of Chicago Press, 1980.

Lambton, Lucinda. *The Queen's Dolls' House*. London: Royal Collection Enterprises, 2010.

Laugier, Marc-Antoine. *An Essay on Architecture*. Trans. Wolfgang and Anni Herrmann. Los Angeles: Hennessey & Ignalls, 1977.

Le Corbusier. *The Chapel at Ronchamp*. New York: Frederick A. Praeger, 1957.

Le Corbusier. *Le Corbusier, My Work*. London: Architectural Press, 1960.

Le Corbusier. *Le Corbusier Talks with Students from the Schools of Architecture*. Trans. Pierre Chase. New York: Princeton Architectural Press, 1999.

Le Corbusier. "Les objets à réaction poétique." In Le Corbusier, *L'Atelier de la recherche patiente*, 209. Paris: Vincent et Fréal, 1960.

Le Corbusier. *Precisions on the Present State of Architecture and City Planning: With an American Prologue, a Brazilian Corollary Followed by The Temperature of Paris and The Atmosphere of Moscow*. Trans. Edith Schreiber Aujame. Cambridge, MA: MIT Press, 1991.

Le Corbusier. *Toward an Architecture*. Intro. Jean-Louis Cohen. Trans. John Goodman. Los Angeles: Getty Research Institute, 2007.

Le Corbusier. *Towards a New Architecture*. Trans. Frederick Etchells. 1931. Reprint, New York: Dover, 1986.

Leatherbarrow, David. "The Image and Its Setting: A Study of the Sacro Monte at Varallo." *RES: Anthropology and Aesthetics*, no. 14 (Autumn 1987): 107–122.

Leatherbarrow, David. *The Roots of Architectural Invention: Site, Enclosure, Materials*. Cambridge: Cambridge University Press, 1993.

Lecocq, Françoise "Les premières maquettes de Rome: L'exemple des modèles réduits en liège de Carl et Georg May dans les collections européennes aux XVIIIe–XIXe siècles." In *Roma illustrata: Représentations de la ville*, comp. Philippe Fleury and Olivier Desbordes, 227–260. Caen: Presses Universitaires de Caen, 2008.

Ledoux, Claude Nicolas, Yvan Christ, Ionel Schein, and Jacques Ohayo. *L'Oeuvre et les rêves de Claude-Nicolas Ledoux*. Paris: Chêne, 1971.

Legrand, J. G. *Collection des chefs d'oeuvre de l'architecture des différents peuples, exécutés en modèles, sous la direction de L. F. Cassas*. Paris: Treuttel & Würtz, 1806.

Lepik, Andres. *Das Architekturmodell in Italien, 1335–1550*. Worms: Wernersche Verlagsgesellschaft, 1994.

Levene, Richard C., and Fernando Marquez Cecilia. *MvRdV 1991–1997: Maas vanRijs deVries*. El Croquis 86. Madrid: El Croquis, 1997.

Lévi-Strauss, Claude. *The Savage Mind*. Chicago: University of Chicago Press; London: Weidenfeld & Nicolson, 1966.

Libeskind, Daniel. "Three Lessons in Architecture: The Machines." In *Daniel Libeskind: The Space of Encounter*, 180–194. New York: Universe Publishing, 2000.

Liddell, Henry. "To the Editor of the Builder." *The Builder* 1 (27 May 1843): 198.

Lieb, Norbert. "Augsburger Baukunst der Renaissance." In *Augusta, 955–1955: Forschungen und Studien zur Kultur- und Wirtschaftsgeschichte Augsburgs*, ed. Hermann Rinn, 229–263. Augsburg: Hermann Rinn, 1955.

Lieb, Norbert. *Jörg Seld: Goldschmied und Bürger von Augsburg*. Munich: Schnell & Steiner, 1947.

Lindsey, Bruce. *Digital Gehry: Material Resistance, Digital Construction*. Basel: Birkhäuser, 2001.

Lipman, Jonathan. *Frank Lloyd Wright and the Johnson Wax Buildings*. New York: Rizzoli, 1986.

Lipsmeyer, Elisabeth. "The Donor and His Church Model in Medieval Art from Early Christian Times to the Late Romanesque Period." Ph.D. diss., Rutgers, the State University of New Jersey, 1981.

Long, Rose-Carol Washton, ed. *German Expressionism: Documents from the End of the Wilhelmine Empire to the Rise of National Socialism*. New York: G. K. Hall; Toronto: Maxwell Macmillan, 1993.

Lovejoy, Arthur O. *The Great Chain of Being*. 1964. Reprint, Cambridge, MA: Harvard University Press, 2001.

Luckhardt, Wassili. "Vom Entwerfen" (1921). In *Brüder Luckhardt und Alfons Anker: Berliner Architekten der Moderne*, 122. Berlin: Akademie der Künste, 1990.

Lupfer, Gilbert, and Paul Sigel. *Walter Gropius, 1883–1969: The Promoter of a New Form*. Cologne: Taschen, 2004.

Lv, Cheng, Deepakshyam Krishnaraju, Goran Konjevod, Hongyu Yu, and Hanqing Jiang. "Origami Based Mechanical Metamaterials." *Scientific Reports* 4, art. no. 5979 (August 2014). http://dx.doi.org/10.1038/srep05979.

MacCannell, Dean. *The Tourist*. Berkeley: University of California Press, 1999.

Maere, R. "De sacramentstorens van Leuven." In *Studia Eucharistica*, 343–348. Antwerp: Nederlandsche Boekhandel, 1946.

Maere, Réne. "Maquette des tours de l'église St. Pierre de Louvain et l'emploi des Maquettes en architecture." *Annales de la Société Royale d'Archéologie de Bruxelles* 40 (1939): 48–88.

Mahlberg, Blanche, and Bruno Taut. "Dandanah der Märchenpalast: Baustein aus massiven Glas." In Speidel, Kegler, and Ritterbach, *Wege zu einer neuen Baukunst*, 86–87.

Malacrino, Carmelo G. *Constructing the Ancient World: Architectural Techniques of the Greeks and Romans*. Los Angeles: J. Paul Getty Museum, 2010.

Mallgrave, Harry Francis. *The Architect's Brain: Neuroscience, Creativity, and Architecture*. Chichester, West Sussex: Wiley-Blackwell, 2011.

Mallgrave, Harry Francis, Gerald Beasley, Claire Baines, and Henry Raine. *Northern European Books, Sixteenth to Early Nineteenth Centuries*. Vol. 3 of *The Mark J. Millard Architectural Collection*. Washington, DC: National Gallery of Art, 1998.

Manetti, Antonio. *The Fat Woodworker*. Trans. Robert L. Martone and Valerie Martone. New York: Italica Press, 1991.

Manetti, Antonio. *The Life of Brunelleschi*. Trans. Catherine Enggass. University Park: Pennsylvania State University Press, 1970.

Marrone, Steven P. *William of Auvergne and Robert Grosseteste: New Ideas of Truth in the Early Thirteenth Century*. Princeton, NJ: Princeton University Press, 1983.

Marshall, Henry Rutgers. "The Architect's Tools." *Architectural Review* 4, no. 7 (November 1897): 55.

Marshall, Percival. *Wonderful Models*. New York: Spon & Chamberlain, 1928.

Martín, A. Jiménez. *La catedral gótica de Sevilla: Fundación y fábrica de la obra nueva*. Seville: Editorial Universidad de Sevilla-Secretariado de Publicaciones, 2006.

Martin, Kathy. *Famous Brand Names and Their Origins*. Barnsley, South Yorkshire: Pen & Sword History, 2016.

Martin, Roland. *L'Agora*. Études thasiennes 6. Paris: E. de Boccard, 1959.

Mauss, Marcel. *The Gift: The Form and Reason for Exchange in Archaic Societies*. Trans. W. D. Halls. London: Routledge, 1990.

McCann, A. M. *The Roman Port and Fishery of Cosa*. Rome: Academy in Rome, 2002.

McCutchon, Kenneth. "Architectural Models." *Architects' Journal* 84 (1 October 1936): 459–461.

McDonnell, Philip. "Models and Their Making." *American Architect* 107, no. 2054 (May 1915): 277–282.

Merkel, Jayne. *Eero Saarinen*. London: Phaidon, 2005.

Merleau-Ponty, Maurice. *Phenomenology of Perception*. Trans. Colin Smith. London: Routledge & Kegan Paul, 1962.

Mertens, Dieter. "Die Herstellung der Kurvatur am Tempel von Segesta." *Mitteilungen des Deutschen Archäologischen Instituts, Römische Abteilung* 81 (1974): 107–114.

Mertins, Detlef. *Mies*. London: Phaidon, 2014.

Michelangelo Buonarroti. *The Letters of Michelangelo*. Trans. and ed. E. H. Ramsden. 2 vols. Stanford, CA: Stanford University Press, 1963.

Mies van der Rohe, Ludwig. "Hochhäuser." *Frühlicht* 1, no. 4 (Summer 1922): 122–124.

Mies van der Rohe, Ludwig. "Two Glass Skyscrapers." Trans. Philip Johnson. In *Mies van der Rohe*, by Philip Johnson, 187. New York: Museum of Modern Art, 1978.

Mikami, Yuzo. *Utzon's Sphere: Sydney Opera House: How It Was Designed and Built*. Tokyo: Shokokuska, 2001.

Millon, Henry A. "Models in Renaissance Architecture." In Millon and Lampugnani, *The Renaissance from Brunelleschi to Michelangelo*, 18–73.

Millon, Henry A., ed. *The Triumph of the Baroque: Architecture in Europe, 1600–1750*. New York: Rizzoli, 1999.

Millon, Henry A., and Vittorio Magnago Lampugnani, eds. *The Renaissance from Brunelleschi to Michelangelo: The Representation of Architecture*. Milan: Bompiani, 1994.

Millon, H. A., and C. H. Smyth. "Michelangelo and St Peter's: Observations on the Interior of the Apses, a Model of the Apse Vault, and Related Drawings." *Römisches Jahrbuch für Kunstgeschichte* 16 (1976): 137–206.

Mills, Criss B. *Designing with Models: A Studio Guide to Making and Using Architectural Design Models*. New York: John Wiley, 2000.

Mills, Criss B. *Designing with Models: A Studio Guide to Making and Using Architectural Design Models*. 2nd ed. New York: John Wiley, 2005.

Mindrup, Matthew. "*Bauspiel* as Immaterial Investigation: Avant-garde Experimentations with Generative Architectural Models." In *Materiality in Architecture and Art*, ed. Sandra Katrina Löschke, 195–212. London: Routledge, 2016.

Mindrup, Matthew M. "Assembling the Ineffable in Kurt Schwitters' Architectural Models." Ph.D. diss., Virginia Tech, 2007.

Mindrup, Matthew. "Kurt Schwitters' Architectural Models." *Journal of the Kurt Schwitters Society* 4 (2014): 23–38.

Mindrup, Matthew, ed. *The Material Imagination: Reveries on Architecture and Matter*. 2015. Reprint, Abingdon, Oxon.: Routledge, 2017.

Mindrup, Matthew. "The Merz Mill and the Cathedral of the Future." *Interstices* 14 (November 2013): 49–58.

Mindrup, Matthew. "The Resistance and Factures in Drawing-out Architectural Constructions." In Mindrup, *The Material Imagination*, 57–68.

Mindrup, Matthew, and Paul Emmons. "Material Models and Immaterial Paradigms." *Journal of Architectural Education* 62, no. 2 (November 2008): 42–52.

Mirot, Léon. "Le Bernin en France." *Mémoires de la Société de l'histoire de Paris et de l'Ile-de-France* 31 (1904): 161–288.

"Model Making by Architects: An Interesting Communication from a Reader Who Strongly Approves the Work Begun at Columbia University." *American Architect* 118 (December 8, 1920): 749–750.

Moholy-Nagy, László. *The New Vision: Fundamentals of Bauhaus Design, Painting, Sculpture, and Architecture*. 1938. Reprint, Mineola, NY: Dover Publications, 2012.

Moholy-Nagy, László. *Vision in Motion*. Chicago: P. Theobald, 1947.

Moon, Karen. *Modelling Messages: The Architect and the Model*. New York: Monacelli Press, 2005.

Morris, Mark. *Models: Architecture and the Miniature*. Chichester, West Sussex: Wiley-Academy, 2006.

Mosser, Monique. "Französische Architekturmodelle im Zeitalter der Aufklärung." *Daidalos* 2 (1981): 83–97.

Motte, Warren F. Introduction to Motte, *Oulipo*, 1–22.

Motte, Warren F., ed. and trans. *Oulipo: A Primer of Potential Literature*. Lincoln: University of Nebraska Press, 1986.

Mulder, Bertus, and Ida van Zijl. *The Rietveld Schröder House*. Trans. Lynn George. New York: Princeton Architectural Press, 1999.

Mundt, Barbara. "Der Zyklus der Chapelle de Rieux und seine künstlerische Nachfolge." *Jahrbuch der Berliner Museen* 9 (1967): 26–80.

Murray, Peter. *The Saga of Sydney Opera House: The Dramatic Story of the Design and Construction of the Icon of Modern Australia*. New York: Spon Press, 2004.

Musmeci, Sergio. "Ponte sul Basento a Potenza." *Industria italiana del cemento* 2 (1977): 77–98.

Mussolin, Mauro. "Il modello ligneo di Baccio d'Agnolo per l'oratorio di San Giuseppe a Firenze." In Frommel with Tassin, *Les maquettes d'architecture*, 87–100.

Myers, Tracy. "'The Possibility of the Exceptional': Lebbeus Woods' Passionate Provocations." In *Lebbeus Woods: Experimental Architecture*, ed. Tracy Myers, 5–23. Pittsburgh: Carnegie Museum of Art, the Heinz Architectural Center, 2004.

Necipoğlu-Kafadar, Gülru. "Plans and Models in 15th- and 16th-Century Ottoman Architectural Practice." *Journal of the Society of Architectural Historians* 45, no. 3 (September 1986): 224–243.

Neder, Federico. *Fuller Houses: R. Buckminster Fuller's Dymaxion Dwellings and Other Domestic Adventures.* Trans. Elsa Lam. Baden: Lars Müller, 2008.

A New Description of Sir John Soane's Museum. 10th ed. Marlborough: Libanus Press, 2001.

Nicholson, Ben. *The Appliance House*. Cambridge, MA: MIT Press, 1990.

Nunn, J. Price. "Models and Their Making." *Builder* 162 (June 26, 1942): 553.

Oechslin, Werner. "Le modèle architectural: 'Idea materialis.'" In Frommel with Tassin, *Les maquettes d'architecture*, 103–120.

OMA/Rem Koolhaas, 1987–1998. Madrid: El Croquis Editorial, 1998.

"On the Proper Display of Models." *The Builder* 1 (1843): 317–318.

Onians, John. *Bearers of Meaning: The Classical Orders in Antiquity, the Middle Ages, and the Renaissance*. Princeton, NJ: Princeton University Press, 1988.

Origen. *On First Principles*. Trans. G. W. Butterworth. Introduction by Henri De Lubac. Gloucester, MA: Peter Smith, 1973.

Osborne, Robin. "Hoards, Votives, Offerings: The Archaeology of the Dedicated Object." *World Archaeology* 36 (2004): 1–10.

Otto, Frei. *Das Hängende Dach: Gestalt und Struktur*. Dresden: Verlag der Kunst, 1954.

Otto, Frei. *Tensile Structures*. [Trans. D. Ben-Yaakov and T. Pelz.] Cambridge, MA: MIT Press, 1973.

Overy, Paul, et al. *The Rietveld Schröder House*. Wiesbaden: Vieweg, 1988.

Pai, Hyungmin. *The Portfolio and the Diagram: Architecture, Discourse, and Modernity in America*. Cambridge, MA: MIT Press, 2002.

Pallasmaa, Juhani, and Andrei Gozak. *The Melnikov House: Moscow, 1927–1929*. London: Academy Editions, 1996.

Panofsky, Erwin. *Idea: A Concept of Art Theory*. Trans. Joseph J. S. Peake. Columbia: University of South Carolina Press, 1968.

Panzanelli, Roberta. “Pilgrimage in Hyperreality: Images and Imagination in the Early Phase of the ‘New Jerusalem’ at Varallo (1486–1530).” Ph.D. diss., University of California, Los Angeles, 1999.

Parent, Joseph-Marie. *La doctrine de la création dans l’école de Chartres*. Paris: Vrin; Ottawa: Inst. d’études médiévales, 1938.

Parker, Edwin S. “The Model for Architectural Representation.” *Architectural Forum* 30 (April 1919): 119–121.

Parshall, Peter W., and Rainer Schoch. *Origins of European Printmaking: Fifteenth-Century Woodcuts and Their Public*. Washington, DC: National Gallery of Art, in association with Yale University Press, 2005.

Passeri, Giovanni Battista. *Vite de pittori, scultori ed architetti: Che anno lavorato in Roma, morti dal 1641 fino al 1673*. Rome: Presso Natale Barbiellini mercante di libria Pasquino, 1772.

Pasteur, Louis. “Dans les champs de l’observation le hazard ne favorise que les esprits reéparés.” Lecture presented at the University of Lille, Douai, France, 7 December 1854. Reprinted as “‘Chance Favors Only Those Minds Which Are Prepared.’” In *A Treasury of the World’s Great Speeches*, ed. Houston Petersen, 470–473. New York: Simon & Schuster, 1954.

Payne, Alina. “Materiality, Crafting, and Scale in Renaissance Architecture.” *Oxford Art Journal* 32, no. 3 (2009): 365–396.

Peck, William H. *The Material World of Ancient Egypt*. New York: Cambridge University Press, 2013.

Peirce, Charles Sanders. *The Essential Peirce: Selected Philosophical Writings*. Vol. 2, *1893–1914*. Ed. the Pierce Edition Project. Bloomington: Indiana University Press, 1998.

Peirce, Charles Sanders. “Excerpts from Letters to Lady Welby (1906–08).” In *The Essential Peirce*, 2:477–91.

Peirce, Charles Sanders. “A Neglected Argument for the Reality of God.” In *The Essential Peirce*, 2:434–450.

Peirce, Charles Sanders. “Pragmatism as the Logic of Abduction (Lecture VII).” In *The Essential Peirce*, 2:226–241.

Penny, Nicholas, Peter Schade, and Harriet O’Neill. *The Sansovino Frame*. Washington, DC: National Gallery, 2015.

Pensabene, Patrizio. “Maqueta de templo en mármol de Luna.” In *Las casas del alma*, 129–132. Barcelona: Fundación Caja de Arquitecto, 1997.

Penther, Johann Friedrich. *Zweyter Theil der ausführlichen Anleitung zur Bürgerlichen Baukunst*. Augspurg: Verlegts Johann Andreas Pfeffel, weil. Kayserl. Hof-Kupferstecher, 1762.

Pérez Piñero, Emilio. “Teatro ambulante.” *Arquitectura*, no. 30 (July 1961): 26–29.

Pérez Piñero, Emilio [as E. P. Piñero]. Three dimensional reticular structure. US Patent 3,185,164, filed 15 November 1961, and issued 25 May 1965.

Phillips, Stephen J. *Elastic Architecture: Frederick Kiesler and Design Research in the First Age of Robotic Culture*. Cambridge, MA: MIT Press, 2017.

Pickering, Ernest. *Architectural Design*. New York: J. Wiley; London: Chapman & Hall, 1933.

Pickering, Ernest. *Architectural Design*. 2nd ed. New York: J. Wiley; London: Chapman & Hall, 1941.

Pietz, William. "The Problem of the Fetish, I." *RES: Anthropology and Aesthetics*, no. 9 (Spring 1985): 5–17.

Pietz, William. "The Problem of the Fetish, II: The Origin of the Fetish." *RES: Anthropology and Aesthetics*, no. 13 (Spring 1987): 23–45.

Pilaski Kaliardos, Katharina. *The Munich Kunstkammer: Art, Nature, and the Representation of Knowledge in Courtly Contexts*. Tübingen: Mohr Siebeck, 2013.

Plato. *Ion*. In *The Dialogues of Plato*, trans. Benjamin Jowett, 1:491–510. 3rd ed. 5 vols. New York: Macmillan, 1892.

Plato. *Plato in Twelve Volumes*. Vol. 1, *Euthyphro; Apology; Crito; Phaedo; Phaedrus*. Trans. Harold North Fowler. Loeb Classical Library. 1914. Reprint, Cambridge, MA: Harvard University Press, 1966.

Plato. *The Republic*. Trans. Paul Shorey. 2 vols. Loeb Classical Library. 1930–1935. Reprint, Cambridge, MA: Harvard University Press; London: William Heinemann, 1969.

Plutarch. "The Dinner of the Seven Wise Men." In *Moralia* 146B–164D, trans. Frank Cole Babbitt, 2:345–449. Loeb Classical Library. London: W. Heinemann; New York: Putnam's Sons, 1928.

Poleni, Giovanni. *Memorie istoriche della gran cupola del tempio vaticano*. Padua: Stamperia del Seminario, 1748.

Pommer, Richard, and Christian F. Otto. *Weissenhof 1927 and the Modern Movement in Architecture*. Chicago: University of Chicago Press, 1991.

Porter, Tom, and John Neale. *Architectural Supermodels: Physical Design Simulation*. Oxford: Architectural Press, 2000.

Postgate, Margaret J. "Architectural Models from Bar Soap." *Pencil Points* 10 (June 1929): 392–396.

Potié, Philippe. *Philibert de L'Orme: Figures de la pensée constructive*. Marseille: Editions Parenthèses, 1996.

Praeger, Frank D. "Brunelleschi's Inventions and the 'Renewal of Roman Masonry Work.'" *Osiris* 9 (1950): 457–554.

Prajda, Katalin. "Manetto di Jacopo Ammanatini, the Florentine Woodcarver-Architect and Pippo Scolari's Castle in Ozora." In *Art and Architecture around 1400: Global and Regional Perspectives*, ed. Marjeta Ciglenečki and Polona Vidmar, 75–79. Maribor: Faculty of Arts of the University of Maribor, 2012.

Puff, Helmut. *Miniature Monuments: Modeling German History*. Berlin: De Gruyter, 2017.

Pye, David. *The Nature and Art of Workmanship*. Cambridge: Cambridge University Press, 1968.

Quatremère de Quincy. *Essai sur la nature, le but et les moyens de l'imitation dans les beaux-arts*. Paris: Treuttel & Würtz, 1823.

Quiccheberg, Samuel. *The First Treatise on Museums: Samuel Quiccheberg's Inscriptiones, 1565*. Trans. Mark A. Meadow and Bruce Robertson. Los Angeles: Getty Research Institute, 2014.

Quicherat, Jules. *Mélanges d'archéologie et d'histoire*. 2 vols. Paris: Alphonse Picard, 1885–1886.

Ramsay, W. M. *The Church in the Roman Empire before A.D. 170*. New York: G. P. Putman's Sons, 1893.

Resch, Ronald D. Self-supporting structural unit having a series of repetitious geometrical modules. US Patent 3,407,558, filed 24 January 1966, and issued 29 October 1968.

Reuther, Hans. “Wesen und Wandel des Architekturmodells in Deutschland—The Origin and Development of the Architectural Model in Germany.” *Daidalos* 2 (1981): 98–110.

Reuther, Hans, and Ekhart Berckenhagen. *Deutsche Architekturmodelle: Projekthilfe zwischen 1500 und 1900*. Berlin: Deutscher Verlag für Kunstwissenschaft, 1994.

Richardson, Margaret. “John Soane and the Temple of Vesta at Tivoli.” *Architectural History* 46 (2003): 127–146.

Rigby, Ida Katherine. “Critics, Artists and the Revolution.” In Long, *German Expressionism*, 173–174.

Riley, Terence. *The International Style: Exhibition 15 and the Museum of Modern Art*. New York: Rizzoli, 1992.

Riley, Terence, and Barry Bergdoll. *Mies in Berlin*. New York: Museum of Modern Art, 2001.

Rivius, Gualtherus Hermenius. *Der Architectur furnembsten, notwendigsten, angehörigen mathematischen und mechanischen Künst*. Nuremberg: Gabriel Heyn, 1548.

Rivius, Gualtherus Hermenius. *Der furnembsten notwendigsten der gantzen Architectur angehorigen mathematischen und mechanischen Kunst eygentlicher Bericht und verstendliche Unterrichtung*. 1547. Facsimile reprint, Hildesheim: George Olms, 1981.

Rivius, Gualtherus Hermenius. *Vitruvius Teutsch*. Nuremberg: Johann Petreius, 1548.

Robison, John. “Arch.” In *Encyclopaedia Britannica: Supplement*, 1:21–38. 3rd ed. 2 vols. Edinburgh: Thomson Bonar, 1801.

Rockstroh, Heinrich. *Anweisung zum Modelliren aus Papier oder aus demselben allerley Gegenstände im Kelinen nachzuahmen, Ein nütlicher Zeitreib für Kinder*. Weimar: Verlag des Landes, 1802.

Roland, Conrad. *Frei Otto—Structures*. Trans. C. V. Amerongen. London: Longman, 1972.

Rook, Royal. “Model Making in the Drafting Room.” *American Architect* 114, no. 2227 (August 1918): 247–252.

Rosa, Joseph. *Albert Frey, Architect*. New York: Rizzoli International, 1990.

Rossi, Aldo. *Aldo Rossi*. Ed. Nakamura Toshio. Tokyo: A & U, 1982.

Rossi, Corinna. *Architecture and Mathematics in Ancient Egypt*. Cambridge: Cambridge University Press, 2004.

Rozestraten, Artur Simões. “Learning with Arkhanes’ Model.” *Acta Scientiarum: Education* [online] 32 (July–December 2010): 263–268. http://dx.doi.org/10.4025/actascieduc.v32i2.9774.

Saalman, Howard. *Filippo Brunelleschi: The Cupola of Santa Maria del Fiore*. London: Zwemmer, 1980.

Saalman, Howard. “S. Maria del Fiore and St. Peter’s.” *Art Bulletin* 57, no. 3 (September 1975): 374–409.

Sakr, Faiza Mahmoud. “New Foundation Deposits of Kom el-Hisn.” *Studien zur Altägyptischen Kultur* 33 (2005): 349–355.

Sandaker, Bjørn Normann. *On Span and Space: Exploring Structures in Architecture*. London: Routledge, 2008.

Sauerländer, W. “Grabmal Heinrichs des Löwen und seiner Gemahlin Mathilde.” In *Die Zeit der Staufer*, 1:325–327. 5 vols. Stuttgart: Württembergisches Landesmuseum, 1977.

Scamozzi, Vicenzo. *L'idea della architettura universale*. Venice, 1615.

Scamozzi, Vicenzo. *L'idea della architettura universale.* At the Sir John Soane Museum Library, anonymous manuscript English translation (ca. 1680).

Scarry, Elaine. *Dreaming by the Book*. New York: Farrar, Straus, Giroux, 1999.

Schaeffer, Jean-Marie. *Art of Modern Age: Philosophy of Art from Kant to Heidegger*. Trans. Steven Rendall. Princeton, NJ: Princeton University Press, 2000.

Schattner, Thomas. *Griechische Hausmodelle*. Berlin: Gebr. Mann, 1990.

Schmutzler, Robert. *Art Nouveau*. London: Thames & Hudson, 1978.

Schoep, Ilse. "'Home Sweet Home': Some Comments on the So-Called House Models from the Prehellenic Aegean." *Opuscula Atheniensia* 20 (1994): 189–210.

Schreiber, Christa. "Das Berlinishe Rathaus: Versuch einer Entsehungs- und Ideengeschichte." In *Das Rathaus im Kaiserreich: Kunstpolitische Aspeke einer Bauaufgabe des 19. Jahrhunderts*, ed. Ekkehard Mai, 91–141. Kunst, Kultur und Politik im Deutschen Kaiserreich 4. Berlin: Mann, 1982.

Schreiner, Ludwig. "Der Lüdenscheider Baumeister Wilhelm Tappe (1769–1823)." *Der Reidemeister*, nos. 49/50 (28 April 1970): 381–396.

Schultes, Axel, and Charlotte Frank, "Leuchtmodelle (Light Models)." In *The Architectural Model: Tool, Fetish, Small Utopia*, ed. Peter Cachola Schmal and Oliver Elser, 260–264. Zurich: Scheidegger, 2012.

Schulze, Franz. *Mies van der Rohe: A Critical Biography*. Rev. ed. Chicago: University of Chicago Press, 2012.

Schumacher, Fritz. "Das Entstehen des baulichen Kunstwerks." In *Handbuch für Architektur*. Part 4, *Entwerfen, Anlage und Einrichtung der Gebaude*, 41–63. Leipzig: J. M. Gebhardt's Verlag, 1926.

Schumacher, Thomas L. *The Danteum: A Study in the Architecture of Literature*. Princeton, NJ: Princeton Architectural Press, 1985.

Schwitters, Kurt. "Die Bedeutung des Merzgedankens in der Welt" (1923). Reprinted in Kurt Schwitters, *Das Literarische Werk*, ed. Friedhelm Lach, 5:133–136. Cologne: DuMont, 1981.

Schwitters, Kurt. "Merz" (1921). Reprinted in Kurt Schwitters, *Das Literarische Werk*, ed. Friedhelm Lach, 5:74–82. Cologne: DuMont, 1981.

Schwitters, Kurt. "Schloss und Kathedrale mit Hofbrunnen" (1922). Reprinted in Taut, *Frühlicht, 1920–1922*, 166–167.

Scolari, Massimo. "Wooden Model of the Dome and Apse Parts of Florence Cathedral." In Millon and Lampugnani, *The Renaissance from Brunelleschi to Michelangelo*, 583–585.

Semper, Gottfried. *Der Stil in den technischen und tektonischen Künsten oder praktische Ästhetik: Ein Handbuch für Techniker, Künstler und Kunstfreunde*. Vol. 2. Frankfurt: Verlag für Kunst und Wissenschaft, 1863.

Shelby, Lon. "Medieval Mason's Tools: The Level and the Plumb Rule." *Technology and Culture*, no. 2 (1961): 127–130.

Shelby, Lon. "Medieval Mason's Tools II: Compass and Square." *Technology and Culture*, no. 6 (1965): 236–248.

Simondon, Gilbert. *L'individuation à la lumière des notions de forme et d'information*. Grenoble: Editions Jérôme Millon, 2005.

Smith, Christine. "Model for S. Giuseppe or S. Marco, Florence." In Millon and Lampugnani, *The Renaissance from Brunelleschi to Michelangelo*, 457, cat. no. 47.

Smith, H. S., and H. M. Stewart. "The Gurob Shrine Papyrus." *Journal of Egyptian Archaeology* 70 (1984): 54–64.

Soane, Sir John. *Description of the House and Museum on the North Side of Lincoln's Inn.* London: James Moyes, 1830.

Soane, Sir John. *Sir John Soane: The Royal Academy Lectures*. Ed. David Watkin. Cambridge: Cambridge University Press, 1996.

"Soleri's Cities on Display." *Progressive Architecture* 51 (April 1970): 29.

"Soleri's Urban Utopia Comes to New York." *Interiors* 130 (August 1970): 6.

Speidel, Manfred, Karl Kegler and Peter Ritterbach. *Wege zu einer neuen Baukunst: Bruno Taut: Frühlicht: Konzeptionskritik H. 1–4 und Rekonstruktion H. 5*. Berlin: Mann, 2000.

Spencer, Brian. *Pilgrim Souvenirs and Secular Badges*. London: Stationery Office, 1998.

Spinelli, Luigi. "Quando l'infrastruttura diventa paesaggio." *Domus* 907 (2007): 78–85.

Spolsky, Ellen. "Doubting Thomas and the Senses of Knowing." *Common Knowledge* 3, no. 2 (1994): 111–129.

Springer, Peter. *Modelle und Muster, Vorlage und Kopie, Serien*. Ex. cat. Vol. 1. Cologne, 1985.

Spuybroek, Lars. *The Sympathy of Things: Ruskin and the Ecology of Design*. Rotterdam: V2_Publishing, 2011.

Stantz, Ludwig. *Münsterbuch: Eine artistisch-historische beschreibung des St. Vincenzen Münsters in Bern*. Bern: J. Dantz, 1865.

Stefani Perrone, Stefania. "La 'Gerusalemme' delle origini nella secolare vicenda edificatoria del Sacro Monte di Varallo." In *Sacri Monti*, ed. Luciano Vaccaro and Francesca Ricardi, 27–57. Milan: Jaca Book, 1992.

Steiner, Rudolf. *Wege zu einem neuen Baustil: Fünf Vorträge gehalten während der Arbeit am ersten Goetheanum in Dornach zwischen dem 7. Juni und 26. Juli 1914*. 1926. Reprint, Stuttgart: Verlag Freies Geistesleben, 1957.

Stevens, Gorham P. "A Tile Standard in the Agora of Ancient Athens." *Hesperia* 19, no. 3 (1950): 174–188.

Stewart, Susan. *On Longing: Narratives of the Miniature, the Gigantic, the Souvenir, the Collection.* Durham: Duke University Press, 1993.

Stocks, Denys A. *Experiments in Egyptian Archaeology: Stoneworking Technology in Ancient Egypt*. London: Routledge, 2003.

Stocks, Denys A. "Scientific Evaluation of Experiments in Egyptian Archaeology." In *Mummies, Magic, and Medicine in Ancient Egypt: Multidisciplinary Essays for Rosalie David*, ed. Campbell Price, Roger Forshaw, Andrew Chamberlain, and Paul T. Nicholson, 446–460. Manchester: Manchester University Press, 2016.

Suger, Abbot. *Abbot Suger on the Abbey Church of St.-Denis and Its Art Treasures*. Ed. and trans. Erwin Panofsky. 2nd ed. Princeton, NJ: Princeton University Press, 1979.

Sulzer, Peter. *Jean Prouvé, Highlights: 1917–1944*. Basel: Birkhäuser, 2002.

Summers, David. *Real Spaces: World Art History and the Rise of Western Modernism.* London: Phaidon, 2003.

Swartwout, Egerton. "The Use of Large Scale Models in Architecture." *Architecture* 24 (1911): 130–133.

Tacconi, Marica S. *Cathedral and Civic Ritual in Late Medieval and Renaissance Florence.* Cambridge: Cambridge University Press, 2005.

Tachi, Tomohiro. "Designing Freeform Origami Tessellations by Generalizing Resch's Patterns." *Journal of Mechanical Design* 135, no. 11 (October 2013): 1–10.

Tachi, Tomohiro. "Freeform Variations of Origami." *Journal of Geometry and Graphics* 14, no. 2 (2010): 203–215.

Tam, Karen. "Dolce & Banana, A Shanzhai Creator's Manual: Production and Consumption of Fake in Contemporary Chinese Art Practices." In *The Changing Landscape of China's Consumerism*, ed. Allison Hulme, 83–106. Oxford: Chandos Publishing, 2014.

Tames, Richard. *Ancient Egyptian Children*. Chicago: Heinemann, 2003.

Tartuferi, Angelo. *Michelangelo Painter, Sculptor, and Architect*. Rome: A.T.S., 1993.

Tassin, Raphaël. "Le rôle de la maquette dans le processus de conception architecturale en France au XVIIIe siècle." In Frommel with Tassin, *Les maquettes d'architecture*, 231–240.

Tatarkiewicz, Władysław. *History of Aesthetics*. Ed. C. Barrett. Vol. 2, *Medieval Aesthetics*. Warsaw: Polish Scientific Publishers, 1970.

Taut, Bruno. "Ein Architektur-Programm." *Mitteilungen des deutschen Werkbundes*, no. 4 (1918): 16–19.

Taut, Bruno, ed. *Frühlicht, 1920–1922: Eine Folge für die Verwirklichung des neuen Baugedankens*. Berlin: Ullstein, 1963.

Taut, Bruno. "Eine Notwendigkeit." *Der Sturm* 4, nos. 196–197 (February 1914): 174–175.

Tavernor, Robert. *On Alberti and the Art of Building*. New Haven: Yale University Press, 1998.

Templar, John. *The Staircase: History and Theories*. Cambridge, MA: MIT Press, 1992.

Tomlow, Jos. "L'esperit del càlcul en l'obra arquitectònica de Gaudí." In Oriol Bohigas et al., *Gaudí 2002*, 176–199.

Tomlow, J. "Die Kuppel des Gießhauses der Firma Henschel in Kassel (1837): Eine frühe Anwendung des Entwurfsverfahrens mit Hängemodellen." *Architectura* 23 (1993): 151–172.

Tosi, Luigia Maria. "La chiesa di San Giuseppe." *Dedalo* 9 (1928–1929): 283–289.

Trachtenberg, Marvin. *The Campanile of Florence Cathedral: "Giotto's Tower."* New York: New York University Press, 1971.

Treib, Marc. *Space Calculated in Seconds: The Philips Pavilion, Le Corbusier, Edgard Varèse*. Princeton, NJ: Princeton University Press, 1996.

Les Trésors des églises de France. 2nd ed. Paris: Caisse nationale des monuments historiques, 1965.

Truesdale, Clifford. *The Rational Mechanics of Flexible or Elastic Bodies, 1638–1788*. Basel: Birkhäuser, 1960.

Tuttle, Richard J. "The Basilica of S. Petronio in Bologna." In Millon and Lampugnani, *The Renaissance from Brunelleschi to Michelangelo*, 522–526.

"TWA's Graceful New Terminal." *Architectural Forum* 108 (January 1958): 78–83.

Überwasser, Walter. "Spägotische Baugeometrie." *Öffentliche Kunstsammlung Basel* 25–27 (1931): 79–122.

Ursprung, Philip, ed. *Herzog & de Meuron: Natural History*. Exh. cat. Baden: Lars Müller, 2002.

Vasari, Giorgio. *Lives of the Painters, Sculptors and Architects*. Trans. Gaston du C. de Vere. 2 vols. 1912–15. Reprint, New York: Alfred A. Knopf: Distributed by Random House, 1996.

Vasari, Giorgio. *Vasari on Technique: Being the Introduction to the Three Arts of Design, Architecture, Sculpture and Painting, Prefixed to the Lives of the Most Excellent Painters, Sculptors and Architects*. Trans. Louisa S. Maclehose. Ed. with an introduction by G. Baldwin Brown. 1907. Reprint. New York: Dover Publications, 1960.

Vasarri, Vittorio. "Il modello della chiesa di San Giuseppe." *Antichità viva* 21, no. 1 (1982): 30–36.

Verdi, Orietta, and Simonetta Ceglie. *La fabbrica della Sapienza: L'università al tempo di Borromini*. Rome: Croma-Università degli Studi Roma Tre, 2015.

Vico, Giambattista. *On the Most Ancient Wisdom of the Italians*. Trans. L. M. Palmer. Ithaca, NY: Cornell University Press, 1988.

Vitrea Dedicata. Berlin: Deutscher Verlag für Kunstwissenschaft, 1975.

Vitruvius. *The Ten Books on Architecture*. Trans. Morris Hickey Morgan. 1914. Reprint, New York: Dover Publications, 1960.

Vitruvius. *Ten Books on Architecture*. Ed. Ingrid D. Rowland and Thomas Noble Howe. Trans. Ingrid D. Rowland. New York: Cambridge University Press, 1999.

Wallace, William. *Michelangelo at San Lorenzo: The Genius as Entrepreneur*. Cambridge: Cambridge University Press, 1994.

Walton, Kendall L. *Mimesis as Make-Believe: On the Foundations of the Representational Arts*. 1990. Reprint, Cambridge, MA: Harvard University Press, 2004.

Waring, Steven H. "Improved Techniques in Architectural Modelling." *Royal Architectural Institute of Canada* 25, no. 2 (February 1948): 58–60.

Weingarten, David, and Margaret Majua. *Monumental Miniatures: Souvenir Buildings from the Collection of Ace Architects*. Norfolk, VA: Antique Trader Books, 1999.

Weinstein, James. "Foundation Deposits in Ancient Egypt." Ph.D. diss., University of Pennsylvania, 1973.

Weinstein, Joan. *The End of Expressionism: Art and the November Revolution in Germany, 1918–19*. Chicago: University of Chicago Press, 1990.

Wesenberg, Burckhardt. "Das Paradeigma des Eupalinos." *Jahrbuch des Deutschen Archäologischen Instituts* 122 (January 2007): 33–49.

Whinney, Margaret. *Wren*. 1971. Reprint, London: Thames & Hudson, 1998.

Whittemore, Thomas. *The Mosaics of St. Sophia at Istanbul: Second Preliminary Report, Work Done in 1933 and 1934: The Mosaics of the Southern Vestibule*. Boston: J. Johnson, 1936.

Whyte, Iain Boyd. *Bruno Taut and the Architecture of Activism*. Cambridge: Cambridge University Press, 1982.

Whyte, Iain Boyd, and David Frisby. "Planning the World City." In *Metropolis Berlin: 1880–1940*, ed. Iain Boyd Whyte and David Frisby, 315–318. Berkeley: University of California Press, 2011.

Wickham, P. R. *Commercial Model Making*. London: Vawser & Wiles, 1945.

Wiedmann, August K. *Romantic Roots in Modern Art: Romanticism and Expressionism: A Study in Comparative Aesthetics*. Old Woking, [Eng.]: Gresham, 1979.

Will, Ernest. "La maquette de l'adyton au temple A de Niha (Beqaa)." In *Le dessin d'architecture dans les sociétés antiques: Actes du Colloque de Strasbourg, 26–28 janvier 1984*, 277–281. [Leiden]: E. J. Brill, 1985.

William, Harvey. *Models of Buildings How to Make and Use Them*. London: Architectural Press, 1927.

Wilson Jones, Mark. *Principles of Roman Architecture.* New Haven: Yale University Press, 2000.

Wilton-Ely, John. "The Architectural Model: I. English Baroque." *Apollo* 88, no. 80 (October 1968): 250–259.

Wixom, W. D. "The Greatest of the So Called Minor Arts." In *The Year 1200*, ed. Florens Deuchler, 2:93–132. New York: Metropolitan Museum of Art, 1970.

Woods, Lebbeus. "Experimental Architecture: A Commentary." *Avant Garde* 2 (Summer 1989): 6–19.

Woods, Lebbeus, and Christoph a. Kumpusch. "A Space of Light." In *The Light Pavilion by Lebbeus Woods and Christoph a. Kumpusch for the Sliced Porosity Block in Chengdu, China, 2007–2012*, ed. Christoph a. Kumpusch, 3–4. Zurich: Lars Müller, 2013.

Wortman, Reinhard. "Hallenplan und Basilikabau der Parler in Ulm." In *600 Jahre Ulmer Münster*, 101–125. Stuttgart: Kohlhammer, 1977.

Wotton, Henry. *The Elements of Architecture*. 1524. Facsimile reprint, Farnborough, Hants.: Gregg International Publishers, 1969.

Wright, Frank Lloyd. "The Cardboard House." In *Frank Lloyd Wright: Collected Writings*. Vol. 2, *1930–1932*, ed. Bruce Brooks Pfeifer, 51–59. New York: Rizzoli, 1992.

Yanagisawa, Jun. "A Utopia Called Model." In *Toyo Ito: Blurring Architecture, 1971–2005*, ed. Ulrich Schneider and Manfred Fenstel, 155. Milan: Edizioni Charta, 1999.

Young, Thomas. *Lectures on Natural Philosophy and the Mechanical Arts*. London: Johnson, 1807.

Zumthor, Peter. *Thinking Architecture.* Baden: Lars Müller Publishers, 1998.

Zygas, Kestutis Paul. *Form Follows Form: Source Imagery of Constructivist Architecture, 1916–1925*. Ann Arbor, MI: UMI Research Press, 1981.

INDEX

Page numbers in italics indicate illustrations.